IFA4, CF5, CeFA®4

INTEGRATED CASE STUDY ASSESSMENT

2006/07 tax year edition

Study Text

IFA/Cert FP/CeF

This **Study Text** provides full coverage for:

- Paper 4 *Investment and Financial Advice* of the Securities and Investment Institute's IFA Qualification

- Paper CF5 *Integrated Financial Planning* of the Chartered Insurance Institute's® Certificate in Financial Planning

- The Module 4 *Holistic Assessment* of the Institute of Financial Services' Certificate for Financial Advisers (CeFA®)

Visit www.bpp.com/financialadvisers for more information

PROFESSIONAL EDUCATION

Contents

First edition May 2006

ISBN 0 7517 2632 X

British Library Cataloguing-in-Publication Data

A catalogue record for this book
is available from the British Library

Published by

BPP Professional Education
Aldine House, Aldine Place
London W12 8AW

www.bpp.com

Printed in Great Britain by WM Print, Walsall

Author: David Wicks, BA, FCII, FPFS
Chartered Financial Planner

Page

Introduction

Chapters

Case Studies

Multiple Choice Case Studies

Written Case Studies

Product List

Tax Tables

Index

Review Form

Using this Study Text

Under the standards for Appropriate Examinations set out by the Financial Services Skills Council (FSSC), it is a requirement that candidates are examined in their ability to **combine and apply knowledge and understanding** of the content of standards to the circumstances of advising on investments which are packaged products. This is achieved by means of an 'overarching' **integrated case study assessment**.

This Study Text has been written for candidates sitting one of the following assessments, all of which meet the FSSC requirements.

- Paper 4 *Investment and Financial Advice* of the Securities and Investment Institute's **IFA Qualification**

- Paper CF5 *Integrated Financial Planning* of the Chartered Insurance Institute's® **Certificate in Financial Planning**

- The Module 4 *Holistic Assessment* of the Institute of Financial Services' **Certificate for Financial Advisers (CeFA®)**

The Study Text contains:

- A list of topics covered in each Chapter
- Clear, concise coverage
- Examples to reinforce learning, confirm understanding and stimulate thought
- A roundup of the key points in each Chapter
- A quiz at the end of each Chapter (except Chapter 9)
- A bank of practice case studies, with answers

We recognise that most students have only limited time for study and that some study material available on the market can be very time-consuming to use. BPP Professional Education has prepared study material which provides you with what you need to secure a good pass in your exam, while making effective use of your time.

Updates to this Study Text

There is a free **Updating Service** for users of BPP's *Financial Adviser Series*. For information on Updates to this Study Text, go to our website at **www.bpp.com/financialadvisers**. If you do not have Internet access, telephone the BPP Customer Service Team on 0845 0751 100 for further information.

Plan your exam practice and your revision

How can you give yourself the best chance of success in your exam? As well as studying the material in this **Study Text** fully, make a **plan** for your **exam practice** and **revision**.

BPP's long experience in preparing students for professional exams shows that **question practice** is a vital ingredient in exam success. Question practice will improve your exam technique and help to build confidence for tackling the exam itself. It can highlight problem areas and remind you of key points. BPP's **i-Pass CDs** each include a bank of objective test questions for you to try at a computer. Feedback is given on answers, and there are flexible ways of using the question banks.

The syllabuses for your examinations, which are based on the standards for Appropriate Examinations published by the Financial Services Skills Council, are wide-ranging. In your **revision** during the run-up to the exam, you will want to focus your revision on ensuring that you can recall what you have studied. BPP's **Passcards** present key facts in a visually appealing style, to remind you of key points.

To order **Financial Adviser Series** Study Texts, i-Pass CDs and Passcards, call 0845 0751 100 or order online at **www.bpp.com/financialadvisers**.

Syllabuses

The syllabuses are set out in turn below for the integrated case study assessments of the **Securities and Investment Institute (IFA Paper 4)**, the **Chartered Insurance Institute (CF5)** and the **Institute of Financial Services (CeFA Module 4)**.

SII's IFA Paper 4: Investment and Financial Advice

The purpose of Paper 4 – the 'integrated' examination – is to examine candidates' ability to combine and apply the knowledge and understanding they have acquired in Papers 1 to 3 to the practical demands of advising clients' on investments which are packaged products.

During their preparation for Papers 1, 2 and 3, candidates will be expected to read the cases related to the subject matter. By this means, candidates will learn to recognise how the different components: regulation, taxation, the broad range of investments, savings and protection products, the ethical and practical considerations involved in the advisory function are drawn together in the provision of competent financial advice.

The examination will focus on providing evidence of candidates' ability to analyse, synthesis and evaluate client and market information, when advising on investments which are packaged products. Questions will require candidates to demonstrate their competence by testing their ability to:

(a)   Interpret a case history from given client information, identifying areas needing clarification or further information and prepare appropriate questions

(b)   Identify and respond to main drivers underpinning a client's financial needs and objectives by prioritising them; meeting the need for income, growth, protection, retirement provision etc. as the client's circumstances require, while complying with their attitude to risk

(c)   Recommend suitable financial advice from client information, including a clear identification of changing needs over time and giving specific consideration to asset allocation, taxation, risk, flexibility, charging structures and affordability and sustainability. [Candidates will be required to recognise both perceived and actual needs and identify appropriate financial services to meet the client's needs. This may involve recognising that some clients' needs should be referred to a specialist.]

(d)   Critically appraise an existing financial portfolio and suggest changes in accordance with defined financial objectives and given economic circumstances, giving reasons why a specific course of action has been recommended. [Candidates will be expected to explain why they have made their recommendations, the advantages and disadvantages of various approaches, how they have taken account of future needs and how they will be handled, including the need for monitoring and review.]

And will involve candidates looking at:

(a)   The impact of life events: birth, employment, marriage, school/university fees planning, empty nesting, divorce, retirement, moving abroad, death, disability

(b)   The need for clients to establish their priorities and budget scarce resources to meet them, particularly the interrelationship between protection and saving, other objectives eg retirement

(c)   The risks and choices associated with borrowing eg paying off the mortgage or saving for retirement.

IFA Paper 4 is an examination at National Qualifications Framework Level 3, testing:

- Application
- Analysis
- Synthesis
- Evaluation

IFA Paper 4: Syllabus content

IFA Syllabus reference	
1	**Gathering the information needed to provide financial advice**
1.1	*Establishing the client - adviser relationship*
1.1.1	Introducing the adviser and identifying the range of services that can be offered to the client
1.1.2	Explaining the purpose of regulation, the firm's regulatory status, the status of the adviser and the implications for the client
1.1.3	Providing the documents disclosing the status of the firm and adviser
1.1.4	Explaining the fact finding process and identifying how this will enable the client's objectives to be met
1.2	*Establishing the client's financial arrangements and objectives*
1.2.1	Plan appropriate questions to identify all relevant personal and financial information
1.2.2	Identifying the client's needs and objectives and the associated timescales
1.2.3	Investigate the client's existing financial provision and investments
1.2.4	Qualify, quantify and prioritise the client's needs, objectives, expectations and timescales
1.3	*Review the performance and suitability of clients' financial arrangements*
1.3.1	Determine the financial performance of the client's existing financial arrangements
1.3.2	Evaluate correctly the suitability of the client's existing financial products/services against new and emerging solutions in meeting the financial requirements agreed previously with the client, bearing in mind the client's attitude to risk
1.3.3	Identify correctly any material factors affecting the appropriateness of the client's financial provision
1.3.4	Identify whether there are any financial needs identified previously, but which were not addressed due to circumstances agreed at the time
1.3.5	Assess the need for any additional information requirements
1.3.6	Appraise the client of the consequences of declining to provide relevant personal and financial information
1.3.7	Investigate the client's current circumstances, any foreseeable changes to their circumstances, and their future needs and aspirations
1.4	*Establish the client's attitude to risk and affordability*
1.4.1	Explain the concept of risk and reward and the concept of correlated asset classes
1.4.2	Investigate whether the client knows and understands the factors which may affect their attitude to risk, the amount(s) that they might pay and the type of investments/savings that they might consider and the returns they can expect
1.4.3	Determine the client's attitude to risk for each objective and timescale
1.4.4	Evaluate the client's budget constraints and requirements and the affordability of products for each area of need for each and every client who might be covered by the advice given

IFA Syllabus reference	
2	**Analyse information necessary to provide financial advice**
2.1	*Review the client's prioritised needs and identify possible solutions*
2.1.1	Assess the requirements of the client and explore any further appropriate potential areas of financial need by evaluating all relevant information available from the client
2.1.2	Investigate and resolve any gaps or possible inaccuracies in the information that will have a bearing on the advice that may be given
2.1.3	Evaluate the client's existing financial arrangements and identify any needs not addressed by these
2.1.4	Identify the appropriate action to take where advice and guidance is required which is outside the adviser's own area of expertise or responsibility
2.1.5	Create an accurate and prioritised assessment of the client's financial needs and possible solutions
2.2	*Determine appropriate financial solutions for the client's financial requirements*
2.2.1	Evaluate possible solutions accurately, including their relative risks and rewards, against the client's financial needs, their identified attitude to risk for each area of need and their current and future tax status
2.2.2	Develop recommendations suited to the client's financial requirements, including relevant solutions, products and, where applicable, providers
2.2.3	Assess whether all recommendations match the client's agreed risk/reward philosophy and are affordable to the client
2.2.4	Confirm that all recommendations fulfil product suitability requirements and the regulatory requirement to provide suitable advice
2.2.5	Identify an appropriate course of action where no suitable product is available
2.3	*Show how one solution/recommendation will affect other client objectives*
2.3.1	Prepare materials for presenting the proposed financial solution(s)
2.3.2	Present information regarding possible solutions to the client, identifying the key features of the proposed recommendation(s)
2.3.3	2.3.3 Identify relevant advantages and any disadvantages to the client regarding the features of the proposed recommendation(s) which will enable the client to make an informed decision
3	**Advise on and progress financial solutions**
3.1	*Review the client's circumstances for any material changes*
3.1.1	Assess any changes in the client's documented information, and where changes are identified, assess and determine their impact upon any recommendations made
3.1.2	Reappraise the client's financial requirements where material changes have rendered proposed recommendations unsuitable and their key features inappropriate
3.2	*Recommend and agree financial solutions*
3.2.1	Investigate and explain to the client where there may be shortfalls in their existing financial provisions relevant to their agreed financial needs and objectives

IFA Syllabus reference	
3.2.2	Evaluate the proposed solutions, explaining their relevant features, benefits and terms and relate these to the specific circumstances of the client, demonstrating how the recommendations meet the client's financial requirements
3.2.3	Provide relevant documentation covering the main aspects of the recommendations and explain disclosure requirements
3.2.4	Explain the implications of any required variance to or any rejection of the recommendation(s) by the client
3.3	*Progressing the accepted solutions*
3.3.1	Ensure that the client understands their right to change their mind, the purpose of the Cancellation Notice and accompanying documents, and the actions that they might take in relation to the Notice
3.3.2	Ensure that, where applicable, the client understands their rights and responsibilities associated with the need for a medical report(s) and the implications of its outcomes for the agreed solutions
3.3.3	Ensure that, where appropriate, proper evidence is obtained of the client's identity for all proposed transactions as required by regulations covering money laundering and report any suspicious transactions to the appropriate authority
4	**Review existing clients' financial arrangements/requirements**
4.1	*Determine correctly the topics for review and the questions to be discussed with the client*
4.2	*Review clients' ongoing financial needs*
4.2.1	Advise the client, where an agreed action is not considered beneficial to them, of the reasons and determine whether they want to proceed
4.2.2	Explain the impact of economic, regulatory, legislative, financial and social change on the client's financial arrangements
4.2.3	Explain the inter-relationship in estate planning between wills, trusts, protection, IHT, CGT and retirement with investment planning
4.2.4	Explain the consequences to the client of changes in their attitude to risk – as a result of changes in: the market, experience, personal and family circumstances

CII's CF5: Integrated Financial Planning

Having completed unit CF5, candidates should be able to apply:

- Their knowledge and understanding of the financial services industry and its regulation
- Their knowledge and understanding of the products and processes tested in CF1-4

Learning outcomes

- Establish the relationship between the client and the adviser
- Gather data
- Identify needs and possible solutions
- Make recommendations
- Monitor clients' circumstances

CF5: Syllabus content

CF5 Syllabus reference	
1	**Establish the relationship between the client and the adviser**
1	Agree client goals, the adviser's responsibilities and terms of business
2	**Gather data**
2.1	Gather information needed to provide financial advice
2.2	Understand the client's risk profile
2.3	Complete accurately a fact-find
3	**Identify needs and possible solutions**
3.1	Clients' perceived needs and their real needs where they are different
3.2	Distinguish between the client's present and future needs
3.3	Analyse the information necessary to provide financial advice
4	**Make recommendations**
4.1	Construct a solution to the client's needs
4.2	Advise on solutions
4.3	Recommend the most appropriate financial services and products for the client's particular circumstances
4.4	Create specific financial package to satisfy the client's needs
4.5	Explain and justify the recommended financial package
5	**Monitor clients' circumstances**
5.1	Review the future needs of the client and make suitable arrangements to discuss these needs at appropriate intervals

ifs CeFA® Module 4: Holistic Assessment

Learning Outcomes and Syllabus

Candidate are required to demonstrate the ability to identify consumers' needs and demands and recommend suitable and affordable investment solutions, using their knowledge and understanding of:

- The UK finance industry, regulation and ethics
- Investment and risks
- Protection
- Retirement planning

The holistic paper will test **analysis, synthesis** and **evaluation**.

Web site links

Organisation	Information included	Website address
Association of British Insurers	Insurance topics	www.abi.org.uk
Association of Investment Trust Companies	Investment trust data	www.aitc.co.uk
BPP Professional Education	Study material and Updates	www.bpp.com/financialadvisers
Chartered Insurance Institute®	Cert FP exam information	www.cii.co.uk
Debt Management Office	Details of gilts	www.dmo.gov.uk
Department for Work and Pensions	State benefits	www.dwp.gov.uk
Financial Services Authority (FSA)	Regulatory information	www.fsa.gov.uk
FTSE	FTSE indices	www.ftse.com
HM Revenue & Customs (Practitioners' area)	Technical information on pensions and other areas	www.hmrc.gov.uk/practitioners
Institute of Financial Services	CeFA® exam information	www.ifslearning.com
Investment Management Association	Unit trust and OEIC/ICVC data	www.investmentfunds.org.uk
National Savings and Investments	NS&I products	www.nsandi.com
Office for National Statistics	Demographic, economic and other statistical information	www.statistics.gov.uk
Pension Service (part of DWP)	Information on state pensions and other benefits	www.thepensionservice.gov.uk
Securities and Investment Institute	IFA Qualification exam information	www.sii.org.uk
Standard and Poor's	Fund databases and ratings	www.funds-sp.com

Examination formats

Each examining body – the SII, the CII and the *ifs* – uses a different examination format, and these are described below.

SII's IFA Paper 4

The **IFA Paper 4** is tested by a **multiple choice** examination of **two and a half hours** in duration.

The examination structure

The examination will comprise three cases. Each case will be tested using between three and five 'vignettes'. Each vignette will comprise a number of questions testing the candidates' knowledge and their skills of comprehension, application, analysis, synthesis and evaluation. Overall candidates will be required to answer 60 multiple choice questions, 30 on case 1 [60 minutes] and 15 on each of cases 2 and 3 [30 minutes each]. Candidates are required to answer all questions.

The case studies

In advance of the Paper 4 examination, candidates will be provided with a set of case studies covering a variety of clients, their financial situations and their financial objectives. The examination will draw on three of the cases but the client's circumstances will be changed slightly. Each case will form the basis of a series of vignettes, each of which will focus on a particular issue - for example calculating a client's tax liability or identifying which investments are unsuitable in a client's new personal circumstances. Candidates will have access to a simple tax table in the examination and product data might be provided.

Levels of attainment

The Unit 4 examination will test application, analysis, synthesis and evaluation.

- Fifty questions testing **comprehension**
- Five questions testing **application**
- Five questions testing **analysis**

What is meant by application, analysis, synthesis and evaluation?

These terms indicate **levels of attainment**, defined in terms of the cognitive skills required to achieve learning outcomes. The table below shows successive levels of attainment, the **abilities** needed to reach each level and the **action verbs** that might be used to frame examination questions and tasks.

Level of attainment	Abilities	Action verbs (examples)
Knowledge	Recall (eg, facts, rules, definitions)	List, State, Define, Outline
Comprehension	Interpret, translate ideas, extrapolate	Explain, Describe, Discuss, Interpret, Identify
Application	Apply general principles/rules in new situations	Demonstrate, Apply, Operate, Illustrate, Employ
Analysis	Break down information and make clear the nature of the component parts and their relationship to each other	Distinguish, Investigate, Analyse
Synthesis	Assemble a number of components in order to generate a new statement or plan	Design, Create, Organise, Plan
Evaluation	Judge the value of methods or materials by comparison with external criteria	Judge, Evaluate, Appraise, Assess

CII's Paper CF5

CF5 is tested by **written case studies**, in an examination lasting **two hours**.

The examination consists of **two** Case Study questions.

- **Question 1** is partly concerned with the process of completing a factfind and carries **50 marks**.
- **Question 2** is based on planning an investment portfolio and carries **50 marks**.

Calculators can be used during the examination, but must be silent battery or solar-powered non-programmable models.

The CII states that the nominal **pass mark** for the CF5 exam is **55%**.

There is no pre-defined quota of passes, but the actual pass mark may be varied depending on the difficulty of the question paper, to ensure that a consistent standard is applied.

Tax Tables will be provided to you in the examination room.

When do changes become examinable?

The CF5 examination will be based on the legislative position in England **eight weeks** before the date of the examination.

ifs CeFA Module 4

The IFS's Module 4 Holistic Assessment is assessed by **multiple choice** questions in a **two-hour electronic examination**.

Past papers have comprised **six case studies**, with **ten multiple choice questions** on each case study, making a total of 60 questions on the paper altogether.

The **pass mark** for the Module is **70%**.

PROFESSIONAL EDUCATION

Tackling MCQs

Multiple choice questions (MCQs) each contain a number of possible answers. You have to choose the **one option(s)** that best answers the question. The incorrect options are called **distracters**.

There is a skill in answering MCQs quickly and correctly. By practising MCQs you can develop this skill, giving you a better chance of passing the exam.

You may wish to follow the approach outlined below, or you may prefer to adapt it to suit your own learning style and needs.

Step 1. **Note down how long** you should allocate to each MCQ or group of MCQs. You will probably not spend an equal amount of time on each MCQ. You might be able to answer some questions instantly while others will take more time to work out.

Step 2. **Attempt each question**. Read the question thoroughly. A particular question might look familiar to you, but be aware that the detail and/or requirement may be different from any similar question you have come across. So, read the requirement and options carefully, even for questions that seem familiar.

Step 3. Read all the options and see if one matches your own answer. Be careful with numerical questions, as the distracters are designed to match answers that incorporate **common errors**. Check that your calculation is correct. Have you followed the requirement exactly? Have you included every stage of the calculation?

Step 4. You may find that none of the options matches your answer.

- **Re-read the question** to ensure that you understand it and are answering the requirement

- **Eliminate any obviously wrong answers**

- **Consider which of the remaining answers** is the **most likely** to be correct or best and select that option

Step 5. If you are still unsure, **continue to the next question**.

If you are nowhere near working out which option is correct after a couple of minutes, leave the question and come back to it later. Make a note of any questions for which you have submitted answers but you need to return to later.

Step 6. **Revisit questions** you are uncertain about. When you come back to a question after a break, you may find that you are able to answer it correctly straight away. If you are still unsure, have a guess. You are not penalised for incorrect answers, so **do not leave a question unanswered!**

Integrated Case Study
Assessment

chapter

1

Gathering information

1 The adviser

1.1 Building the relationship

The relationship between an adviser and the client is vital to the process of **giving financial advice**. If this advice is to be **suitable**, and if it is to be presented to the client in a way which will **motivate him to take action**, the process must be conducted in an **environment of trust**. From an early stage, therefore, the client needs to understand exactly what he can expect from the adviser, and can start to develop that trust.

Professional financial planning advice is an **important and valuable service**, and the client should be aware, for example, that the process is a lot more than someone just trying to sell a particular product. Without an **overall understanding**, it may be difficult for the client to appreciate why such lengthy factfinding is needed, and why so much information which he regards as **confidential** is necessary as a **preliminary**.

The adviser will want to **introduce himself** personally (assuming the client is new to him) and as part of this, there may also be a **reminder** of the way in which the contact with the client was initiated. For example, it may be as a result of the client responding to an **advertisement**, or there may have been a **referral** from an existing client. (Where there has been a referral, mentioning this should make it easier to ask the new client for referrals at a later stage.) To some extent this will also form part of the **ice-breaking** process which must occur at the start of any meeting, so there will be ordinary conversation linked into this part of the meeting.

The **range of services** on offer and the approach which will be taken by the adviser will be discussed at this stage. For example, does the firm **specialise** in advice in a particular area or provide a **full financial planning service**? Are there areas on which advice is **not offered**, for example direct equity investment? Are there other areas of **potential interest** such as general insurance advice? Might the initial meeting lead on to the adviser introducing a **specialist** to deal with certain parts of the client's needs, for example pension planning? As the financial services world becomes increasing complex and as clients recognise that advice in most cases needs to take an **holistic view** (in other words take into account all the client's financial circumstances) this initial outlining of scope is a necessary first stage.

The **regulatory position** should also be covered at this point. The client needs to understand whether the client and his firm are **independent**, or **tied** to a particular product provider (or, with the abolition of **polarisation**, whether they are **'multi-tied'** to a number of providers). The client must also understand what this means in terms of the service being offered.

Regulatory requirements also need to be observed during the early part of the meeting. This means giving the client a **business card** and a copy of the firm's **Initial Disclosure Document** and **Terms of Business**. Different firms have **different strategies** in relation to the terms of business. Some provide this to the client by post before the meeting, and others rely on the adviser passing it over during the meeting. In any event, the **content** should be **explained** so that the client can relate it to his particular circumstances and can view the advice which is eventually given in context. Similarly, as well as simply giving the client a business card, the arrangements for **contacting the adviser**, if necessary, should be made clear.

1.2 Introducing the factfind

The **purpose** of any meeting will reflect the stage which has been reached in the process of giving advice. The **initial meeting** is likely to be primarily focused on **factfinding**, in other words collecting the information which the adviser needs in order to give **suitable advice**. From the client's point of view, the time taken for the adviser to factfind may seem long – the process can often take a couple of hours or more. Unless the client understands the importance of the process, he is unlikely to be willing to spend the necessary time, and indeed may be inclined to **abbreviate** answers or even **leave out** information entirely in order to reduce the time involved. This in turn may **affect the ability** of the adviser to formulate appropriate and attractive recommendations.

The adviser will therefore need to **explain** that by the end of the meeting he needs to have built up a **complete and accurate** picture of the client, including his **current circumstances** and his **future objectives**. It is the difference between where the client is currently and where he would wish to be in financial terms that determines his **needs**. Without full factfinding, needs cannot be fully identified and solutions put forward may not be the most appropriate.

Most firms use a form to allow the adviser to ensure that he collects the necessary information. This may be called a **factfind**, factfinding form, a financial planning questionnaire, a personal financial questionnaire, or similar. The detailed **structure** of the factfind form will vary from firm to firm, but this will be more to do with order and layout than content. However, forms will generally **reflect the markets addressed** by different firms. A firm which deals primarily with young couples with limited means and usually limited existing assets may have a form which focuses more on protection needs than anything else. On the other hand, a firm which targets **older individuals** with an emphasis on **investment** will focus on this area. This does not mean that advisers should only ask questions which are prompted by the form. Instead, they need to be **alert** to the need to build a **complete picture** and to explore all **relevant areas** in detail. The form should therefore act more as a **prompt** than as a script for the meeting, and indeed if the adviser simply goes through the form asking the questions as printed, this will make the factfinding process seem like an interrogation. In reality, the best factfinding occurs in a **conversational** manner and this makes it easier for a client to provide information.

From a **regulatory** point of view, remember that the **obligation** on the adviser is to take the steps necessary to **know the client**. This means that although completing the factfind form may allow **sufficient information** to be obtained in many cases, it may not do so in all cases, and in more **complex** circumstances there may be the need to collect significant amounts of **additional information**. It will certainly not meet the regulatory objectives simply to complete a factfind form without further thought, and neither will this be the right approach from the client's point of view.

An example of a factfind form (Financial Planning Questionnaire) is given at the end of this Chapter.

2 Questioning technique

2.1 Open and closed questions

Advisers need to adopt a good questioning technique. There are various different types of question, and it is useful to consider particularly the use of **closed questions** and **open questions**.

Closed questions are those which are designed to elicit a **specific** piece of **information**, such as a date of birth, or an income figure. Here are some examples.

- Could you please tell me your date of birth?
- Are you married?
- How many children do you have?

The answer to a **closed question** will usually take the form of a **single word**, or a **short phrase**. Very often, the answer could simply be 'Yes' or 'No'. Closed questions can gather a lot of information in a **short time**, but the person answering the questions will feel as if he is being cross-examined, and will soon become **disinterested** in the process as a whole if faced with a **long sequence** of questions of this type.

Open questions give the client the opportunity to **express his views**, or his **feelings**, and invite a **longer response** which will usually require more thought. Examples are:

- What are the schools like in this area?
- How do you feel about investments which can go down as well as up in value?

Questions of this sort provide information which can help to **identify the considerations** which are **most important** to the client and can give clues as to how he would react to different recommendations.

A further variation on the open question is the **probing question**. There are many occasions in everyday conversation where the answer to a question seems **incomplete** and needs to be extended in order to ensure that the meaning is conveyed accurately. Sometimes during a conversation, it may seem that there is something unsaid which would explain a comment in more detail, perhaps **explaining** why a person has a **particular opinion**. In factfinding for a financial adviser, it is important that such areas are **probed** to improve the overall understanding of the adviser.

For example, suppose the adviser asks the client the question set out above about his feelings in relation to **investments** that can go down as well as up in value. Suppose the client replies: 'Oh, I wouldn't touch anything like that any more.' The adviser could simply take this at face value and note that the adviser appears to have a **cautious attitude to risk**. However this would fail to take advantage of the **opportunity** to probe the comment to get more information about his attitude and perhaps the **origin of his concern**. The adviser might therefore say: 'I see. Have you had investments that you have been unhappy with in the past?' Finding out what a client wishes to **avoid**, and why, will often play a major role in helping to identify what **investments** would be **appropriate**.

Probing questions can be very simple, for example as follows.

- Could you just explain that in a bit more detail please?
- So how does that affect your view of your current situation?

In **everyday conversation** all these question types arise and are used **naturally** and **normally**. There is nothing different about the way in which a factfinding interview should be conducted, except perhaps the existence of a **defined overall objective**.

The use of different questioning styles also affects the **tempo** of the meeting. **Open questions** take **longer** to answer (and to think about the answer). They therefore **slow progress** down, whilst **closed questions** can be handled much more **quickly**. Using different styles of question can therefore be a useful tool in **controlling the pace** of questioning too.

2.2 Phrasing and ordering questions

If an adviser asks a self-employed client 'What are your net relevant earnings?' he is unlikely to **understand** what he has been asked unless he is an accountant by profession. There is no point asking questions which are not understood by the client, and although this is essentially an obvious point to make, even experienced advisers find it easy to **lapse into jargon** at times. As in most fields which require expertise, technical terms and abbreviations abound in financial services, and discipline is required to ensure that **questions** are **phrased** so that the client understands what is being asked. If not, the client will sometimes ask what adviser means, but could **misunderstand** and give the wrong answer, or could **leave out** something which is relevant.

Although the adviser should always make a **conscious effort to avoid jargon**, it is important to take into account the **client's level of knowledge** and awareness of financial matters so that the client is not irritated by explanations of basic matters with which he is already familiar.

The **order and progression** of questions is important too. For example, if an adviser asks:

- Have you got enough life cover?
- Are you happy with your investments?

The client is likely to answer 'Yes'. If the client believed otherwise, he would presumably have done something about it. Alternatively, the client might answer that he is **not happy** with the **current situation** and that this is why the adviser has been contacted. In neither case has the adviser learnt anything from the question, and may indeed have **lost ground**.

On the other hand, a **sequence of questions** might be more effective. For example:

- If you were to die, how would your family's outgoings alter?

- So what level of income, after tax, would be needed to cover them?

- How much income would be available from your pension scheme or from other sources?

- You have some life assurance, which could be invested to provide further income. What interest rate do you think we could safely assume this might earn?

- So, there would be a shortfall in their income of £x, if you were to die. Is it important to you to provide for that shortfall?

This sequence of questions is **simplified** and **condensed**, but it shows how the client can be **helped** to **recognise** and **understand** his needs, at the same time as going some way to **quantifying** them. This is a result of asking questions in a **logical order**, and in an **understandable** manner.

2.3 Factfinding areas

It is difficult to provide an exhaustive list of all the areas in which questions may need to be asked as part of the factfinding process. As already discussed, the adviser always needs to be alert to identify areas where questioning can usefully be extended. However the main areas are as follows:

- **Personal details**. This will include obvious items such as name, address and contact details. Date of birth, sex and smoker or non-smoker status could also be recorded at this stage. It is important to collect information regarding **dependants**, and at this initial stage, similar details might also be included in relation to the client's **partner**, who may also be in attendance at the meeting. It is usually advisable to meet with both partners if possible. The necessary details are considered in more depth below. Further

BPP)))
PROFESSIONAL EDUCATION

points might also be included at this point, for example a comment about the individual's **general health**, perhaps any history of **health problems within the family**, and also softer information, regarding the individual's **hobbies and other activities**. These aspects may provide some insights into the client's **attitudes**, and also give the opportunity to establish a **conversational basis** for factfinding.

- **Dependants.** This should include details of **dependent children**, including their ages. For teenagers, the adviser should try to ascertain if possible the **period** for which the children are **likely to be dependent**, for example through a planned **university** education. Parents may also wish to contribute to their children's' future financial well being, for example by providing a **new car** or a **deposit for a house**. Older children may also be included in this section of the factfind because although they may not be dependent, they may still be important from the point of view of the parent's **financial planning**. A further important point is to identify any **other individuals** who might be **wholly or partially** dependent on the client. For example there may be an **elderly relative** for whom the client is providing some financial help, possibly by meeting all or part of the **fees for a nursing home**. Such aspects can make an important difference to the client's **priorities and needs**.

- **Occupational details.** Details should be collected of the **source** of any **earned income**, including whether it arises from **employment** or **self-employment**. This is the time to discuss the **security** and **consistency** of the income, and aspects such as whether any **promotions** are to be expected. Details of **benefits in kind** for employees can be important since these may affect the individual's personal needs, for example where the employer provides a car, and the individual therefore does not need to finance one personally. There may also be aspects such as **share options** which may contribute to the individual's overall financial situation.

- **Previous employment.** Employment history may be important, particularly if there are benefits such as **preserved pensions** which relate to past employments. This may also help to give the adviser an **impression** of the client's **career** as a whole, and for example whether he tends to move quickly from job to job or is more likely to remain with one employer for a long period.

- **Income details.** It is important to establish **how much income** the client and his partner, if applicable, receive. This may be partly from **earned** income, partly from **pensions** or **other benefits**, and partly from **investments** or other sources. Income here should focus on net income after tax, or should provide sufficient details for the adviser to calculate what the net income after tax would be. The extent of any income over expenditure will determine the **ability** of the client to **fund regular amounts**, for example premiums to life assurance policies or regular contributions to pension arrangements.

- **Outgoings.** In some cases clients will be able to identify their **total outgoings** and hence their **available spendable income** quite straightforwardly, but in other cases it will be necessary to go through the client's expenditure **item by item** in order to get a satisfactory picture. The factfind form is likely to include a **template** which allows information on outgoings to be collected. It is important to take account of necessary outgoings, for example the cost of heating and lighting, rent or mortgage payments, but also account needs to be taken of **voluntary expenditure**. There will be expenditure on hobbies and pastimes, clothing, travel and so on, which is not always in the category of necessary expenditure, but nevertheless the client would wish it to continue. A financial adviser's recommendations **cannot ignore** these wishes. It is also important to take account of **regular contributions** to existing financial products as part of this exercise.

- **Assets.** A **snapshot** of the client's **current asset position** will be relevant from a number of points of view. Most obviously it provides part of the picture of where the client currently is from a financial point of view. Existing assets will also give the adviser some information as to the client's **investment experience**, and perhaps give an insight into his **attitude to risk**.

- **Liabilities.** The **largest liability** for many people is their **mortgage**, and this will need to be protected in the event of the client's **death or incapacity**, so it will influence **protection needs**. There may be **other loan arrangements**, for example hire purchase agreements or credit cards, which should also be taken into account in assessing protection needs. These assets will also give an insight into the **lifestyle** and **priorities** of the client or clients.

- **Insurance policies.** Details should be collected of existing **life insurance** and other protection policies such as **permanent health insurance** (income protection insurance) **critical illness** cover, **private medical insurance** and so on. This should include details of the amount of cover, and any options, in particular **increase** options. Some policies will be earmarked for particular purposes, for example protecting a mortgage, and this should also be recorded. If the policy is for a fixed **term**, this also needs to be recorded so that the date on which cover ends may be important.

- **Regular savings.** This might include **endowment policies** or regular contributions to an **ISA** or **regular savings plan** linked to unit trusts etc. In each case the adviser should establish details of the type of savings arrangement involved, and the method of its investment, as well as the **level** of saving and **current value.** In some cases the client may not know the current value, for example in the case of an endowment policy, in which case details of the start date should be recorded as a minimum. The actual value can be **checked** later. Some arrangements, in particular endowments, have a **fixed term** and may not be accessible without significant **penalties** prior to the maturity date and this is also relevant information. Once again some arrangements might have **specific purposes** and these should also be noted.

- **Pension arrangements.** Pension arrangements might be in the form of membership of an **occupational pension scheme** or personal arrangements such as **personal pensions.** Full details of benefits should be collected, including **related benefits** such as life assurance, spouse's pensions and so on. In the case of an occupational scheme, particularly if it is on a defined benefit basis, the client may have an **explanatory booklet** which will give a useful summary of the benefits provided, and the adviser may well find it useful to have sight of this booklet and perhaps take a copy of it. The information collected should not relate just to the current pension arrangement, but should also include details of **preserved pensions** from previous employments and any arrangements such as personal pensions to which the individual is no longer contributing. There may also be **pension transfer vehicles** which have taken the place of benefits which would otherwise have been preserved, for example, under an occupational scheme.

- **State pensions.** Few clients will know precisely what their **expectation** of State benefits is, but it is useful to find out whether there are any particular circumstances which could reduce the benefits which might otherwise be expected, for example prolonged periods of **self-employment** which would reduce the entitlement to **S2P/SERPS** benefits. Particularly for clients who are quite close to retirement, it will be useful to suggest to the client that he obtains an **estimate** of State benefits from the DWP (a simple process which can be completed on paper or via the Internet) or to assist the client in obtaining such an estimate.

- **Estate planning.** Some clients will have made specific estate planning arrangements, details of which should be recorded. The adviser will also want to check whether the individual has made a will, and if so whether it is **up to date** and continues to reflect his **current intentions.** If there is a will, details of its provisions should be requested, and it may also be useful to obtain details of the **executors**, particularly if they might also be involved as **trustees** in relation to any financial planning solutions.

- **Inheritances and trusts.** Much wealth is passed down from generation to generation through inheritances and an **expectation** may affect an individual's **attitude** to long term aspects of financial planning. Sometimes an individual will have rights which can be readily identifiable under a trust, and which are therefore more certain, and these will also be part of the factfinding exercise.

As already discussed, no factfind form can on its own be certain of covering **all areas** which are relevant to particular individuals. The intention behind the design of most forms is to provide the **basis** for the information which is **most likely** to be necessary and relevant in typical cases. Nevertheless there may be considerable amounts of **additional information** required in some cases. An obvious example is where an individual owns his **own business**, or a substantial **shareholding in a private company**. This situation is likely to be discovered when obtaining details of the individual's earned income (and other income if dividends are involved). However details of the **value** of the business and extent of the individual's ownership will need to be explored in some detail. Because of the **difficulty** in valuing businesses without actually agreeing a sale, the basis used to determine any assumed value should also be discussed in some detail. The adviser can then make a **judgement** as to the extent to which the value is **reliable**, and how easy it will be to dispose of the business or the shares when necessary.

2.4 Analysing information

So far, we have considered **collecting** information, but it is then important that the adviser considers and **analyses** the information thoroughly. This will occur partly during the factfind process itself and may prompt the adviser to ask further questions. For example, where the individual has a partner of the opposite sex, it will be important for the adviser to establish whether the couple are **legally married**. It is often the case that couples within a long term relationship choose to remain unmarried for various reasons. The client may not realise the importance of **marital status** from a financial planning point of view, and the adviser may need to approach the subject with sensitivity. However, there are many ways in which this is relevant, for example:

- Legally married spouses automatically have **insurable interest** in each other

- A gift from one spouse to another is **not regarded as a disposal** for CGT purposes, whereas a gift between unmarried individuals is

- A transfer between spouses (which might occur if investments are transferred in order to improve their income tax treatment) is **exempt from IHT**

- Similarly, **on death**, any amounts left to a legal spouse are **entirely exempt from IHT**

This list is not exhaustive, but shows the extent to which marital status may impact on an evaluation of the individual's situation and the options open to them. Note that parallel provisions apply to registered **civil partners**, but not to other same sex partners.

Amongst other areas which may repay further probing are the following.

- The position of **adult children**, who may be intended to **inherit** on the client's death, and to whom transfers may usefully be made during the client's lifetime in order to **reduce** the potential **inheritance tax** on death

- Other family members, for example **grandchildren**, may also be intended to benefit in the long term and there can be tax advantages in making provision for them sooner rather than later

- If there are **existing investments**, a consideration of the risk involved in them may not only give an indication of the client's **attitude to risk**, but may also highlight a need for **reorganisation**

- The existence of **liabilities** may well point to a need for **protection**, but also it may be that existing protection policies which are not specifically earmarked against those liabilities would in reality be needed to deal with them, leaving the client rather **less protected** than he believes

- In addition, although many people protect their **mortgage** with a **life assurance policy**, it is significantly less common for other risks, such as the inability of the individual to work as a result of **incapacity**, to be covered

- Where a **will** has been made, the **inheritance tax implications** should be considered and thought given to whether the will is as tax efficient as it could be

Once again this list is by no means exhaustive, but it does given an indication of areas where further probing may be necessary, and the extent to which an alert adviser may need to **extend questioning** beyond the routine contents of the factfind form.

3 Needs and objectives

3.1 Real needs and perceived needs

Having collected all relevant information from a client, the next stage in the process is to identify accurately the **needs** which should be addressed as part of the financial planning process. Although this sounds as if it should be an easy process, there is much to be taken into account.

First of all, the needs which a prospective client might readily identify might not really be the needs which are most pressing. Many people would like to be rich, and to be able to live in style, without the need to work, and without any financial worries. This may be a **desire**, and therefore a **perceived need**, but there are often more pressing concerns to be dealt with. For example, **protecting** the family's financial position in the event of the **death or disability** of the breadwinner is certainly a real need and indeed an immediate need. It is perhaps less exciting, and even less palatable to address, but for **most people** this must be considered a **first priority**. Real needs are therefore not always the same as perceived needs, and an important part of the adviser's role is to help the client to **identify** his real needs and to **prioritise** them in terms of **objectives**.

The factfinding process will provide the necessary information for this task, but identifying the needs will need skilful **evaluation** of that information. It will be the client who must decide what his needs really are, and who must place a priority upon them, but it will be the adviser who **guides** him to his **conclusion**.

3.2 Current and future needs

It is also necessary to build up a picture of the client's **current** and **future needs**. Saving money for a later date, for example in the context of **retirement planning**, comes under the heading of future rather than current needs. Future needs are those which involve **long term planning**; current needs are essentially those which derive from the answers of the 'what if?' variety. For example:

- What would happen if the breadwinner died?
- What would happen if you were disabled?
- What would happen if your partner were no longer able to look after the home or the children?

These are circumstances which can arise **suddenly** and without warning, and **protection** against these circumstances is of **great importance**. This is not to say that future needs are unimportant, but current needs may be **more pressing**, and when we come to discuss **prioritisation** below, one of the things which must be taken into account is whether any particular need is current or future.

4 Quantifying and prioritising needs

4.1 Shortfall

Quantifying needs is really a matter of identifying any **shortfall** which exists between the client's current situation and the position in which the client would like to find himself. The client is not therefore just one of examining factual information relating to existing provision, but it must also take into account the client's **financial objectives**. Then once his needs have not only been identified, but also have been quantified, the process of **prioritisation** can begin.

4.2 Capital or income needs

It will also be necessary to consider whether each **need** is best met by the provision of a **lump sum**, by the generation of an **income**, or by a combination of the two.

A **lump sum** generally gives more **flexibility**. It can be invested to provide income, but it would be possible to retain the ability to **draw on the capital** should this become necessary or desirable.

On the other hand, the **level of income** which can be provided will **depend** on conditions (particularly **interest rates**) at the time the money is invested. It may, depending on the way the investment is made, **fluctuate** as conditions change. Also, as capital is withdrawn, this will reduce the prospect of future income. All of these factors mean that there is an element of **uncertainty** if an individual relies on a lump sum to provide a given level of income in the future. For example, suppose someone wanted to **estimate** what would be a reasonable **interest rate** to assume could be achieved on investing a lump sum in a secure environment like a deposit account. Their answer ten or even five years ago might have been considerably **different** to their answer today, when inflation and interest rates are at a **relatively low level**. The uncertainty also means that it is **unwise to underestimate** the capital which would be needed to meet a given income need and any assumptions made should be **conservative**.

A further factor to consider is that some allowance should be made to protect the value of the income from **inflation** over the period for which it is required. Otherwise an income level which **started** off at an **adequate** level will gradually be **eroded** in terms of its spending power with the result that the provision becomes inadequate. This is particularly important where the period of time for which the income is required is **lengthy**, or indefinite.

Where arrangements are made to provide an income directly, this may provide more certainty, but the fact that the income is **guaranteed** may make it **expensive** to provide. However, where the income is provided only for a specified period, this is likely to be less costly.

An example of this is the **family income benefit** policy, which pays a **regular income** in the form of instalments of the sum insured following the **death** of the life insured, through to the **end of the original term**. This type of arrangement can be very useful, and certainly it provides **low cost cover**, but its limitations must be fully understood.

Advantages and disadvantages of Family Income Benefit

Family Income Benefit cover is designed for a situation where an income would be required to cover the period between the death of the life insured and, for example, an estimated point in time when dependants (typically children) will become financially independent.

The cover has advantages and disadvantages compared to term assurance cover, which would generate a cash sum which could be invested to provide income.

Advantages

- Low cost
- Certainty of agreed level of income
- Can build in increases to income level (selected at start of cover)
- Can exchange income benefit for lump sum at time of claim

Disadvantages

- No possibility of extending benefit term
- Basis of alternative lump sum is generally at discretion of insurer
- No access to capital if benefits taken as income
- Income basis pre-selected and inflexible

Particularly when dealing with life cover needs, it is **generally preferable** where possible to look towards the provision of a **lump sum**, because of the **control and flexibility** that this brings. In addition, while the needs of a family are perhaps at their greatest while any children are dependent, the **timescale** over which the situation persists can be **difficult to predict**, particularly if the likelihood of the children progressing to university or college education is uncertain.

In other situations where the need is to **replace a source of income**, it may be more natural to provide **benefits in income form**. Examples of this are **income protection insurance** (IPI, also known as **permanent health insurance** or PHI) and **pension arrangements** of various sorts.

So far we have only considered situations where the need is to provide for an **income**, and discussed whether the needs should be met by means of a **lump sum** or a **specific income benefit**. It is important however also to give consideration to any potential **lump sum requirements**. This might include **debt repayment**, but this is by no means the only such need. For example, a person who suffers an accident and becomes **disabled** will certainly need to have a source of income which is not dependent on their working. However, there could also be other needs, for example **modifying the home** to allow for a wheelchair, or meeting the **costs of convalescence**. These may be best dealt with by means of a **lump sum**.

This underlines the fact that **IPI** (which provides an income) and **critical illness benefit** (which is payable as a lump sum) should **not be seen as alternative** means of providing the same cover. They fulfil **different needs** and often an individual would ideally have both types of cover in force to provide fully for his needs.

Similarly in **retirement** a **lump sum** may be needed, or at least be desirable, as well as an income. This could, for example, pay for **'the holiday of a lifetime'**, buy a new car, or help towards the cost of renovating and furnishing a dream **retirement cottage**. Later in this study text we consider various products in relation to needs, and the adviser needs to match them to his client's circumstances with care.

5 Calculating the shortfall

5.1 Basic approach

Whatever the need being considered, the process of calculating any **shortfall** will follow a similar path, which can be summarised as follows:

- Calculate the **requirement** for income or lump
- Take into account **existing arrangements**, including State benefits where applicable
- Calculate the **shortfall** between existing provision and what is required

There are a number of factors which can complicate this calculation, however, and we consider the most important of these in the remainder of this section.

5.2 Inflation

Some allowance will need to be made for inflation in two senses. First, if the need being considered is a **future need**, for example retirement income or future school fees, it will be necessary to **estimate the amount** which will be **needed** at the relevant time. If no allowance is made for inflation, the amount provided will certainly be too little.

Second, where the need is for income (whether provided specifically, or intended to be generated by a lump sum), the **value of that income** will be eroded by inflation whilst it is being paid. The calculation should therefore allow for the income to **increase during payment**.

To illustrate the importance of this, simply consider an individual who retires at age 60, with a **level pension** of £10,000 pa. By the time he reaches 85, assuming inflation has been running at a constant annual rate of 3%, the value in **real terms** of his pension will have **more than halved**, to around £4,800 pa. In some circumstances, income may be automatically protected from inflation, fully or partly. For example, **State pensions** are **automatically inflation proofed** in line with the RPI, and sometimes increase more quickly if the Government so decides. Pensions arising from occupational pension schemes will also increase in a number of circumstances, and in particular if they were accrued after 6 April 1997 under a defined benefit scheme, through the requirement for **Limited Price Indexation (LPI)**. This inflation proofing may not fully protect the income from inflation however.

Limited Price Indexation (LPI)

The LPI requirement applies under defined benefit occupational schemes and requires that benefits accrued from 6 April 1997 increase in line with the RPI, subject to a limit of 5% pa for benefits accrued between 6 April 1997 and 5 April 2005, or 2.5% for benefits accrued from 6 April 2005.

Under the Pensions Act 2004 (which introduced this reduction in the limit from 5% to 2.5%), the requirement for LPI increases to benefits arising under defined contribution schemes was abolished entirely for benefits coming into payment from 6 April 2005.

Note that different requirements apply to contracted out rights in the form of Guaranteed Minimum Pension (GMP) benefits, though there is now no requirement for increases in relation to Protected Rights coming into payment from 6 April 2005.

The **need for inflation proofing** is generally considered in the light of the need to maintain the **purchasing power** of the income concerned. This is a clear need, but it is worth considering whether further provision is desirable, particularly if the income is to be drawn for a long period of time. **Living standards** for the average person or family tend to **increase** over the years, largely as a result of the fact that their income is usually derived largely from **earnings** which tend to **increase faster** than prices. This means that someone whose income is increasing only in line with prices is likely to gradually fall behind the increase in living standards which other members of the community enjoy. This is one of the reasons why there has been considerably controversy in recent years relating to the fact that **State pensions** are only automatically linked to **prices**, whilst many people believe they should be linked to **earnings**. Clearly however, this would substantially **increase costs** from the government's point of view.

5.3 Growth

For **savings and investment** arrangements, some allowance will need to be made for the **growth** which is expected to be achieved. The basis on which **projections** can be given is of course **regulated**, but generally there will be three figures based on different growth assumptions which will give the individual some idea of the effect that different levels of growth can have, and an idea of the **range of possible benefits** (though the final outcome could be more or less than the highest and lowest figures given in the projection). In practice, it is important that the **actual growth** achieved is **reviewed** rather than reliance being placed in the long term on **projections**. Again in planning terms, it is likely to be advisable to **err on the side of caution** in expectations of growth.

5.4 Short term and long term needs

Some needs are likely to be **immediate cash needs**, whilst others will require **income in the long term**. These differences will also need to be allowed for. For example, in considering life assurance, if the breadwinner of the family dies, there will be a need for immediate cash to provide for the **payment of debts**, and for **funeral expenses**.

In addition, **income** will be needed to meet the **ongoing expenses** of the family. Part of this income will be needed only in the relatively short term, for example to cover the additional expenses that arise **whilst children are dependent**. Some will be needed in the long term, particularly to **support the surviving partner**, or contribute to the income needs of the partner if he or she has some income in their own right.

5.5 Interest rates

A further important assumption is the **rate of interest** which could reasonably be anticipated on the investment of a lump sum where this approach to the provision of income is adopted. Where the investment is intended to provide income to meet basic needs, it will **not be appropriate to take risks**, and as a result, a modest rate of return needs to be assumed. In current conditions, perhaps 3.25% pa net of basic rate tax would not be unreasonable. The assumption needs to be **agreed with the client**, but the adviser will have an important role in ensuring that the client **does not make unrealistic assumptions** and as a result underestimate the lump sum needed.

6 Shortfall calculation on death

6.1 Basis of calculation

As already discussed, the first part of calculating a **shortfall** is to determine the level of income and/or lump sum required. The **basis** of the calculation will depend on the **circumstances** concerned, and in this example we consider the position which could arise on **death**. Although the basis of the calculation will be **similar** for other circumstances, for example a family member becoming **incapacitated**, the particular factors which need to be considered will differ.

In this case we will consider in turn:

- Immediate cash requirements
- Short term income needs
- Longer term income needs

We will consider the basis of this calculation in relation to a **young couple** called Martin and Sylvia. They are in their 20s, married with a young son, Matthew, who is just one year old. Like many young married couples, before Matthew was born they had **not paid much attention to life assurance**, although their **mortgage** is covered by a **term assurance policy**. They have **no other policies** in existence.

We will assume that Martin earns **£24,000 basic salary**, and also receives about **£4,000 pa in overtime** payments. He is a **member of an occupational pension scheme**, which provides him with **life assurance cover** of £48,000 (twice salary) and would also provide a **widow's pension** of £8,000 pa which is **inflation proofed**.

Sylvia does not currently work outside the home, and has **no preserved occupational scheme benefits**.

We will consider the **situation** which would arise **if Martin were to die**.

6.2 Immediate cash requirements

As with all elements of the calculation, factfinding will give the adviser information as to the areas in which needs will arise. No generalised list can therefore be sure of dealing with the actual needs of particular clients.

The most obvious and probably the largest need will be to **repay the mortgage**, but this, we are told, is already covered by a **term assurance policy** in this case. The adviser should check that this is **adequate**. In the past **lenders** have usually **required** life assurance to be arranged to cover any mortgage, but these days they are **less insistent**. This can mean that in some cases mortgages are arranged with **no life assurance protection**, with the lender having the property as security, but leaving the surviving family unprotected if the ongoing mortgage payments cannot be met.

Where life assurance is arranged at the same time as the **mortgage**, it is likely to be for an **appropriate amount** and for an **appropriate term**. However, mortgage arrangements are frequently **changed**, particularly with the high level of activity in the re-**mortgage** market, and if a mortgage has been moved from one lender to another, it is not unusual for the amount of the loan to be **increased**. Problems then may arise if the amount of life cover in force is not adjusted in the same way. We will however assume for the sake of this example that the mortgage is fully covered.

Other borrowings may need to be repaid and could be substantial. This could include **credit card balances**, a bank **overdraft** and other credit agreements, for example **hire purchase** arrangements. It can be very important from the point of view of the financial security of the survivors that these arrangements are dealt with through life assurance cover.

Funeral expenses will also need to be met and may involve costs running into several thousand pounds.

There is also likely to be a need for an **emergency fund** which can be drawn on to meet **unforeseen costs**. As a general rule, somewhere between three and six months' income should be allowed, though this may vary, particularly if there is an emergency fund already in existence.

In some cases, there may also be an **inheritance tax liability** to consider, but in this case we will assume that Sylvia will inherit the bulk of the estate which will therefore be an exempt transfer from an inheritance tax point of view. This is an illustration of the importance of determining the **marital status** of clients during the factfind process, since an inheritance tax liability could easily arise if the couple were not legally married.

The amounts of these requirements must be determined in the light of the circumstances of the couple, and with their agreement. Here we will assume the following.

	£
Credit card balances	600
Overdraft	Nil
Other credit agreements	800
Funeral expenses	2,000
Emergency fund	7,500
Total	10,900

6.3 Short term needs

Matthew is likely to be **dependent for at least 15 years**, and perhaps longer, so an income should be provided to meet the associated costs through this period. A starting point for this calculation is the **current cost**, but certainly the allowance for expenses needs to take account of the fact that they are likely to increase as children get older. This is not just a result of inflation, though this is relevant, but follows from the **enlarged range of activities** likely to be followed as Matthew gets older. In addition, a **single parent** is likely to need to spend more on **childminding**, simply because there is no partner with whom to share the responsibility.

Further costs would arise if **school fees** were likely to be needed, and **intentions** in this respect should be determined during **factfinding**. For the purposes of this example, it is assumed that the parents expect Matthew to attend State school. In this case, a reasonable estimate of **short term income expenses** associated with Matthew might be £4,000 pa. As always, careful factfinding is necessary to determine the needs of specific clients.

6.4 Longer term income needs

These will largely revolve around the **living expenses** of the **surviving spouse**. The net income of the family is a good starting point here, allowing for any part already taken into account for short term income needs.

Martin's **take home pay** would be around £1,500 per month, after allowing for **tax** and **National Insurance**, as well as his **overtime**. The exact figure will depend on such things as pension contributions, and the adviser should check recent payslips as the best guide.

If Martin died, his income would be lost entirely. **Some outgoings** would **reduce** too, particularly in this case the **mortgage repayments**, since the debt will have been discharged by the proceeds of the life assurance arrangement. Some of the income will currently be used to cover expenditure which is classified under short term income needs for our purposes, and this should also be taken into account.

Suppose that this means that the **long term need for income replacement** is around £500 less than Martin's take home pay. This gives a figure of £1,000 per month net of tax.

6.5 Other sources of income and capital

The **life assurance policy** covers the mortgage and this has already been **taken into account** in our calculation. If Martin dies, the **pension scheme** will provide a cash **lump sum** of £48,000, and an **income for Sylvia** of £8,000 per year before tax. There will be a widowed parent's allowance payable from the State, which currently would be £4,380 pa before tax. Taken together, the income from the pension scheme and the widowed parent's allowance will provide a net income of around £920 per month. This assumes Sylvia claims the single person's **income tax personal allowance**, but has no further tax allowances.

It is assumed that there are **no other sources of income or capital** which would arise in this situation.

6.6 The shortfall

There is an **immediate cash requirement** of £10,900. No provision has yet been made for this need, and this will therefore need to be covered by means of **life assurance**.

The **pension scheme** will pay out a **lump sum** of £48,000, but this is set against long term needs in the calculation. This is because there could be a **delay in payment of benefits**, and although this should not occur, a **personal life assurance** arrangement would be **more reliable** to deal with short term needs.

The **short term income shortfall** is £4,000 pa net of tax. Once again, the pension scheme benefits are set against long term needs, partly in case there is a delay in their payment, but also because the benefit is **payable throughout Sylvia's life**.

The **long term income needs** come to £1,000 per month, from which we can **deduct** the **State benefits** and **pension scheme income** which total £920 per month. This gives a long term income shortfall of £80 per month net of tax.

This shortfall can be met by **investing the lump sum** from the pension scheme. If the **interest generated** net of basic rate tax is 3.25% pa, the income produced would be £1,560 pa, whereas the long term income shortfall in annual terms is £960 pa. This therefore leaves a **surplus** of £600 pa. This can be used to reduce the short term income need, leaving £3,400 pa still required.

7 Converting the need to a lump sum

In the example, needs have arisen in various forms, and we have identified a **shortfall** in terms of a **requirement for immediate cash**, a need for **short term income** and a need for **long term income**.

Provision could be made for the **short term income requirement** through a **family income benefit arrangement**, or by providing a **lump sum** which can be invested to provide that income.

Calculating the **necessary lump sum** is a matter of **assumption**, and the **calculations** will need to be **reviewed** as investment conditions change. For short term income needs, a simple approach would be to multiply the income requirement by the years over which it is required. The capital invested would produce **interest**, and this would allow for the amount drawn to **increase** through the term. Although **approximate**, this is a reasonable rule of thumb approach to the problem.

For **longer term needs**, it is safest to rely only on the **interest** to provide **income**, rather than assuming that the capital will be drawn down. This reflects the fact that it is **difficult to be sure of the period** for which the income will be required, and if the capital is drawn down, there is a risk that it will be **completely consumed** at a time when Sylvia is still alive and has a continuing income need. It is also **prudent to increase the lump sum** to allow for **inflation**, otherwise the value of both income and capital will decline in real terms over the years.

The extent to which an **adjustment** needs to be made for **inflation** is greatest for younger people because there is a **longer period** over which the income will need to be protected. It is **difficult to be precise** about the extent of any

necessary adjustment, but given the long period involved here, it might be **reasonable to increase** the capital requirement by 50%.

In the example above, therefore, the calculation of the lump sum necessary to provide for their remaining income needs on Martin's death would be as follows:

	£
Immediate cash requirement	10,900
Short term income need (£3,400 x 20 years)	68,000
Total	78,900

This may be **higher than you might have expected** at first sight, and at least in the short term it may not be within the couple's means to provide for this in addition to other needs, for example to provide **protection against Sylvia's death**, or the **incapacity** of either parent. It is precisely because the needs of most people are beyond what they can comfortably afford that the **prioritisation** of benefits is so **important**.

8 Prioritisation

An **adviser's relationship** with a client is a **long term** one, and **financial planning** is in itself a **gradual process**, partly because of changes which occur during the individual's lifetime, but also because of the **constraints of affordability**. Most clients therefore need to prioritise their needs and deal with the most pressing needs first.

The process of **prioritisation** will enable the client to **establish a plan** which allows **some needs** to be addressed (wholly or partly) **immediately**, whilst others will be **deferred**. The existence of such a plan helps to ensure that the needs which are deferred are **not left indefinitely** but are **reviewed** at a later date. Prioritisation is therefore important both from the client's and the adviser's point of view in setting out future expected strategy.

Bear in mind that **needs and priorities will change** over the years, and that the **relative priorities** of different areas of financial planning must be **revisited** at each review meeting, so that decisions are made based on **current circumstances**, and not on those which were expected to apply when the framework was originally established.

Making **priority decisions** is not an easy process, if only because, having recognised his needs, the client will realise that **they all should be dealt with**. However, given that **affordability** considerations will prevent this in almost all cases, priority decisions are required.

These decisions will **vary** from client to client, but it is fair to say that, in general, **current needs should be addressed before future needs**. Current needs are those which provide protection against events which could occur immediately, and perhaps unexpectedly, such as **death** or **disability**.

Current needs must therefore figure **high in the priority order**. On the other hand, the need for **retirement planning and other future needs** is also pressing, because even when retirement seems a long way ahead, it is important to recognise that building up resources over a **long period** of time is **considerably easier** than trying to do so at the last minute. In many cases, therefore, the final outcome of the prioritisation process will be a **combination** of plans designed to address a number of needs, with emphasis placed on current needs, but with some provision being made which is directed towards future needs.

FINANCIAL PLANNING QUESTIONNAIRE

1. Personal details

	Client	Partner
Surname		
Forenames		
Address (Home)		
Tel Number (Home)		
Address (Work)		
Tel Number (Work)		
Preferred contact method Home/Work Day/Evening		
Date of Birth		
Sex		
Marital Status		
Smoker/Non-Smoker		
General Health		
Any health problems in family background?		
Hobbies/Activities		

Notes

2. Immediate family and other dependants

Name	Relationship	Age	Sex	Occupation	Comments - Health, extent of dependency etc

Notes

3. Occupational Details

	Client	Partner
Employed/Self employed		
Occupation (and position)		
Regular Earned Income		
Review date or accounting period		
Bonus/Overtime etc		
Benefits in kind (eg car, medical insurance etc)		
Share options		
Security/Prospects		
Time in this job		
Any other current source of earnings?		

4. Previous Employment

	Client	Partner
Previous employment or self-employment		
Dates		

Notes

5. Other Advisers

	Client	Partner
Accountant		
Solicitor		
Stockbroker		
Bank Manager		
Doctor		
Financial Advisers		

Notes

6. Income

	Client		Partner		Total	
	Per month	**Per year**	**Per month**	**Per year**	**Per month**	**Per year**
Earned Income						
Income from deposits						
Income from gilts etc						
Income from shares/unit trusts etc						
Rents etc						
Other investment income						
Pensions or annuities						
State benefits						
Total monetary income						
Taxable benefits						
TOTAL INCOME						

Notes

	Client	Partner
Tax allowances		
Tax & NI		
Net income		

7. Outgoings

	Client		Partner		Total	
	Monthly costs	**Annual costs**	**Monthly costs**	**Annual costs**	**Monthly costs**	**Annual costs**
Rent or mortgage						
Utilities						
Council tax						
Repairs/maintenance						
House & contents Ins						
Phone						
Housekeeping						
Miscellaneous						
Car costs						
Other travel expenses						
Papers & magazines						
Holidays						
Clothing						
School fees etc						
Professional subs						
Professional fees						
Loan payments						
Credit cards						
Pension conts						
Life policies						
Other policies						
Regular savings						
Other expenditure						
TOTALS						
				TOTAL OUTGOINGS		

Notes (eg anticipated changes or major expenditures)

8. Assets

	Client	Partner	Joint
Residence			
Other property			
Bank accounts			
Building Society Accounts			
Gilts/Bonds etc			
Life assurance	See Section 10.		
PEPs			
ISAs			
Unit trusts			
Investment trusts/OEICs			
Quoted shares			
Offshore investments			
Unquoted shares			
Child Trust Fund			
Other items (eg antiques/collectables etc)			

Notes

9. Liabilities

	Loan 1	Loan 2	Loan 3
Lender			
In whose name (or joint)?			
Amount outstanding			
Purpose			
Started			
Remaining term			
Interest rate			
Monthly payments			
Fixed/variable etc			
Repayment method			
Associated policies			
Premiums			

Notes

Are there any other outstanding liabilities, such as income tax or CGT liabilities?

10. Life Assurance Policies

	Policy 1	Policy 2	Policy 3	Policy 4
Ins Co				
Life Insured				
Type				
Own life/life of another				
In trust?				
Started				
Maturity				
Sum Insured				
Premium				
Frequency				
Special terms				
Purpose				

11. Other Insurance Policies - (IPI, PMI, Critical Illness etc)

	Policy 1	Policy 2	Policy 3	Policy 4
Ins Co				
Type of policy				
Life Insured				
Benefits				
Other features (deferred period, escalation etc)				
Started				
Term				
Premiums				
Purpose				

12. Regular Savings other than life assurance policies

	1	2	3	4
Institution				
Type				
In whose name				
Contribution				
Frequency				
Investment area				
Other features				
Started				
Term (if applicable)				
Purpose				

Notes

13. Occupational Pension Arrangements

	Client	Partner
Does employer have a scheme?		
Are you eligible?		
Have you joined?		
Date of joining		
Basis of pension benefits		
Current expectation or fund value		
Scheme retirement date		
Expected retirement date		
Life Assurance		
Spouse's/Dependants' Pensions		
Contracted-out?		
Member contributions		
AVCs/FSAVCs		
Preserved pension details from earlier employment		

14. Preserved Pensions

	Client	Partner
Employer		
Benefits/Fund		
Retirement age		

15. Personal Pensions

	Client	Partner
Provider		
Type		
Contribution		
Frequency		
Details of waiver if included		
Investment area		
Other features		
Started		
Current fund		
Selected Pension Age		
Expected retirement age (if different)		
Contracted-out?		
Details of any associated life cover		

Notes

16. State Pensions

	Client	Partner
Basic Pension		
SERPS/S2P		
Graduated Pension		
TOTAL		

17. Estate Planning

	Client	Partner
Will?		
Date made		
Is it up to date?		
Beneficiaries and details		
Any special provisions?		
Executors		
Any planned changes?		

18. Inheritances

	Client	Partner
Are you expecting any inheritance(s)?		
Details		
Are you a beneficiary of any trusts?		
Details		
Any gifts expected or received?		
Details		

19. Attitude to Risk

To what extent are you prepared to accept investment risk?

20. Record of Case

Action	_	Notes
Initial contact date		
Factfind completed		
Terms of business issued		
Meeting dates		

Information outstanding

Declaration

All information will be treated in strict confidence. It will be used to prepare financial planning recommendations, but with no obligation to act upon those recommendations.

Signed

Client

Partner

Financial Adviser

Date

Key chapter points

- At the start of the relationship with a client, a financial adviser needs to ensure that the client is fully aware of the nature of the service he offers.

- It is important to complete the regulatory requirements, such as giving the client a business card and a copy of the firm's Initial Disclosure Document and Terms of Business.

- The initial meeting is likely to focus on factfinding, to ensure the adviser has all the information necessary to provide suitable advice.

- The purpose of factfinding needs to be explained carefully to ensure that the client is not tempted to abbreviate or leave out some details.

- If details are not provided fully, it may mean that the advice given is not complete, or even is not suitable.

- Most firms use factfind forms, but advisers need to be alert to the need to ask additional questions where necessary.

- This is important in terms of the regulatory requirement to 'Know the Client', but it is also a prerequisite of the advice process.

- Questioning technique is an important aspect of factfinding, and advisers should ensure that they used open and closed questions effectively.

- Questions should be asked in a logical order, and in a conversational manner as far as possible.

- The factfind form will guide the various areas which need to be explored, including personal details, and income and outgoings.

- Occupational details should include employment status and any benefits provided as part of the remuneration package, for example, pension benefits.

- Care should be taken to establish the extent to which income is available for financial planning as a result of income, net of tax, exceeding outgoings.

- Assets and liabilities are also important in establishing a client's current position.

- Advisers need to distinguish between real and perceived needs, and current and future needs in guiding the client's priority decisions.

- Quantifying needs requires the shortfall between the current and desired position to be identified in relation to each need.

- An important decision in dealing with income needs is to consider whether it is best to provide specifically for an income benefit or a lump sum which can be invested for income.

- Inflation is an important consideration in dealing with any future need.

- Prioritisation is a necessary aspect of financial planning for most people, because of the difficulty of trying to meet all needs at any one time. It also proves the basis of a plan for the future.

- However, advisers must take account of the fact that needs and priorities do change over time.

- Priority order must be decided by the client but the adviser should guide the client in making these decisions.

Chapter Quiz

1   What is the difference between open and closed questions, and how should they be used?............. (see para 2.1)

2   Why might be important to have details of a client's previous employments?... (2.3)

3   In what ways might the marital status of a client and his partner be important for financial planning purposes? ....(2.4)

4   Are current or future needs likely to be the most immediately important in giving suitable advice to a client? ....(3.2)

5   To meet an income need, what advantages does the provision of a lump sum which can be invested to provide income have over directly providing an income? ....(4.2)

6   What are the stages of a shortfall calculation?...(5.1)

7   What immediate cash requirements might arise on death? ....(6.2)

chapter

2

Existing arrangements

Chapter topic list

1 Collecting information

2 Arrangements to consider

3 Purpose and suitability

4 The effect of change

5 Matters deferred

Key chapter points

1 Collecting information

1.1 Influence on factfinding

Factfinding was discussed in Chapter 1, and this made clear that **extensive factfinding** is an important **prerequisite** of giving proper and **suitable advice** to the client. One of the most important areas to consider is the **information** obtained regarding **existing arrangements**. If this is not tackled in a full and effective way, it is likely that the advice process as a whole will be flawed.

In this chapter, we particularly focus on information relating to the **existing financial arrangements** of the client, and how the adviser should deal with this.

1.2 Range of information

As part of this consideration, it is important to be aware that the **range of information** required here is **wide**, because the **range of existing financial arrangements** is also wide. It includes not only financial products such as life insurance, unit trusts, pension arrangements and so on, but also **other resources** such as the client's **house**, other **property** and **cash** held on deposit or in **NS&I products**.

In addition, **pension** and **other benefits** relating to the client's **employment** will also have an impact on his overall position and financial planning needs.

As with all aspects of factfinding, the adviser must ensure that he has **sufficient information** to assess the **impact of the existing arrangements**, and this may mean going beyond the fixed questions on a factfind form in some cases.

2 Arrangements to consider

2.1 Main residence

For many people, their **major asset** is the **property** in which they live, in other words their **main residence**. Details of the type of property (which may merely be confirmation of your own observation) are important, as well as an indication of the client's estimate of its value. If the property is **leasehold**, as is common with flats in particular, the period of **time remaining** on the lease can be a significant factor also.

Where the client is living in **rented accommodation** at present, there may be **plans to buy** a property in future, or he may expect to **continue renting** in the long term.

The extent to which the property (where owned) has already been used to **secure a loan** will **influence** both the client's **outgoings** and the extent to which the property could be used as **security for further finance** if and when required.

The **mortgage arrangements** themselves will also often be significant. In some cases it may be possible to **rearrange the mortgage** on a more favourable basis, or perhaps gain the benefit of a better interest rate. The method of loan repayment needs to be taken into account in the overall financial plan, and in some cases, it may be appropriate for the repayment basis to be modified.

The **value** of the property (where owned) may **contribute to future financial planning** if it is intended eventually to **trade down** to a cheaper property, so **liberating cash** for an alternative use, for example, the provision of income in retirement.

Advantages and disadvantages of property investment

Property is a popular investment, but there are both advantages and disadvantages, including the following.

Advantages

- No CGT on gains on disposal of main residence
- Investment property generates income (rent) as well as gains
- If bought with a loan, interest can be set against rental income for tax purposes
- Useful diversification if other investments are equity based

Disadvantages

- In case of main residence, the individual cannot treat the property purely as an investment because of the need for somewhere to live

- Difficult to achieve diversification because of size of investment

- Partial disposals are not possible with a single property

- CGT liability likely to arise with property other than a main residence

- Valuation is difficult to be sure of until a sale is agreed

---

2.2 Other property

If the client owns **other property**, either in the UK or abroad, this will also affect the structure of his overall financial planning. For example, a **property overseas** may **reduce holiday costs**, and could even generate a **rental income**.

The **capital value** of the property will also be relevant if the property is to be sold at some point, though it will be important to take account of the need to repay any borrowing, and deal with any **CGT liability that would arise**. (There is no CGT exemption for a second property.)

However the property will be regarded as **part of the client's estate on death**, even though it is located overseas, and could lead to a significant **inheritance tax liability**, for which arrangements may need to be made.

Remember that there may also be a mortgage associated with a second property, and this liability also needs to be considered, both as regards its repayment, and the need to protect the loan in the event of incapacity or death.

2.3 Deposits and NS&I products

Some clients may have no bank or building society accounts whatever, while some will simply have a **cheque book account** for dealing with day to day financial transactions.

In other cases, there will be a number of accounts, ranging from a cheque book account to other accounts intended for **saving or investment**, possibly including some requiring notice periods, or with tax advantages such as a **cash ISA**.

In other cases, there will be holdings in various **NS&I products**. The range of products is wide but **security** is very much to the fore. Some products such as **Savings Certificates** can be very **tax efficient**, particularly for **higher rate taxpayers**.

The extent to which the client has invested on a deposit basis will also start to give an insight into his **attitude to risk**, and the extent to which he seeks **accessible investments.**

Limits on tax advantaged deposit investment

- The cash mini-ISA limit is currently £3,000 per person per tax year

- This limit will remain in place until April 2010 (it was expected to reduce to £1,000 in 2006/07 but the existing higher limit was extended to 2010 in the 2005 Budget)

- Up to £15,000 per person can be invested in each current issue of NS&I Savings Certificates

- There are four current issues (2 and 5 year Fixed Rate and 3 and 5 year Index-linked) giving a total possible investment of £60,000 per person

- A new limit will apply each time a new issue is introduced

Both the cash component of ISAs and NS&I Savings Certificates offer tax free interest payments.

2.4 Life assurance and protection arrangements

Life assurance policies will in some cases be orientated towards **protection**, and in other cases towards **investment**. It is important that the type of policy be identified, and its purpose, as well as details such as the **premium** level, the **term**, and the **potential benefits** both on death and maturity.

In many ways the most illuminating piece of information here is the **purpose for which the policy was established**. In some cases, the client may not have a clear idea of exactly what that purpose was, or perhaps the original purpose is no longer relevant (for example, to deal with a loan which has since been paid off). In others, **particular policies** will be firmly linked to **specific future requirements**. From the answers to questions on this point, the adviser will develop an awareness of the extent to which the client **understands** his existing provisions and the degree to which they deal with his needs.

A further vital piece of information when dealing with existing life assurance policies is whether the policies are **written in trust**. If not, they may in themselves create or increase a liability to **Inheritance Tax (IHT)**.

Importance of trusts

If a policy is written on an own life, own benefit basis, and the life insured dies, the proceeds of the policy will form part of the estate for IHT purposes. If the nil rate band is already used elsewhere and the benefit is not covered by an exemption (for example the inter-spouse exemption) this will mean that 40% of the benefit will be absorbed by the additional IHT liability resulting from the sum insured itself. For example, if the sum insured is £100,000, and the proceeds fall into the estate, the extra IHT liability will be £40,000, leaving a net benefit of only £60,000.

If the policy is written under trust, the proceeds fall outside the estate, and are not subject to IHT, so the beneficiaries receive a net benefit of the whole £100,000.

In addition, if the policy falls into the estate, the proceeds will not be accessible to the beneficiaries until the grant of probate (or letters of administration if the individual dies intestate), and the resulting delay can be several months. This can cause a lot of inconvenience and sometimes even financial hardship in the meantime. If the policy is written in trust, the benefits can be paid to the beneficiaries as soon as they are received from the insurer.

If the policies are in trust, **details of the beneficiaries** may help the adviser identify at least some of those for whom the client feels provision should be made.

The Budget in March 2006 announced changes to the IHT treatment of trusts, which means that additional care will be required in dealing with trust cases in the future.

Other protection policies should also be considered, including:

- Income Protection Insurance or IPI (also known as Permanent Health Insurance or PHI)
- Critical Illness insurance
- Personal accident, sickness and redundancy insurance
- Private medical insurance

2.5 ISAs and PEPs

Many clients will have existing investments in ISAs (Individual Savings Accounts) and PEPs (Personal Equity Plans). These have proved popular investments because of their combination of **flexibility**, **access** and **tax advantage**.

The investment returns within an ISA are **free of tax on income** (except that **dividend tax credits cannot be reclaimed**) and on **capital gains**.

The **range of investments** that may be held within an ISA is wide. There are two separate **components**:

- Stocks and shares
- Cash

Until 2005, there was also a **life insurance component** but this did not prove particularly popular and has effectively been **absorbed into the stocks and shares component** from 6 April 2005, with limits adjusted accordingly.

The **investments** permitted within a **PEP** are the **same** as those allowed within the **stocks and shares component of an ISA**. These include **direct holdings of shares**, provided they are quoted on a recognised stockmarket (though this is not restricted geographically), and related **collective investments** such as unit trusts, OEICs and investment trusts. **Gilts** and **corporate bonds** are also allowed, provided there is at least **five years** remaining until redemption at the time they are purchased.

Note that it is **not permitted to switch money between components**, which can limit flexibility in practice.

2.6 Equity investments

Equity investments (ie **shares** and related **collective investment vehicles**) are particularly **tax efficient** if held within an **ISA** or **PEP**, but are also worthwhile investments where held directly by the individual concerned. Substantial **capital gains** can be achieved (though there is also a risk of loss) and **income**, in the form of dividends will also be generated and can grow if the company or companies in which the investment is made prosper.

Taxation of dividends

Dividends are paid net of a tax credit of 10%, which recognises that dividends are paid from the profits of the company concerned, and these profits have already been subject to corporation tax.

The tax credit fully discharges the tax liability of starting rate and basic rate taxpayers, but cannot be reclaimed by non-taxpayers. Higher rate taxpayers have a further liability to bring the total to 32.5% (of which 10% is discharged by the tax credit).

For example, if a dividend of £180 is received, this represents £200 of gross income, paid net of a tax credit of £20. There is no further liability (nor ability to reclaim)for non-taxpayers, or those subject only to starting or basic rate.

Higher rate taxpayers must pay a total of 32.5% of £200 = £65, of which £20 is covered by the tax credit. They therefore have a further liability of £45.

This treatment of income applies to investments in direct shareholdings, and to holdings in equity based collective investment vehicles such as unit trusts, OEICs and investment trusts.

Details are again important. The adviser will need to determine whether the investments are in **direct shareholdings or collective investments**, and whether there is a **spread** of holdings. Specific details of the holdings should be obtained. A spread of investments is vital in order to reduce risk through **diversification**. We return to the subject of diversification in Chapter 3.

From a tax point of view, details of the **time** and **cost** of purchase should be obtained, to see what **gains** or **losses** have arisen over what period. This can influence decisions in relation to any possible restructuring of the portfolio, because a disposal of a holding could trigger a **CGT liability**.

A **related question** which may not always figure on the factfind form (these vary greatly from firm to firm and you should make sure you are familiar with the one in use at your firm as well as the example given at the end of Chapter 1) is whether there have been any **disposals** so far in the **current tax year**. If so, all or part of the **CGT annual exemption** may already have been used, or perhaps a **loss** has arisen which could be offset against other gains.

2.7 Pension arrangements

One of the major areas requiring financial planning is **provision for retirement** and it is important to obtain as much information as possible regarding **existing arrangements**, both relating to **current employment** or **self-employment**, and to **previous periods**.

In the case of an **occupational scheme** provided by the employer, it may be possible to obtain from the client a **statement of benefits**, or a booklet describing the scheme. This will be an important source of information. Often however you will still need to obtain further information, for example the **length of service** which is taken into account, and you will need to check whether all of the individual's **earnings** are taken into account for pension purposes.

Occupational scheme variations

It is important to understand that occupational schemes are not all the same. Variations often occur in areas such as:

- **Definition of earnings**. Although schemes are allowed to pension virtually all taxable earnings from the employment, many only take account of basic salary, which simplifies administration. Some reduce earnings by a deductive item to allow for the State basic pension.

- **Service**. Most schemes base benefits on service as a member of the scheme, but some give benefits in respect of earlier service with the employer, perhaps whilst completing a waiting period (a minimum service qualification before joining the scheme).

- **Dependants**. Schemes often provide pension benefits for the spouse or registered civil partner of a member who dies, but some extend this to other dependants, such as children, common law spouses and other same sex partners.

There are many other variations too, so only a consideration of the details of a specific scheme can be relied upon. Advisers must be careful not to jump to conclusions about the benefits provided.

Some schemes promise a specific level of benefit at retirement, generally linked to earnings at or close to retirement (these are known as **defined benefit (DB)** schemes or **final salary schemes**). Others are based on a known level of **contribution**, with benefits dependent on the investment growth achieved, and ultimately the annuity rates available at retirement. These schemes are known as **defined contribution (DC)** schemes or **money purchase** schemes.

Remember also that pension schemes will usually include **life assurance benefits** and provision for pensions to be paid to a surviving **spouse**, and sometimes to dependent **children** and **other dependants**.

However much information you gather regarding the scheme, it is invariably useful to find out the **extent** to which the client feels that his **income needs** in retirement will be **provided for** by the scheme. Many scheme members do not have an accurate picture of the benefits they will receive. If they have **misunderstood** what is available, this will affect the way in which they approach financial planning and the **prioritisation** of their needs.

Some employees may pay **additional voluntary contributions (AVCs)** or **free-standing additional voluntary contributions (FSAVCs)** to supplement their pension provision, and details of these should also be gathered.

Remember that **members** of occupational schemes are also **eligible** to contribute to **personal pensions** under the **simplified pension tax regime**, effective from 6 April 2006, and where such contributions are being paid, full details should be gathered.

For employees who are **not included** in an occupational scheme, it is important to find out if they expect to become **eligible** at some time **in the future**, for example, after meeting a **minimum service** requirement (often known as a waiting period) before entry. If so, this expectation should be taken into account.

Employees not included in an occupational scheme may have benefits under **personal pensions**. These are always on a **defined contribution** basis, but might be arranged through the workplace (often called a **group personal pension**), and may include an **employer contribution**.

The **self-employed** necessarily rely on themselves, and cannot therefore belong to an occupational scheme, but again may have **personal pension** benefits.

When gathering information about pension arrangements, advisers should always remember the following points.

- There may be **several arrangements** in force at the same time, for example, an employee may belong to a **group personal pension** through the workplace, but also contribute to **another arrangement personally**

- There are sometimes arrangements relating to **previous periods** in an individual's working life, for example, benefits under a **personal pension** arrangements established when an individual was **self-employed**, but with contributions suspended when they entered an occupational scheme. (Although most employees can continue to contribute to a PP under the **concurrency rules**, affordability considerations will sometimes rule this out.)

- Similarly there may be **preserved pension rights** under the occupational scheme of a former employer, or under a **s32 buy-out policy** or **personal pension** which has been established to receive a **transfer** from such a scheme

These points will need to be considered if a **full picture** of the client's existing pension arrangements is to be obtained and is to be built up.

State pensions can also be important. Only employees and those within the category of **'carers'** qualify for benefits above the basic pension, so **factfinding** should establish whether benefits under **S2P** are available. Those eligible may also be **contracted out**, so all or most S2P benefits will have been given up, and benefits from an occupational or personal pension scheme will be provided instead.

2.8 Other investments

The range of **other investments** which could be in existence is virtually **unlimited**, so at some stage in the factfinding process, it will be necessary to ask a question which is aimed at identifying **anything which has so far not been specifically mentioned**. It is often useful to prompt recollection of anything which may have been forgotten by mentioning either specific **types of investment** or specific **purposes**, for example 'Is there anything else on which you could draw if anything unexpected happened?' or 'Do you have any investments which are specifically earmarked for your children?'

3 Purpose and suitability

3.1 Identifying the purpose

In many cases, existing investment arrangements have been put in place for a particular **purpose**, although this is not by any means always the case. Where it is, the adviser should ensure that the investment is, and remains, **suitable**, both in relation to its **intended purpose**, and in the context of the client's **overall affairs**.

Often there will be **no single precise purpose** behind a particular investment, but again its suitability should be considered in relation to the client concerned.

Changes in purpose

There are many situations where an investment initially established for a particular purpose needs to be reconsidered. For example:

- **Savings arrangements** might have been put on place to build up provision for financial help to a child when attending **university**. In the event, the child may not continue in education. The savings arrangement could then be **reconsidered**, and might fulfil a **new function**, such as providing a house deposit for the child, or could meet a need of the parents' instead.

- A **life insurance policy** might have been established to provide for **mortgage** repayment in the event of death. If the policy is still in force after the mortgage is paid off, it might be **superfluous**, or perhaps the cover may be worth **maintaining** for other purposes.

- An individual might have a **personal IPI** arrangement, but later enters an employment where a **group IPI** scheme is available, and the personal cover is **no longer needed**. (Limits imposed by insurers mean that it is unlikely that both arrangements could pay out in full unless the cover levels were very low.) The amount being paid in premiums to the personal IPI policy could then be **re-allocated** to other needs.

Advisers need to **probe** in this area. Where a particular financial product was established, there should be a **reason** for doing so (which should have been set out in the **suitability letter** issued at the time). Sometimes probing this might **reveal information** which the client had forgotten to give in other parts of the factfinding process. For example, if a life insurance policy is written for a **specific term**, there may have been a specific reason why that term was chosen; it could have been linked to a **liability** expected to **persist** for that period, and if so, the adviser should ensure that he has **details** of the liability as well as the cover.

Similarly, a **savings arrangement** may have been established for a **known period**, and might then have been aimed at a **specific objective**.

3.2 Determining suitability

There are various aspects to consider when looking at the **suitability** of existing arrangements, including the following.

- **Adequacy**. In the case of a protection arrangement, this means considering how the cover provided compares with **current needs**. Increase options may be included, and these should be considered in the light of the way in which the need is expected to change, for example, because of **inflation**. If the need is outstripping the cover, further action will be needed, not just immediately, but on a regular ongoing basis. For savings and investment arrangements, there will need to be an estimate of the eventual **target value** (if known) and **progress** to date will need to be checked to see if the arrangement is on track.

- **Timescale**. Where there is a particular purpose, the timescale is usually defined by that purpose, but the timescale may have **changed** since the arrangement was put in place, and this may therefore require further action. Sometimes **investment performance**, if it has been disappointing may mean that the original timescale has become **unrealistic**. On the other hand, some arrangements may carry **tax penalties** if the timescale is shortened, for example in the case of a **qualifying policy** which is surrendered earlier than originally intended.

- **Commitment**. Some arrangements carry a commitment, for example the payment of **premiums** to a life assurance policy through the term, and this may or may not be appropriate to current circumstances.

- **Affordability**. Sometimes affordability may be an issue, particularly if circumstances have **changed** for the worse, and plans may need to change to reflect this. Equally, in some cases income may have **improved**, allowing **increased arrangements** to be made to cover more needs, or to accelerate the expected achievement of existing targets. Even without change, the individual may have initially **over- or under-estimated** the amount he could reasonably devote to financial arrangements.

- **Risk**. The degree of risk associated with any particular arrangement should not be viewed in isolation, but rather in the **context** of the client's **overall situation**, and also in relation to **each particular objective**. We return to the subject of risk in Chapter 3.

- **Diversification**. Allied to consideration of risk is the issue of diversification. **Over-concentration** of investment in a small number of areas is likely to **heighten risk** (though it also means that strong performance will impact to the greatest possible extent). Sometimes diversification should be considered in relation to one particular **objective**, for example retirement planning, which is likely to require a number of different components. It should in addition always be considered over the individual's position as a whole.

- **Flexibility**. Dealing with **change** is an important part of financial planning, and particularly for **long term arrangements**, it is important to allow sufficient flexibility to adjust.

- **Tax efficiency**. The tax efficiency of arrangements reflect the individual's current position, and arrangements made in the **past** may or may not still be tax efficient for them now. Their position may have **changed**, or the relevant **tax legislation** itself may have changed, making existing arrangements less appropriate.

- **Possible alternatives**. The issue of suitability needs to be considered in the light of the **alternatives** that are available. An existing investment may be suitable, but another might also be suitable and **more attractive** in some way, for example being an equivalent but lower cost option. However, replacement of one arrangement with another needs care and is **often inappropriate**. **Protection** arrangements may be replaced if there is a **cheaper alternative**, provided that there is no reduction in any aspect of cover, or, if there is such a reduction, the client understands the difference and still feels the new product is **preferable**. Even then, the existing arrangement must not be cancelled until the new one is **in place**, to avoid a gap in cover and to prevent difficulty if cover is refused on health grounds, or risk rates in general change.

For investment products, **penalties** might arise, and there could be **tax** consequences. Also, there are usually **costs** involved, whilst improved performance **cannot be guaranteed**. (These points are considered in Chapters 6 and 8.) This does not mean that investments and investment products should never be replaced, but it does mean that considerable care is needed, and that the justification for the change must be thorough.

3.3 Completeness of information

Throughout the factfinding process, the client should realise the **importance** of ensuring that the information he has given is both **complete** and **correct**. This is highlighted in the context of considering existing arrangements, because these may not seem appropriate if the **reasons** that they are in place are not made clear. Similarly some may seem appropriate where, if the adviser had complete information, they would not be so.

An example might be where a client does not wish to give an adviser details of all his **investments**, perhaps in order to save time. However, assessing whether the **portfolio** is suitable in the light of the client's **needs** and **attitude to risk** requires consideration of the portfolio as a whole, not just some of its components. The result may be that the advice given is not as beneficial as the adviser (and the client) would wish.

Clearly, if an adviser is **aware** that the client is not giving complete information, he should **emphasise** the **advantages** of doing so. If the client still **declines**, the advice should be accompanied by a **caveat**, stating that only the information given could be taken into account, and that other, undisclosed information might have **altered the advice** given.

It is clearly **inappropriate** for an adviser to **encourage** a client not to give full information, even if the adviser feels that the recommendations he is giving are focused on a single, self-contained area. The client should always be given the **opportunity** to give **full information**, and should be made aware of the **importance** of doing so. From an adviser's point of view, he must still give full information about products and cover risk fully. The client giving limited information does not reduce this obligation at all.

3.4 Specific investment types

In section 2 above, we discussed **various investment types** which might arise when considering a client's existing investments. We will consider each of these further in Chapter 5, when dealing with recommendations. However, some of the issues which will need to be considered in **reviewing** existing investments are discussed in this section. At this stage, these necessarily concern aspects **specific to the investment type** as distinct from the client's **objectives**.

- **Main residence**. The first thing to understand in relation to the main residence is that its main purpose is **not as an investment**, but rather to provide a **home**. A home will always be needed in most cases, so its value will **not be wholly available** for investment purposes if sold, and its **suitability** cannot be judged only in investment terms. What can be considered is whether the client is relying to an **excessive extent** on the property to provide cash, for example on the basis that he will **trade down** at some future date. The future of the **property market** cannot be predicted accurately, and sometimes the market can be 'slow', making it difficult to dispose of the property at the desired time. The asset **cannot usually be split** into smaller components either, so the investor is fully exposed to market movements until the time the sale is actually made. This creates a **high degree of risk**. Nevertheless, if the individual has other investments, property provides a useful **diversification**.

- **Other property**. Other property, whether in the form of a **holiday home** or a **'buy to let'** investment property gives rise to many of the same points as the main residence, although the need to use it as a home does not apply. Having several properties gives some **flexibility**, particularly as regards spreading the timing of **disposal**. Nevertheless, the values are all dependent on essentially the **same market place**, though **geographical spread** gives some genuine diversification within the property market.

- **Deposits and NS&I products**. Almost everyone needs some investment in **cash**, to cover **day to day expenditure** and to meet **emergency needs**, as well as providing a secure base for investment generally. **Tax efficiency** is important here, particularly for higher rate taxpayers, and tax free arrangements such as **cash ISAs** and **NS&I Savings Certificates** are often attractive. Higher interest rates can also be achieved for **larger deposits**, which may mean that investing a large sum in one account rather than spreading it between several is most effective. If the sums involved are fairly substantial, it can be attractive to place some money in a **notice account**, where a higher interest rate is available in return for having to give a minimum period of notice before making a withdrawal. The main issue with cash is that **long term**, returns are likely to be **modest**, and the **opportunity cost** of holding too much money in cash can be high – the opportunity to invest in assets with a potentially higher return is being missed.

- **ISAs and PEPs**. These are tax advantaged vehicles and **shelter gains from CGT**, which can be very important in the long term. **Income** is not subject to any tax, except that dividend **tax credits** cannot be reclaimed. This means that equity related investment through ISAs and PEPs is attractive for higher rate taxpayers, and those who would otherwise be subject to CGT. The **attraction** for others is **modest**, but it is unlikely to be wise to move out of ISAs and PEPs except on investment grounds. Investments other than cash do carry a **relatively high risk factor** however, which is suitable for some investors, but not for all. (There is an issue as regards **inheritance tax** in some cases, since the ISA and PEP funds are paid out to the **estate** on death, and it can make sense to reconsider these investments in an overall review of **estate planning**.)

- **Equity investments**. Again these investments offer the prospect of **good long term growth**, but carry **risk** too. The **term** involved will be important in determining the suitability of these investments, together with the client's **attitude to risk**. Tax efficiency plays a part here too, because much of the return is usually expected to arise from **capital gains**, so allowing use to be made of the various **CGT reliefs and exemptions** including the **annual exemption**.

- **Pension arrangements**. The tax advantages of registered pension schemes mean that they will be important in financial planning for most people during their working careers. Those with the opportunity of joining **occupational or personal pension schemes** to which their **employer** will **contribute** gain an additional advantage. However, **restrictions** on the **timing** and **form** of benefits will result in some inflexibility, which in turn suggests that their use will be as **part** of retirement planning, rather than as a complete strategy.

4 The effect of change

However well an individual's **existing arrangements** may have met their needs at the time they were arranged, **change** is always likely to occur. Although its nature is uncertain, the fact that changes of some sort will occur is virtually **inevitable**.

The **consideration** of the **existing portfolio** therefore needs to **take into account** this change. The purpose is not to determine whether the arrangements were suitable when recommended, but instead whether they are suitable now.

Changes could have occurred in many areas, including:

- Income and expenditure
- Marital or civil partner status
- Number of dependants
- Employment status
- Health
- Objectives
- Attitude to risk
- Wealth (for example, as the result of an inheritance)

Factfinding should have revealed the **current situation**, and where existing arrangements seem **unsuitable**, probing will often uncover a **change** which has occurred, creating this position.

Change can also occur in **external circumstances**, for example in tax legislation, economic environment including interest rates, employment benefits and so forth. These also need to be taken into account.

5 Matters deferred

In Chapter 1, the need for clients to **prioritise** was discussed. When giving recommendations, advisers should always be aware that clients are unlikely to be able to deal with all their needs immediately, and must therefore decide which are most pressing. It follows that when their existing arrangements are considered, there are likely to be gaps, because at the time they were established, they dealt with the client's **priorities at the time**.

The prioritisation process creates an **agenda** for the future, and when reviewing a client's position, this will provide a useful starting point. However, the adviser should **not assume that priorities are the same** as they were when the priorities were last considered. Any changes in the individual's situation and in the external situation impact on **priorities** as well as **needs**. For example, starting a family is likely to greatly increase the priority of protection arrangements relative to savings and investment.

Discussing the **priorities** as **identified** in the past and what **changes** have occurred is a further important aspect of the factfinding process.

Key chapter points

- Gathering information about existing arrangements is a very important part of factfinding as a whole.

- The range of information is potentially very wide, and needs to include aspects such as residential property, NS&I products and cash as well as more traditional financial products.

- The main residence is a major financial asset for many clients, and there is often a major associated liability in the form of a mortgage secured on the property.

- There may be other property, either in the UK or overseas, and sometimes this may produce income in the form of rent.

- Property investment can be very attractive, but over-concentration in this (or any other single investment area) carries significant risk.

- Deposit arrangements are necessary to an extent for almost everybody, and there are tax efficient options such as cash mini-ISAs and NS&I Savings Certificates, which will appeal particularly to higher rate taxpayers.

- Many clients will already have life insurance arrangements in place for protection purposes.

- From an inheritance tax point of view, and from the point of view of convenience, the use of trusts should be considered in relation to such protection policies.

- Other protection policies such as IPI (PHI), critical illness benefit etc must also be considered in the light of overall needs.

- ISAs and PEPs often figure and are tax efficient investment vehicles.

- Equity investments give the potential for significant growth and allow the use of CGT exemptions and reliefs, though they involve a relatively high degree of risk.

- Pension arrangements are important in relation to retirement planning needs, particularly where there is an employer who is prepared to contribute.

- State pension benefits will also contribute to retirement planning needs though it is important to determine whether there are long periods of self-employment in respect of which there will be no S2P benefits.

- Similarly, if an employee has been contracted out for long periods, this will reduce the amount of additional S2P benefits provided by the State.

- Suitability of existing arrangements needs to be considered in the light of current needs and priorities, which may have changed since the arrangements were established.

- In some cases, the original need for which an arrangement was made may have passed, and the arrangement may no longer be required, but in others, the need may have increased in size or have become a higher priority.

- Risk needs to be considered as part of an assessment of suitability, but needs to be considered in relation to each objective, rather than in isolation.

- The consideration of existing arrangements is an area where clients are often tempted to limit the information they give, and advisers should emphasise the importance of completeness in order to allow them to formulate suitable recommendations.

- It is important to take account of change in the client's circumstances, because such changes can have a significant effect on needs and objectives.

- Similarly the external environment will affect what a clients wants and needs to tackle in terms of his personal financial planning.

- Aspects which were previously deferred on grounds of priority will also give an insight into what needs to be done now.

- However, advisers should not assume that those deferred needs necessarily remain relevant today.

Chapter Quiz

1   Why is it important to consider a client's existing mortgage when dealing with existing arrangements as a whole? .... (see para 2.1)

2   If a client owns a property overseas, would this affect the potential IHT liability on his death? .... (2.2)

3   What are the advantages of writing a life insurance policy in trust? .... (2.4)

4   List some of the areas in which variations often arise in the benefit structure of occupational pension schemes .... (2.7)

5   How could an individual seek to improve the return he achieves on deposit based investments? .... (3.4)

6   List the main areas in which changes could occur in a client's personal circumstances which would impact on his financial planning needs and priorities.. (4)

7   What changes in the external environment might have a similar effect?.. (4)

chapter

3

Attitude to risk

1 Risk and reward

1.1 Background

There is an **inevitable relationship** between **risk** and **reward**. In general terms, the greater the potential reward, the greater the associated risk is likely to be. Ideally, most clients would want to achieve the **highest possible return**, but with the **lowest possible risk**, and this is **not achievable**. It is therefore important that clients understand this, and that, with the help of advisers, come to understand what is the right **balance** of risk and potential reward within their own portfolio.

1.2 The market

The operation of **market forces** is what creates and maintains the relationship. Put simply, if there were two investment opportunities, both carrying the prospect of the **same potential return**, but one involving a **greater degree** of risk than the other, the one with the **lesser risk** will be **most popular**. As a result, market forces would **push up the price** of the lower risk investment, which would reduce its potential return. The two investments would then offer a choice of (relatively **high risk/high potential reward** or **low risk/low potential reward**. This is the only situation in which there are likely to be both willing buyers and willing sellers for both investments.

Similarly, if two investments carried the **same level of risk**, but one offered a higher potential return, it would be the most sought after and its price would increase as a result, lowering the yield until a balance was reached. Once again, this is the situation in which there would be both willing buyers and willing sellers for each investment.

The **market** therefore ensures that this **basic relationship** between risk and reward operates and as a result, those who seek security must accept that this will mean accepting **lower potential growth**, whilst aiming for the greatest potential returns will mean accepting risk.

1.3 Meaning of risk

The term 'risk' can mean different things to different people, so before we go further in this discussion of risk, we should give some consideration to its **meaning**. For example, to some, risk means the possibility of the value of an investment **falling** in monetary terms, whilst to others it means the possibility of the investment **failing to keep pace with inflation**. Others consider risk in the context of **accessibility**, and the value of the investment not being available at the time it might be required.

Probably the best way of thinking about risk is in terms of the potential for a particular investment to **fail to perform in the way expected**. For example, suppose an individual wishes to earmark some money to pay an **income tax liability** which will arise in, say, **six months' time**. He might reasonably choose to place this money in a building society account, where the capital value is **secure**, and some interest will be earned, albeit that the rate of interest may be variable, and therefore not entirely predictable. If the amount invested is the amount needed to meet the tax liability, then his provision is secure (barring the small possibility of the building society itself failing). On the other hand, if he placed the money in an **equity-linked** investment, then **fluctuations** in value, particularly in the short term, may mean that there is insufficient available for him to meet his tax bill.

It would be possible for him to invest **slightly less** than the amount needed to pay the tax bill, to allow for the **investment return** which will be achieved during the investment period. With the building society account, an allowance would be made for **interest**, and although the interest rate may be variable, the likelihood of a significant divergence from what is expected is small. On the other hand, with the **equity**-related investment, a **very significant divergence** could occur if investment conditions change markedly.

This means that the degree of **risk** involved with the **equity** investment is much **higher** than with the building society account, and given the necessity of having sufficient money to deal with the tax liability at the time it falls due, a high degree of **risk is unlikely to be acceptable** in relation to this investment. (We return later in this chapter to the subject of the relationship of risk to particular objectives.)

1.4 Volatility

An important concept when considering risk is **volatility**, as measured by the **standard deviation** of returns. Volatility is essentially the extent to which the value of an investment may **fluctuate** from time to time, and so **vary from expectation**.

The diagram below illustrates the performance of **two funds** which, over a given period, have achieved the **same investment return**. One fund (Fund A) has done so by a relatively **smooth** progression in price, whilst the other (Fund B) has **fluctuated significantly** through the period, sometimes having a price considerably in excess of the first fund, sometimes significantly below.

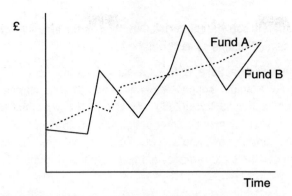

If the investments are held **throughout the periods** illustrated in the diagram, the investor will have done **equally well** whichever fund he used. However with Fund B, there is a much greater chance of **variation** from expectation if the units are encashed or if withdrawals are made at a different point in time.

The **standard deviation** is a measure based on **statistical techniques**, which allows the **volatility** of different funds to be **compared**. The higher the standard deviation, the greater the volatility. Over recent years, standard deviation data has increasingly figured as part of fund performance information. In the diagram above, the standard deviation of Fund B would be greater than that of Fund A.

Underlying the use of standard deviation and a consideration of volatility generally is a basic thought which is difficult to argue against. This is that, if the overall **expectation** of performance from two funds is **similar**, it is **hard** for an investor or adviser to **justify the choice** of a **more volatile** fund rather than a **less volatile** fund, because of the greater risk that expectations of performance will not be met. To put this another way, if results are similar, the manager of a more volatile fund is taking a higher degree of risk in terms of his investment strategy without there being a **compensating improvement in performance**.

2 Diversification and correlation

2.1 The principle of diversification

Although the **broad concept** of diversification is understood by most people, it is necessary to realise that there is more to diversification than simply including a **range of different assets** within a portfolio. The intention of having a range of assets is that there should be some **protection** from a situation where the **entire portfolio** is placed at **risk** through essentially one event or one change in attitude within the market.

The most obvious lack of diversification is where an individual has the whole of his portfolio invested in the shares of a **single company**. In recent times, an example of how **disastrous** this can be would be shares in Marconi, which fell from a price of around £10 at one time to a low point of just a few pence. If the whole portfolio is invested in these shares, the effect would be dramatic.

Although a portfolio can be diversified to an extent by having shares in a range of different companies, thought needs to be given to whether this diversification is **effective in reducing risk**, and if so to what extent. For example, having shares in three companies rather than one reduces the risk to the portfolio as a whole of a market **downrating** of the shares of **one** of these companies. However, if the three companies all operate in the **same sector**, there is a risk that the factors that can cause a problem at one company will also cause a problem at one or both of the others. This would be true of a **change in demand** for their particular products or services, for example as occurred for a number of major airlines following the September 2001 terrorist attacks in New York.

Even if the **shares of one company** are affected by events **specific** to that company, there can still be an effect on market sentiment towards the sector as a whole. There will always be factors that **differentiate** the shares in one company from those in another, but companies operating in a similar fashion in similar markets will **tend to move in the same direction** as a result of external factors. Shares which tend to move in the same direction are said to show

positive correlation, or to be **positively correlated**. Correlation, then, is the extent to which the values of different investments tend to move in the same direction as each other.

Shares which tend to move in **opposite directions**, perhaps because their interests are served by opposing events, are said to be **negatively correlated**. For example, suppose there were two different companies, one manufacturing gloves and scarves, whilst the other manufactures lightweight clothing suitable for use in hot weather. If the long range weather forecast is good, this will favour the manufacturer of lightweight clothing, but if the forecast is bad, then this would favour the company manufacturing gloves and scarves. The factor which is **favourable** for one company would be unfavourable for the other, and the share performance of these companies might be expected to be negatively correlated.

If an individual holds both shares, therefore, he could **reduce or remove** the extent to which the value of his investment portfolio was influenced by the weather, and might therefore expect **overall performance** of the two shares taken together as likely to provide a return in line with average stock market movements.

In reality, there will be **many more factors** which influence these share prices, and it is extremely unlikely that the effect would be as dramatic or as precise as a downward movement in one share being exactly balanced by an upward movement in the other.

The **extent of correlation** is therefore measured on a **scale** which ranges between -1 and +1. A correlation of +1 would mean that the shares in each company always moved in the same direction to the same extent. A correlation of -1 would mean the reverse, ie that an upward movement in one share was always accompanied by a balancing downward movement in the other.

A **zero correlation** would mean that there was **no particular relationship** between the movements in one share and the movements in the other, but instead, the movements were entirely **independent**.

In order to truly **reduce risk**, the construction of a portfolio would need to make use of different **assets** which are **negatively correlated**. This would reduce the risk to the portfolio of significant downward movement, because as some assets fell in value, others would increase. It follows also that there is **less chance of a significant upward movement** (relative to the market) because the existence within the portfolio of negatively correlated assets will dampen the increase in value of successful stock selections. However avoiding classes of assets which are negatively correlated to each other essentially means taking a firm view that the prospects for the asset classes chosen are extremely positive and that no safety factor is necessary.

2.2 Methods of diversification

There are a number of ways in which diversification can be achieved across a portfolio. Although we have illustrated the concepts of diversification and correlation largely with reference to equity investment, the reality is much wider. Amongst the methods of achieving diversification are:

- **Diversification within an asset class**, for example by means of purchasing a large number of different shareholdings rather than a single shareholding, or by investing through an equity unit trust or similar collective investment vehicle rather than through direct holdings in shares

- **Diversification of asset classes**, for example by investing in gilts and property as well as in shares

- **Diversification by market or geographical area**, for example by investing in equities quoted on the Japanese market as well as in equities quoted on the UK market

- **Diversification over time**, by purchasing investments at different times and therefore at different prices, so reducing the risk of purchasing all the assets within the portfolio at what might eventually be seen to have been an historically high price

The last point is an interesting one and should be considered where an individual is saving on a **regular basis**. An example of this might be through a unit trust **regular savings plan** where regular monthly contributions purchase units at the prices available month by month. If the unit price falls, the monthly contribution will buy additional units, and assuming that the price recovers over time, this will give the investor an advantage. With a lump sum investment, the issue of the timing of the investment is far more important, and a significant loss can result if an investment is made shortly before the price falls.

Pound cost averaging

Suppose the current price of units in a particular unit trust is £1.00. Suppose that the price subsequently falls to £0.60, and then recovers to £0.80.

Take first the case of a lump sum investor, who invests £12,000 in units at £1.00 each. He buys 12,000 units, and at the end of the period being considered, these are worth £9,600 (12,000 × £0.80).

Now consider an investor who invests £6,000 in units at their initial price of £1.00 and a further £6,000 when the price has fallen to £0.60. At the time of the first purchase, he buys 6,000 units, and at the time of the second purchase, a further 10,000, giving him a total holding of 16,000 units.

At the end of the period, the value of this holding is £12,800. Interestingly, although the unit price is at a lower level than was the case at outset, the regular investor has made a modest gain, whilst of course the lump sum investor has made a loss.

By purchasing units whilst the price is relatively low, the regular investor tends to reduce the average cost of the units he buys. Here, the combination of buying 6,000 units at £1.00 and £10,000 units at £0.60 gives an average purchase price of £0.75 per unit, and the investor will show a gain if unit prices recover to exceed this level.

Note however that if the unit price had increased, and then fallen back, the regular investor would have purchased relatively expensive units, and would do poorly. For example, if the price at the time of the second purchase was £1.20, he would then have bought 5,000 units for £6,000. His total holding would be 11,000 units, which would be worth £8,800 at the end of the period. His loss would therefore be worse than that of the lump sum investor.

Because more units are purchased when prices are low than when they are high, the advantages to the regular investor tend to outweigh the disadvantages if the fund is volatile and fluctuates both upwards and downwards from its average performance.

As a result of the effect of pound cost averaging, it may be **acceptable** for the investor to choose a **higher risk** (more volatile) fund where he is making **regular contributions** than he would be prepared to countenance if making a lump sum investment.

Care still needs to be taken over a period of time. If regular contributions are made over a fairly long period, then the **capital value** of the investment will grow, and the effect on the capital value of a downturn in unit price will significantly **outweigh** any advantage obtained through the **purchase of new units** at a low price. It may therefore be appropriate to reconsider the investment over time and in particular to consider whether **part of the accumulated fund** should be **moved to a less volatile investment** even if future contributions remain linked to the original choice of fund.

3 Asset classes

3.1 Range of assets

Before considering products, it is important to consider the extent to which the client's overall investment position should be spread across **asset classes**. Once this decision is made, the task of finding **suitable individual products** can then be made in context.

The main asset classes are:

- **Cash**
- **Fixed interest securities**
- **Equities**
- **Property**

The essential features of each of these classes is considered in the following paragraphs.

3.2 Cash

Of all the investment classes, **cash** (for example, on deposit)provides the **greatest security of capital**, but at the same time, long term **growth prospects are modest**.

Cash is unlikely to be effective therefore as a long term holding in most portfolios, though an element of cash allows **short term needs**, for example payment of investment management charges, to be dealt with. In addition, it may provide a **temporary holding area** for money which is later to be committed to a different asset class.

Although investment in cash is low risk, it is **not entirely without risk**. The major risks are:

- **Institutional failure**: banks and building societies do not commonly fail, but it is possible for them to do so, and although compensation arrangements are usually in place, these may not protect the whole of the amount invested. (Compensation arrangements also vary if the deposits are held outside the UK.)

- **Inflation**: security of capital alone does not protect the purchasing power of an investment, and the interest rate achieved may not keep pace with inflation, particularly in the long term, and particularly if inflation rates increase from current levels.

Many people are attracted to cash in order to give their portfolio a **secure foundation**, but if the proportion held in cash is too great, the individual's financial situation is likely to suffer in the **long term**. This is because the returns achieved are likely to be less good than they would have been with investment in other areas. In particular, the **possible erosion** of the value of the money held in cash by inflation is a major issue.

There is also the risk that interest rates will change, affecting future return and income.

Given that there are **tax efficient cash** vehicles available, for example through cash mini-ISAs and NS&I Savings Certificates, it is easy to be tempted by tax efficiency rather than to consider the investment merits and demerits. The division of assets by **asset class** in the light of the client's objectives should be the first consideration, after which making the investments as tax efficient as possible is the next step.

3.3 Fixed interest securities

This asset class includes **gilts**, **corporate bonds** and **PIBS**, amongst other things. Fixed interest securities provide **certainty of income**, and can provide **certainty of capital** if the particular security is **held until redemption date**. If **traded** before redemption date, the capital value will be **affected by market conditions**, in particular **interest rates**.

Fixed interest securities can provide **growth** in the long term, though the **greater degree of security** than is present than with, for example, equities, means that the **growth potential is rather less** in the long term. However, these investments provide **effective diversification** for the portfolio because prices are **less volatile than equities**, and at times, fixed interest securities may be holding their value or increasing in value whilst equities are falling.

Various risks are involved, most notably the following.

- **Capital value**: as already discussed, the capital value may fall as well as rise.

- **Failure of issuer**: although gilts are highly secure, because they are backed by the UK government, other fixed interest securities are less so, and security of both income and eventual capital redemption will reflect the credit standing of the company or building society involved.

- **Re-investment**: an important point is that the majority of fixed interest securities are issued for a known term, and when income or capital repayments are received, they must be re-invested, and the terms on which this is possible cannot be predicted in advance.

- **Inflation**: because both income and capital redemption value are fixed, high levels of inflation can seriously erode their value, particularly over the long term.

- **Interest rates**: if interest rates increase, the capital value of fixed interest securities will generally fall, and interest rates by their nature are unpredictable.

Fixed interest securities are useful to add **diversification** to a portfolio, and also have specific importance in situations where income is required. For example, those in retirement will often identify the need for a **secure income** as their first priority, and fixed interest securities can provide this.

They also have a special position in relation to pension planning, because **capital values will tend to increase if interest rates fall**. If an individual has a pension arrangement and wishes to **consolidate gains**, probably made through other assets, in the period **immediately before annuity purchase**, a transfer to cash would not be appropriate, because this does not give any protection from **variations in annuity rates**. On the other hand, an investment in **fixed interest securities** does. If interest rates fall and annuity rates therefore become more expensive, it is likely that the capital value of the securities will increase and this will provide some compensation (though the protection will not be absolutely precise).

3.4 Equities

It is generally accepted that equities provide the **best long term growth prospects** of all the asset classes, with the **possible exception of property**. They provide a return consisting **partly of income** in the form of **dividends** distributed by the companies concerned. The dividend stream should increase over the years if the company prospers.

In addition, the **capital value** of shares will also reflect the **growth of the companies** and should **increase** over time. This **combination of returns** provides the opportunity to outperform inflation which will always be a major consideration where the aim is growth over a long period of time.

Various risks are associated with equity investment, including the following.

- **Company failure**: however carefully the selection of shares is carried out, there is a risk that a company chosen may fail, or may suffer a reduction in profitability which can reduce or eliminate the flow of dividends, at least temporarily, and depress the share price.

- **Market conditions**: as well as the risk of particular companies getting into difficulties, it is also possible that market conditions generally may be disappointing, perhaps as a result of economic conditions, or sometimes political factors.

- **Inflation**: although equities give the investor a good chance of outperforming inflation, this is by no means certain, particularly in the shorter term, and particularly if inflation rates are high.

- **Volatility**: of all of the investments considered here, equities are the most volatile, and this places a great deal of pressure on the timing of both investment and disinvestment.

Equity investment requires **considerable skill** in terms of deciding **overall strategy** and also in **selecting** the particular shares into which investment will be made. Most **smaller investors** will not personally possess this skill, or indeed the **research facilities** which are required to back it up, and for this reason the various **collective investments** discussed in Chapter 5 have been developed.

3.5 Property

As with equities, **property** can generate a return in two ways, through **rental income** and through an **increase in capital value**. In the case of an individual and the investment inherent in the purchase of his own residential property, although there is no rental income, there is the **additional value** received from the use of the property as a home. Without the property, the individual would face an additional outgoing in the form of **rent**.

Property therefore provides a good opportunity for a **return in excess of inflation** and also provides **diversification** for a portfolio which is partly **invested in equities**. Historically, movements in **property prices** have **not shown a high degree of correlation** with equities, so property prices may be increasing when equity prices are reducing and vice versa. Across a portfolio, this therefore tends to **reduce risk**.

Once again there are risks involved in property investment, of which the main aspects are as follows.

- **Lack of diversification**: it is difficult for individuals to achieve diversification in property investment, simply because of the size of the investment required but lack of diversification exposes the individual to variations in value resulting from the features of a particular property.

- **Concentration**: the size of the investment generally needed in a property might mean that the portfolio as a whole becomes over-concentrated in this area, because there may be little scope to invest in other assets such as equities.

- **Valuation**: the valuation of the property is inevitably a matter of the opinion of the valuer until and unless the property is actually sold, and it may be difficult therefore to track the progress of the investment if held for a long period.

- **Rental income**: where property is rented out, there is a risk that rent will not be paid, either because the property is vacant, or because of financial difficulties experienced by the tenant.

- **Physical hazards**: property is susceptible to problems such as subsidence, fire and wear and tear, although to some extent the effect of these problems can be alleviated by adequate insurance and maintenance.

- **Maintenance costs**: following on from this therefore, the investor needs to take account of the costs of maintenance and insurance, which will eat into the overall return. There may also be costs involved in the use of a letting agent to find tenants and collect rent where a property is let, particularly on a residential basis.

- **Disposal**: if the property is to be sold, it is necessary to find a suitable buyer, and given the individual nature of properties generally, this may or may not be straightforward.

Large investors may be able to achieve **diversification** in property, and it is also possible to reduce risk by investing in a property **fund**, or indeed in the **shares of a property company**. Nevertheless, this does not and **cannot entirely eliminate risk.**

4 Relative risk rating of products

4.1 Background

Any attempt to produce a **classification** of the risk involved in different investment products is **fraught with difficulty**. There are a number of points which need to be borne in mind, including the following:

- Any such categorisation **cannot be a complete answer** to the consideration of risk, but can only be a **very broad guide**. For example, it is reasonable to separate unit trusts into broad bands, relating to the UK and overseas, with the latter being higher risk because of the potential exposure to **exchange rate fluctuations** as well as changes in asset values within the overseas market. Although this is true in general terms, within any such division there will always be **widely varying degrees of risk**. It could be, for example, that a smaller companies fund investing in the UK market carries a higher degree of risk than a fund investing in major companies quoted on an overseas market. (This is where aspects such as the measurement of **volatility** through **standard deviation** can be of considerable value.) Some funds **hedge** the **currency risk** through the purchase of suitable derivatives, and this reduces the risk rating of the fund, but also reduces the potential return (because of the cost of the derivatives).

- Some product types offer both **income** and potential **capital growth**, and the risk relating to each aspect could differ. For example, the **income on gilts** is subject to a **negligible risk**, because of Government backing, but the **capital value** prior to redemption **fluctuates** on the market, and therefore represents a higher risk. This also illustrates that different investors may use investments in different ways – gilts are very secure if held to redemption, but if the investor's intention is to actively trade them on the stock market, rather than hold them to redemption, then the risk is considerably greater.

- The point has already been made that the effect of investing on a **regular monthly basis** in potentially volatile assets is to **dampen the risk** involved. This means that in general terms, investments made through regular amounts carry lower risks than an investment in the same product type made as a lump sum.

Also, it is crucial to **interpret risk** in the context of the **particular clients** involved and the **objectives** for which any particular investment is made. This was briefly alluded to at the start of this chapter, and is covered in more detail later.

4.2 Product design

Any categorisation of products can only take into account the **basic design** of each one. There are almost **limitless permutations** available in the market place, and it may be that certain investment types which would generally be classified as quite high risk can be packaged together with an **element of guarantee** which would reduce the risk.

The reverse can also be true. A **with profits policy** has generally been regarded as a low to medium risk investment vehicle, and a similar policy on a unit linked basis might be regarded as carrying higher risk. However, depending on the **range of available funds** under the unit linked product, it may be possible to **switch** from an asset backed situation to a deposit situation to lock in the gains as the time for encashment approaches.

It is also usually possibly to run on a unit linked contract **beyond its planned maturity date**, and this will tend to **reduce risk**, because the investor has the opportunity to allow his investment to ride out any short term reduction in asset values which may occur at or around the time of maturity.

On the other hand, a **with profits policy** is generally much **more difficult to extend** in this way. Although it may be possible to leave the investment with the life office, it is often the case that the level of **terminal bonus** will crystallise at the expected maturity date. Thus if a market downturn has led to a reduction in terminal bonus levels, or indeed has prevented a terminal bonus being paid at all, there may be no escape for the investor.

The trend in recent years for terminal bonuses to represent a **significant proportion** of the total policy proceeds (sometimes as much as half) has meant that the **risk** associated with traditional with profits policies has **increased substantially**.

4.3 Product classification

The table which follows gives a broad classification of products by risk.

	Negligible risk	Low risk	Low/ Medium risk	Medium risk	Medium/ High risk	High risk
Deposit based and similar investments	NS&I Savings Certificates	Bank or Building society deposit Annuities Premium Bonds	Offshore deposits			
Gilts etc	Gilts (income) Gilts (redemption)	Index-linked gilts	Gilts (pre-redemption capital value)	Undated gilts PIBS Corporate bonds		
Life insurance linked		Non-profit	With profit	Unit-linked (managed) Unit-linked (UK funds)	Unit-linked (overseas funds)	
Equity investment				Unit trusts (UK) Investment trusts (UK) OEICs (UK)	Single UK fully quoted equities Unit trusts (overseas funds) Investment trusts (overseas) OEICS (overseas)	AIM shares Unquoted shares Specialist unit trusts, investment trusts and OEICs (eg emerging markets)
Derivatives						Futures Options
Other investments				Residential property	Commodities Enterprise Zone Trusts Antiques Collectables	EIS Enterprise Zone property

5 Client understanding

5.1 Communication

Because of the importance of risk in investment terms generally, it is very important to ensure that there is a **full understanding** between the **adviser** and **client** regarding risk. This means both the **client's attitude to risk**, and also the **risk involved in any recommendations** which are made. Similarly it is sensible to check the client's understanding of risks involved with **investments** which **he already holds** within his portfolio.

The terms **'high risk'**, **'medium risk'** and so on are difficult to define. They provide a **shorthand** method of describing the **broad category** of risk into which an investment fits, but cannot alone communicate the risk satisfactorily to a particular client.

For example, 'high risk' might be interpreted by one client by meaning that the value of the investment **can go down as well as up**, whilst another might understand it as meaning that the value **can reduce to nothing**. 'High risk' might also mean that not only could the value of the investment fall to nothing, but it could even require **additional funds** from the investor.

None of these definitions is right or wrong in absolute terms. They simply illustrate that the use of **jargon** is not a substitute for providing the client with a proper **explanation**. When an adviser makes recommendations therefore, he should include not only a description of the degree of risk involved in each investment under consideration, but also details of what this actually means. It is useful to relate this to the client's **particular circumstances** and any past **experience of investment** which he may have had.

The client's **attitude to risk** will determine how far the adviser's recommendations can go in building risk into the portfolio. It will however always be important to maintain **balance**. Even the client who is prepared to take the risk that an investment will lose its value entirely is unlikely to be well served by a portfolio consisting entirely of high risk investments. It will always be important to **include investments of lesser risk**, and in particular, in almost all situations, a certain amount of cash should be available on an instant access basis to provide an emergency fund.

5.2 Zero risk

Some clients might suggest that they are not prepared to take any investment risk whatsoever. In reality, a 'no risk' or 'zero risk' situation is **virtually impossible** to achieve, and advisers should be prepared to **communicate** this to clients by discussing what the expression actually means.

In discussing asset classes above, we identified **risks involved with the various classes**. For example, a deposit account which many clients may consider carries no risk in fact carries two important risks:

- The (admittedly small) risk that the institution might fail
- The risk that the value of the investment might not maintain its purchasing power

There are investments which carry **low risk**, for example, **NS&I Index-linked Savings Certificates**. However, the extent to which these can be used is limited by the **maximum investment levels** imposed by the Government through the NS&I terms. Also, the **investment period** is fixed, and although it is perhaps unlikely that something as established as these certificates would be entirely withdrawn, it is not impossible that this could occur.

In addition, even matching **price inflation**, or exceeding it by a known amount, as in the case of the savings certificates mentioned above, is arguably still not a 'zero risk' investment. Some might argue that someone whose capital only increases in this way will still **fall behind** other individuals who are invested in a more adventurous manner and achieve higher returns.

5.3 Comparisons

One way in which clients can often be assisted in understanding risk is by means of **comparisons**, which illustrate the **nature of risk in different situations**.

The following are examples.

- **Shares in a single company** tend to be higher risk than a **portfolio of different shares**, because the shares of the single company are affected by matters relating to that specific company as well as factors affecting the market as a whole.

- **Shares in smaller companies** tend to be higher risk because they are generally less financially secure than **larger companies** and their business may be concentrated in a few specialist areas. They may therefore be worse affected by a change in market conditions.

- **Long-dated gilts** (ie those with a long period remaining to redemption) may be more volatile in price than **short-dated gilts**, because their price is affected to a greater extent by interest rate changes. This is because the price is essentially the present value placed on the future stream of income and the eventual capital redemption. The longer the period over which this will be received, the greater the influence of interest rates.

6 Relating risk to objectives

6.1 Timescale

An individual's attitude to risk is very **far from being an absolute function** of their own psychological makeup. Although there is an element of this, in practical terms, the acceptable level of risk is likely to **vary from investment need to investment need**. One of the main determining factors is the **timescale** involved.

Earlier in the chapter we mentioned the fact that where an individual is putting money aside to meet a **known liability** which will arise in the **short term** (in our example, a liability to pay income tax) there would be **little justification** in taking a **high level of risk**. Over a period of a few months, there is little scope to generate a substantial investment return, and even if investments do well, the difference between the return generated and the interest that could have been achieved on a deposit account will not be great, particularly after taking account of **investment costs**.

In this example there were in fact **two separately identifiable time-related aspects** which tended to favour a **low risk** approach. These were:

- The **short term** involved
- The **fixed time** when the liability would arise.

The fact that the **due date** for the payment of income tax is **fixed** reduces the investor's flexibility, which has already been limited by the short timescale. For example, if an investment is made in assets such as unit trusts which tend to **fluctuate** in value, there is **no flexibility** to delay encashment in order to ride out a short term downturn in values, because the tax liability needs to be met on the fixed date and **penalties and interest** will apply if this does not occur.

Where the timescale is **longer**, the investor has **more choices**, and may be able to accept the risk of fluctuations in investment values in the short term in order to gain the **advantage** of a higher potential long term return. For example, suppose a self-employed individual in his 30s is considering **retirement planning**. At this stage he is not sure when he will want to retire, but expects this to be some time between the ages of 60 and 65. As he approaches this age, he feels that he may choose to gradually **reduce the work** that he does, and he therefore likes the idea of a **phased retirement**, under which he will gradually draw income benefits from the pension arrangement, to supplement his gradually reducing earned income.

This is a situation where investing in **asset-backed investments** such as equities or associated collective investment vehicles would be appropriate. Over the long term, it would be expected that equities would **outperform** investments such as **deposits** and **fixed interest securities**, and short term fluctuations should not create difficulties because the intention is to invest the money for a period of close to 30 years. Indeed, the opportunity to purchase additional investments whilst prices are low, perhaps through regular monthly contributions, could in fact improve his overall position, as illustrated earlier in this chapter.

As the individual grows older, the **remaining investment term reduces**, and the **balance changes**. It is a commonly used strategy to move money gradually from equity investment to more secure areas such as fixed interest securities over a period of perhaps five years leading up to retirement. This is often known as **lifestyle investment planning**.

Through this process the **gains** made in equities are **gradually consolidated**, and the **exposure** to the volatility of equities is **gradually reduced**.

So, for **long term investments**, **potential performance is likely to be more important** than short term fluctuations, whilst an objective with a **short term timescale** will usually be met by a **more secure** form of investment.

This therefore is one of the reasons why a client's **portfolio** is likely to contain a **mixture of investments**. **Deposits** provide for **immediate cash needs**, or needs which may arise, perhaps because of an unexpected event such as storm damage to the client's home, necessitating a repair, which would require money to be available instantly or near-instantly.

In the **middle range**, there may be a good opportunity to use investments such as **fixed interest securities** with a **known redemption date** when a defined amount of capital will be produced on a basis which is guaranteed (in the case of gilts) or reasonably certain (as in the case of good quality corporate bonds).

Zero dividend preference shares may also have a role to play in this area, particularly where income from the investment is not required. These shares, which are issued as a class of share in a split capital investment trust, provide a **specified cash sum** on a **known date**, subject to the assets of the trust as a whole being sufficient to cover this liability. The shares (often known simply as '**zeros**') are **not risk free**, because the assets of the trust may turn out not to be sufficient to allow for repayment, but if a trust is selected with a significant level of assets and a moderate period to the date when the trust will be wound up (which is when the zeroes will be repaid) the risk may be small. However, the position of the trust and its asset value can change rapidly, particularly if the trust employs gearing to a significant degree.

When assessing the approach to be taken to each of the client's objectives, the timescale and the flexibility of the timescale will therefore both figure as important factors.

6.2 Nature of objectives

A further point to consider is the nature of the objective in the sense of how definite it is. This may encompass whether the objective is likely to **come to fruition at all**, and whether the **exact amount** involved is known.

To give some examples, objectives which **will arise** (barring earlier death) might include:

- Building up resources for **retirement**
- **Mortgage repayment**

Objectives for which it is reasonable to plan, but which in the event **may or may not occur**, could be:

- Potential costs of **university education** for young children
- Cost of a child's **wedding**

In most cases, these objectives are also **uncertain in amount**, though mortgage repayment will be for a known amount.

Where the amount required is known, there may be a tendency to try to build in a level of **guarantee** that the **required amount** will be available. This could be done in various ways, particularly by once again **switching assets** from relatively high risk to lower risk investments as the end of the timescale for achieving the objective comes closer.

Objectives where the amount required is uncertain are generally those where the effect of **inflation** creates the **uncertainty**, at least in part. For example, **university costs** can be estimated currently, but it is very hard to predict ahead the amount which may be required for a child who is perhaps 10 or 15 years away from the point where these costs will have to be met. University fees are perhaps a good example of a particularly **difficult objective** to fund for. Not only is the effect of inflation uncertain, but the **highly politicised** nature of funding higher education means that there could be a considerable change to the basis of funding and the extent to which individuals and their families are expected to meet the costs involved.

All of this means that any investment portfolio needs to be **reviewed frequently** in order to adjust to **changing circumstances**, and indeed **changing priorities**. We deal in more detail with the review process in Chapter 7.

Key chapter points

- **In general, the higher the potential reward an investment offers, the greater will be the level of risk that must be accepted.**

- **Conversely, if an investor seeks a low exposure to risk, the potential investment reward available is likely to be modest.**

- **Market forces operate to maintain this situation, which is necessary if there are to be both willing buyers and willing sellers across the range of investments.**

- **Risk may mean different things to different people, for example the possibility of a fall in value, or a reduction in value to nothing, or a failure to keep pace with inflation.**

- **Arguably the best definition of risk is the potential for an investment not to perform in the way that was expected.**

- **Volatility measures this and allows different investments to be compared on a statistical basis, through the measurement of standard deviation.**

- **Diversification of a portfolio is necessary in order to reduce risk, though it will also reduce the possibility of significant outperformance compared to the market.**

- **Diversification will only be really effective if assets which are not positively correlated to a high degree are included.**

- **Correlation is the tendency for the values of different assets to move together, as might be the case with the shares of two different companies operating in the same market.**

- **Diversification can be achieved in various ways, including within a single asset class, across different asset classes, by market or geographical area, or over time.**

- **Pound cost averaging may allow an investor to choose a higher risk, more volatile fund for regular investments as compared to lump sum investments.**

- **The spread of a portfolio over the asset classes of cash, fixed interest securities, equities and property should be considered before the selection of individual products.**

- **Cash is likely to be required within almost all portfolios, and is a secure (though not entirely risk free) investment, but offers relatively low long term growth prospects.**

- **Fixed interest securities offer a fixed level of income and (usually) a known capital sum on a pre-determined redemption date.**

- **The degree of risk involved depends to a significant extent on the credit status of the issuer, but capital values are also affected by interest rates.**

3: ATTITUDE TO RISK

- Gilts are very secure if held to redemption, because both income and redemption value are fixed and backed by the UK government, but capital values still fluctuate prior to redemption date.

- Equity investment gives the opportunity for high potential gains, and provides the prospect of increasing income, but it involves a significant degree of risk.

- The skill required to be successful in equity investment is not accessible to most smaller investors except through collective investment vehicles such as unit trusts.

- Property investment also offers the opportunity of income and capital growth, but again involves risk, particularly because of the difficulty of achieving effective diversification.

- The relative risk rating of product types can only be approximate, and must be considered in the light of the particular aspects of each individual product.

- The understanding of risk by clients is a very important aspect of advice, and requires good communication on the part of the adviser.

- The level of risk which is acceptable will vary according to the objective concerned, with the least risk related to objectives which are short term and which have a fixed, inflexible timescale.

Chapter Quiz

1   What does standard deviation measure in relation to an investment fund? .... (see para 1.4)

2   If two assets have zero correlation, what does this mean? ....(2.1)

3   What is meant by diversification over time in investment terms? ....(2.2)

4   What are the major risks inherent with an investment in cash? ....(3.2)

5   What particular risks are related to the valuation of property as an investment? ....(3.5)

6   Why does the available timescale impact on the level of risk which is likely to be acceptable in relation to the achievement of a particular objective? ....(6.1)

4

Analysing information

1 Assessing requirements

1.1 Background

When the adviser has collected the **information** he needs in order to **prepare recommendations**, it is important that he **assesses** the information **critically**. When we discussed factfinding earlier, the point was made that no factfind form can ever be designed so that it is absolutely certain to collect all of the information that could possibly be relevant in a particular client's case, and that advisers need to be **alert** to ask any **additional questions** which are pertinent.

Once the factfind information has been collected, then the information should be considered carefully by the adviser to see whether any further information could usefully be collected at the time. Sometimes it may be clear from an **examination of the information** recorded that there seem to be **gaps** in information, or **inaccuracies**, and these are looked at in some detail below.

1.2 Further needs

The discussions with the client will have **identified areas of need**, and will have agreed with the client at least some areas which need to be addressed. However, a further consideration of the information given might suggest **additional needs** which the client had not raised, and which had not occurred to the adviser at the time of the factfinding meeting.

For example, it could be that possible provision for **school fees** for young children was discussed, but that the conversation had not developed on to the possibility of **university education** being required. This would certainly be something which should be taken into account in quantifying and prioritising needs.

There could be a **mortgage** which was covered by **term assurance**, but in looking at the information in more detail, the adviser might see that the **original loan** had been **increased** at the time of **re-mortgaging**, but that no further adjustment was made to the life cover in force. This could also highlight a **further need**.

Great care is always necessary in assessing information given by clients, simply because they are unlikely to **fully appreciate** the need for **completeness** both in the factual base upon which recommendations are made, and in the consideration of needs which derive from them.

2 Gaps and inaccuracies

2.1 Incorrect and incomplete information

Where information is **incorrect** or **incomplete**, this can be the result of a number of different circumstances. One possibility is simply that the information requested has been **refused** by the client. There is of course **nothing which compels** a client to provide the information requested, but if he does choose not to do so, any **recommendations** which the adviser offers **may be affected**. It is therefore important that this situation is recorded and acknowledged by the client as well as by the adviser.

Sometimes information may have been **given** by a client, but it is **still not fully complete or correct**. Occasionally this may be **intentional**, but most often it is the result of **misunderstanding** or **lack of knowledge** and advisers should always be on the lookout for such situations. One of the most important services the adviser can provide is to ensure that the understanding which a client has of his overall financial position is as accurate as possible.

Sometimes too, correct information may be **recorded incorrectly** or an aspect of a particular situation may be **assumed** by an adviser where it should be checked. There may also be **inconsistencies** in the information provided by clients. We consider this in more detail below.

2.2 The consequences

Any **recommendations** which are based on information which turns out to be wrong, or where some relevant part of the information has been omitted, are likely to turn out to be **less than ideal**, and indeed in many circumstances will be entirely **inappropriate**.

Suppose the client has **declined** to give certain information, for example full details of his **income** position. Although the advice given may still be affected, at least the **client** is in a position to **judge** the extent to which this is important, and will be able to consider the recommendations made in the light of the **further information** available to him, but not to the adviser. Nevertheless, the advice may turn out to be unsuitable, through no fault of the adviser's.

Example: Incomplete information

A client has earned income, but also has an investment portfolio which generates a considerable amount of investment income. He decides not to reveal the investments to the adviser during the factfind, because he only wants advice on protection and retirement planning. Amongst the ways in which advice could be affected might be:

- **Over-emphasis on IPI (PHI)** arrangements to protect earned income against the possibility of incapacity, when in reality, the individual could support himself to a large extent from his investment income

- **Underestimation of the need for estate planning** as the investment portfolio would probably increase any IHT liability

- **Incorrect calculation of retirement planning needs** because the investment portfolio might go some way to providing the required level of income in retirement

- **Possible incorrect assessment of tax position** and therefore the importance of tax reliefs on pension contributions

- Expectation that **CGT annual exemption is currently not used**, resulting in recommendations designed to utilise it in future

- **Unsuitable investment recommendations** for retirement planning because of the inability to take account of the way in which the existing portfolio is invested to achieve an appropriate level of diversification within the parameters of acceptable risk

There could be various other areas, depending on the detail of the recommendations. What is already striking however is the **wide range of areas** which could be **affected** by the client's decision not to give full information.

The adviser might realise that information might be missing if, for example, there seems to be a large excess of income over expenditure, which in reality is being invested, but there is no indication of how this is being used in the information given. Alternatively, there might be a mention in the conversation of the receipt of a large inheritance, but no indication of what became of it. These factors should therefore **prompt** the adviser to **seek further information**.

Even just knowing that the client is not giving details of an investment portfolio helps considerably more than being unaware that anything is being withheld.

Where the problem is an error or omission of which the **client is not aware**, then clearly he will not be in a position to judge the recommendations properly, and the results may accordingly be more damaging. The **adviser** must therefore **take responsibility** for ensuring that the client has provided all the information which the adviser needs and that any part of the information which seems to be incorrect or incomplete is **queried and checked**.

2.3 Updating information

A very important aspect of this is to ensure that the information gathered about a client and his circumstances is and remains **current**. The process of finalising financial planning recommendations may be **lengthy** and the **continued validity** of information held should be confirmed before the recommendations are implemented.

Similarly on **reviewing** a client's position, perhaps a year after implementation, the **starting point** of the process must be to **confirm existing information** and to identify **areas of change**. The review process is discussed in Chapter 7.

Some of the information likely to need updating is fairly obvious. For example, an employed client may have received an **annual salary review**, or **outgoings may have increased** simply as a result of inflation. There may be other **less obvious factors**; perhaps a health problem has arisen, or the client's job has become less secure.

It is easy to treat the updating of information as a **routine**, quickly accomplished exercise, but it actually deserves **as much care and attention** as the initial factfinding undertaken with the client.

2.4 Possible problems

It is not possible to list all the areas in which information related problems could arise. Having said that, it is possible to identify **certain situations** where problems are most **common**.

First of all, it is useful to identify the fact that the problems broadly break into **two categories**, namely **inconsistencies** and **errors**. Although this division is not entirely scientific, and certainly there are grey areas between the two, the analysis is nevertheless useful to help the adviser to identify them.

2.5 Inconsistencies

Inconsistencies arise when two or more pieces of information appear to **conflict**. It may be that both or all of the pieces of information viewed in isolation are perfectly feasible, but taken together, they do not make sense.

For example, an individual may give details of his **income**, and may also mention the **highest rate of tax** which he pays. If the stated income, perhaps from employment, is below the higher rate tax threshold but the client indicates that he pays tax at 40%, then this is an inconsistency which clearly **needs to be addressed**.

Similarly the client might indicate that he is **cautious** in his attitude to investment, but the factfinding process might reveal that he has investments which would normally be associated with a much more relaxed **attitude to risk**.

Another possible area where an inconsistency can arise is in the **current value of investments**, particularly those which have been built up from regular contributions. Where the **current value or surrender value** of a savings vehicle appears to be considerably **higher or lower** than one would normally expect, then further details should be sought either to explain the divergence or to correct the information gathered.

These areas concern **misunderstandings** on **matters of fact** but further inconsistencies can arise because of **conflicting views**. It may for example be that the adviser's interview is conducted with a couple rather than with an individual, and different, conflicting statements may be gathered from each individual. Sometimes **different individuals** have **different priorities** and this situation not only needs to be identified, but also must be handled with considerable tact.

Even **one individual** may have a number of **conflicting priorities**. People often identify **needs** in a number of areas and may describe many of them as being **extremely high** or **top priority**. In reality, it will be necessary to determine a more **accurate priority order** in most cases since generally, it will not be possible to deal with all needs immediately.

Importance of inconsistencies

Suppose a couple gives an adviser an inconsistent view of their priorities. For example, one partner might say that they intend to send their children to State schools, which are good in the local area. The other says that one of their priorities is to provide the best possible education for their children, even if this means paying for it.

It is not the adviser's role to get involved in a conflict between the partners, but he does need to know whether his recommendations need to take account of a possible need to save for school fees, and/or a need to provide protection through life insurance and IPI to ensure that fees can be provided for however long they might be needed.

His recommendations cannot therefore be finalised until he knows whether the issue needs to be addressed. This might be approached by asking the extent to which he needs to make allowance for education costs, and then probing the responses which are given.

The adviser should always seek to **clarify** matters which appear **inconsistent**, but once again, he should be careful **not to jump to conclusions**. There are usually a number of different possible explanations for any apparent inconsistency, and indeed, there may not, on closer inspection, be an inconsistency at all.

2.6 Errors

Errors are often easier to identify than inconsistencies because they involve **statements** which are definitely **factually incorrect**. They can arise in various areas and most commonly reflect the fact that most **clients** are relatively **inexpert** in financial matters and cannot be expected to understand all the conditions and taxation implications of financial products.

There are many potential problem areas. **Taxation** often figures in one form or another and, for example, the **tax treatment of contributions** to or **benefits** from various investment products may be involved.

We now examine a number of more common errors in detail.

- **PP contributions**. A client or prospective client may state that he is paying contributions to a **personal pension** or **stakeholder pension** arrangement on a **gross** basis. This cannot be correct because an individual would pay such contributions **net of basic rate tax relief**.

  There could be various explanations. He could be contributing to an old **retirement annuity contract** where contributions are still paid gross (until April 2007), and he would have to claim relief through his tax return. On the other hand, perhaps he is paying contributions net of basic rate tax to a personal pension **without realising** that his personal pension is being **credited** with the gross amount and that the pension provider is reclaiming tax relief on his behalf.

- **Occupational scheme benefits**. Problems can arise in relation to **occupational scheme benefits** too. A client may state that he expects a benefit under the scheme of **2/3rds final salary** at retirement. If the scheme booklet indicates that benefits are **1/60th of final salary for each year** of scheme membership, and the client's service will only amount to, say, 20 years at retirement, then clearly something is wrong.

  It could be that the client has simply **misunderstood** what he is entitled to. The scheme booklet might refer to a **maximum benefit of 2/3rds**, and this may have been read as if it applied to everyone. Alternatively, the client may have been granted **special benefits**, not described in the booklet, perhaps at the time he was recruited, as an inducement to leave a previous employer or for some other reason, such as a transfer payment being made from a previous employer's scheme.

  (Note that many schemes will continue to apply a limit in this form, even though the basis of HMRC limits is now different.)

- **Guarantees**. Clients are sometimes mistaken about the **terms of contracts** they have. For example, a potentially fluctuating unit trust or unit linked contract may be stated as being subject to a **guarantee** of a minimum rate of return, or at least a **return of capital invested**.

  This **could be correct**, but may not be, and such a guarantee would be likely to **affect other terms of the contract** too, in particular the ability of the investor to access his investment. A guarantee of an **unusually high return** is likely to indicate an **error** or misunderstanding on the part of the client.

- **Investment contracts**. There can sometimes be errors relating to the **type of contract** in which a client invests. For example, a unit trust savings plan may be said to have **built-in life assurance**, or a **fixed maturity date**. These are features which are associated with unit-linked life insurance policies rather than unit trust savings plans.

- **Taxation**. Errors often occur in a **client's understanding** of taxation too, both generally and specifically in relation to financial services products. For example, a client might state that **no tax is deducted** from the interest on his Building Society **Instant Access Account**, although he is a **taxpayer** otherwise.

  Unless he has mistakenly completed a form to state that he is not a taxpayer, **20% tax will be deducted at source**, although the client may not have realised this. Similarly errors can arise regarding the taxation of life insurance policies, PEPs, ISAs and almost all other types of investment and investment product.

Of course, no list of possible errors or inconsistencies could claim to be complete, but the items covered here should help to pinpoint some of those which most commonly arise. Inevitably these are in the **more complex areas** of financial services, where the **average client** could not be expected to have as full an understanding as a professional financial adviser would have.

2.7 Dealing with errors and inconsistencies

Sometimes the adviser will **identify** an error or inconsistency during the meeting, and if so, should normally **clarify the situation** there and then. On other occasions, he will identify the problem later, perhaps as he prepares his recommendations. If it could affect them, he will need to **seek clarification** immediately, perhaps by phone, so that he can be sure that the recommendations will be sound.

If the error or inconsistency is not immediately relevant to them, he should still seek to clarify the situation, but may choose to do so when he **next meets** the client. Remember that part of the service provided will be to help improve the **client's awareness** of his financial situation generally, and he would not be fulfilling this aspect of his role if he did not seek to **correct** any misunderstanding the client might have.

Just as with questioning technique, the adviser should consider how best to deal with the error or inconsistency. If the client feels 'caught out' in some sense, then he may become **disaffected** with the financial planning process as a whole.

2.8 Completing information

Although it may be unwise, some clients will choose to **withhold certain information** from the adviser. Sometimes this will be done knowingly, sometimes through oversight. Sometimes it will be done openly, with the client saying that he is not prepared to answer certain questions, and sometimes the question will be answered, but the adviser will not have been given the full answer.

As discussed earlier, any **missing information could affect the overall picture** the adviser builds up of the client, and could therefore **affect his recommendations**. He should therefore try to identify areas where information seems incomplete, so he can try to gather the missing facts. Part of this will be done through identifying apparent errors or inconsistencies in the information given. Often **clarifying** these will produce **additional information**.

However, such inconsistencies cannot always be easily identified. For example, a client who does **not disclose** all of his income to **HMRC** may well not disclose it to the adviser either, and may be at pains to ensure that there are **no obvious signs** of the excess.

The adviser should ensure that his client is aware of the information he has used in preparing his recommendations. It is a good idea to **give the client a copy of the factfind** for this purpose, and perhaps also because it highlights areas that he agreed should be looked at again at some future date.

The adviser should also ensure that whatever the arrangements are into which the client enters, they are **consistent** with the **information collected**. If a client insists that he can afford a **regular investment plan** which seems to be **well beyond his surplus income**, the adviser should seek clarification of how future payments will be afforded.

If he does not do so, he runs the risk of the arrangement proving beyond the client's means and **lapsing**, which may well have **disadvantageous financial implications** for the client and probably for the adviser. But this is not the only concern. Such actions could raise questions with regard to the **money laundering regulations** too, which could have very serious consequences.

3 Specialist advice areas

3.1 Other advisers

Because of the wide nature of the field, there will always be areas where any one adviser's **knowledge** and **experience** is **insufficient** to offer advice in which the adviser himself and his client can have confidence. On these occasions, it may be appropriate for the adviser to seek **assistance** from others or indeed to **refer** a client to someone else. This is part of maintaining a **professional approach** to clients and is a sign of strength rather than a sign of weakness.

These situations can be broken down into a number of areas:

- **Competence**. If the advice involved relates to a **technical aspect** of a product or its application, the adviser may seek a more experienced adviser within his own organisation or look to the **expertise** offered by relevant **product providers**. If on the other hand it is a separate area of expertise, outside financial services, such as the law, it may be appropriate to consult a **specialist** or to **advise the client to do so**.

- **Licensing**. In some organisations, advisers are licensed to deal with **certain product areas** and not others. Where a client's requirements exceed the level of licensing the adviser currently has, then **another adviser**, appropriately **trained**, should be called in.

- **Experience**. There may be situations which, although strictly within the adviser's competence, could nevertheless **benefit** from the **experience** of others. Technical knowledge and classroom learning are necessary, but experience adds considerably to this and drawing on the experience of others is one of the best ways to **ensure that the client gets the benefit** of the best advice possible.

- **Second opinion**. Similarly, even if the adviser is experienced in a particular area, it is often a good idea, particularly in complex cases, to ask for a second opinion. There can be few people active in financial services who have not, at some time, overlooked a particular aspect of a case in drawing up their recommendations, only to find that it turned out to be of great importance. The involvement of a second person may pinpoint this much earlier in the process than would otherwise be the case.

  On other occasions, although the adviser may draw up **recommendations** which he believes are **appropriate**, he may still have a feeling that there is room for **improvement**. If he is struggling to identify where that improvement could be made, it is surprising how often a fresh look at the details by someone else can be enlightening.

3.2 Range of advisers

It is important to keep an open mind as to the range of people who might be involved.. These could include **other advisers** in the same organisation, **experts** employed by product providers, **external consultants**, **solicitors**, **accountants** and **actuaries**, amongst others. The adviser must always be sufficiently aware of his client's needs to **recognise** situations where his own expertise does not provide a complete answer and then to fill in the gap as appropriate.

Many clients will have already have advisers to whom they might turn for help in various areas. Particularly in the case of an **accountant**, but with other advisers too, these areas will sometimes **overlap** with those which are relevant to the financial adviser.

It is always important to **acknowledge the expertise** of others and the importance of their relationship with clients. It is therefore advisable to **build a co-operative relationship** with those existing advisers rather than a competitive one. The making of **justified recommendations** which are in the client's best interests should never lead to conflict with other advisers.

4 Prioritisation

4.1 The need to prioritise

As discussed in Chapter 1, there will almost always be a **need to prioritise** the needs of a client, because in practical terms it is extremely unlikely that most individuals will be able to make provision to cover all of their needs within an **affordable budget**. Prioritisation is **not an exact science**, and ultimately it will be the client's view of which areas are of the greatest immediate importance which will decide the approach to be adopted. However, the adviser has a responsibility to help the client reach **sound conclusions** in this important area.

There will generally also need to be a balance between dealing with immediate and longer term needs. **Immediate needs** are likely to be the **highest priority**, but unless some provision is made for **longer term needs**, for example retirement planning, these may become **extremely difficult or impossible to deal with**.

For example, an individual **approaching retirement** with no retirement planning provision may find it **impossible** to reserve **sufficient money** to provide for a reasonable standard of living in retirement. Nevertheless, it is broadly true that, for most people, **protection needs** such as life assurance, income protection insurance (also known as permanent health insurance) should be **considered first**.

Advisers should also bear in mind that individuals will be **motivated** in different ways towards dealing with **different needs**. They will recognise the need to provide for **protection**, for example if they have dependants, but may find it more motivating to start to make provision for **savings for their own future**. It is inevitably more pleasant to think ahead to a time when they will be spending their savings than it is to imagine a situation when they may become **incapacitated**, and therefore reliant on an insurance arrangement, or where they have died, and financial **provision for others** is necessary.

4.2 Life stages

Most people will go through a number of **life stages**, and their needs and priorities will **change** to reflect their current circumstances. It is however rather **simplistic** to assume that everyone passes through the same fixed stages of life, during which their needs and objectives will fit in with a universally applicable model.

Nevertheless, it is clearly true that the priorities of a **young single person** will differ from those of the **married couple** with a **young family**. However this is less to do with the progression through life stages than to do with other influences on **needs and priorities**. It is therefore those influences, rather than life stages, that we examine in more detail.

Amongst the most important influences are the following.

- **Age**. Although different people will progress in different ways, it is true that a person's age **influences their financial planning** needs to a significant extent. At very young ages, a child will probably not be involved at all, but may nevertheless be affected by the planning made (or not made) by others, particularly those on whom the child is dependent.

  Increasing age brings **independence**, and initially, the priority is likely to be to **save**, probably for the short term future, and later for longer term needs such as **retirement**. In the 'twilight years', priorities are likely again to change with increasing emphasis on **income needs** and possibly on the creation or preservation of an **inheritance** for the next generation.

- **Family situation**. It is not so much the **marital status** of the client which is important, at least in terms of priorities, but more the extent to which others are **dependent** on him. Dependants may mean **children**, a **spouse** or **partner**, but can also include others such as **elderly relatives**, particularly those in reduced circumstances or who might be in poor health.

  Those with dependants will therefore need to give a **high priority** to the need to **protect** the financial position of those dependants. The essential division of financial planning into arrangements for oneself and arrangements for others is a **continuing theme** throughout financial planning and is one which can sometimes create problems of prioritisation.

- **Income level**. The level of income enjoyed by an individual is also an influence on priorities. For example, the extent to which **State benefits** will replace income in retirement, or in the event of incapacity, is proportionately much greater at lower income levels, since the State seeks only to provide the means for a relatively **modest level of existence**.

  Also, there may be some concern in relation to **means-tested benefits** that provision made by the individual in some areas may **reduce or remove** entirely part of the provision which would otherwise be made by the State. At the other end of the scale, those on extremely high incomes may not need to replace so great a proportion of income since not all of that income will be strictly **necessary**.

- **Source of income**. Income which derives from a **job** or from **running a business** may be reduced or completely removed by the **death** or **incapacity** of the person involved. On the other hand, if the income arises from investments, those investments are likely to continue to produce exactly the same income, irrespective of the health or survival of their owner.

  The importance of arrangements such as **permanent health insurance** and indeed **retirement planning** will have to be considered in the light of the extent to which income will continue.

- **Employment status**. Employees are generally dependent on their employer for the continuation of income during their working lifetime and this may provide a source of **security or insecurity**. It is important to take account of any likelihood of change in the employee's position, particularly where there is an expectation of such change, and where it could be completely beyond the control of the employee himself.

  It may in particular be necessary to reconsider priorities if an employee **changes jobs**, and finds that the **benefits provided**, for example pension arrangements, IPI arrangements and so forth are entirely different. The self-employed on the other hand have much more control, but the level of **State benefits** provided is considerably **lower**, particularly as regards pension benefits. This is therefore likely to mean that retirement planning has a higher priority for the self-employed than for employees.

- **Business owners**. Those who own and work in their own business will have to take account of this in determining their priorities. It can be very **attractive** to enjoy the **control** which such a position brings, and also have a **potentially valuable asset** to eventually sell when retirement is reached. However, it is often the case that individuals **overestimate** the extent to which they can rely on the sale value of their own business when they reach retirement. This may make it especially difficult to quantify needs in such cases.

  Many factors contribute to this position, including the fact that much of the ability of the business to **generate profit**, and therefore value, may in fact be **dependent** on the continued involvement of the individual himself. Advisers should therefore ensure that clients are **realistic** in their expectations in this area, and also ensure that they do not rely on their business entirely to provide for their needs – over-reliance on any one asset is always a **high risk strategy**.

- **Existing arrangements**. We have discussed existing arrangements in various parts of this text, and inevitably the existence or otherwise of such arrangements will have a **major impact** on priorities. It is also important to consider whether there is a need to **restructure** the client's **existing holdings** if their priorities have changed. We will consider this in more detail in Chapter 7.

- **Liabilities**. Those with the greatest liabilities need the largest degree of **protection**, if only to avoid the potential problems which would result from those liabilities being left behind. Although the majority of people provide some **life insurance** cover to provide protection against major liabilities such as **mortgages**, far fewer provide any protection for the effect that **incapacity** would have.

Although the mortgage will usually be the client's **biggest** liability, there can be others of significance too, and all need to be considered. This is a good example of a situation where the adviser may need to increase the understanding of the client of his needs in order to ensure that a **rational view** is taken of the **prioritisation** process.

- **Health**. Those in **poor health** may have a greater need for, and therefore place a higher priority on, **life insurance** and other **protection products**, but at the same time the premiums for those products may be higher, or they may be completely unobtainable. This may therefore **limit the choices** available and may mean that the individual needs to make **other arrangements** as far as is possible.

  Bear in mind also that those in ill-health may be able to obtain **preferential terms** in relation to some products, in particular **annuities**. Enhanced annuity rates may be available if the health problem is such as to diminish the expectation of life. Such annuities are commonly called **'impaired life annuities'**.

Each individual's circumstances, and each individual's attitudes, are different, and the comments above can only be general in view. However, they indicate the wide range of factors which the adviser needs to consider in discussing priorities with clients and ultimately in presenting recommendations to the client.

Key chapter points

- After collecting information during the factfinding process, the adviser must assess the information critically.

- Part of this process must be to assess whether there are any additional needs which have not so far been identified and which should be considered in the preparation of recommendations.

- The information should also be considered from the point of view of accuracy and completeness, without which the recommendations may not be suitable.

- Clients sometimes fail to give accurate and complete information because they do not fully appreciate the importance of doing so and the adviser needs to ensure that the client understands the consequences.

- It is also important to ensure that the information gathered during the factfinding process is still up to date when recommendations are made and eventually acted upon.

- Advisers should also check for inconsistencies and errors which appear to have been made in the information collected.

- These may be the result of the client providing incorrect information knowingly or by mistake.

- In some cases they may also arise from incorrect recording of information given.

- Such aspects of information should be clarified as soon as possible, and where relevant to recommendations, this may mean a further client contact, perhaps by telephone.

- Errors often arise as a result of the client not fully understanding technical aspects of taxation, products or investment, particularly in more complex areas of financial services.

- There is commonly difficulty for clients in the interpretation of the provisions of pension arrangements, whether occupational or personal.

- Providing the client with a copy of the factfind is a useful way of confirming the information which has been used in the preparation of recommendations.

- Clarifying inconsistencies and errors is often a good way of uncovering extra information that may have been overlooked in the original factfinding process.

- Advisers may need to bring in others if advice is required in areas with which the adviser is not fully conversant.

- Clients may already have advisers with other specialist fields, for example an accountant or a lawyer.

- An actuary might be involved if there is an employer sponsored occupational scheme.

- A consideration of life stages in examining needs can be over-simplistic, but there are various influences which are likely to dictate the most pressing needs for individuals. These include age and family situation, amongst other things.

Chapter Quiz

1   What are the possible consequences of advice being prepared on the basis of information which is not accurate and complete? .... (see para 2.2)

2   Why is it not always adequate to rely on a scheme booklet for details of the benefits under an occupational pension scheme. ....(2.6)

3   What situations might give rise to an adviser needing to involve a colleague in the advice process for a particular client? ....(3.1)

4   What impact does employment status have on the likely needs of a client? ....(4.2)

5   What particular factor can make it difficult to quantify needs in the case of a business owner?.......................(4.2)

6   In what area of financial planning are preferential terms available to those who are in ill heath? ....(4.2)

Recommendations

1 Evaluating solutions

1.1 Background

The adviser needs to consider the **possible solutions** to each of a client's needs and this will mean a consideration of **various products**. In this chapter we consider a range of needs and the products which are most likely to come into consideration, looking at the **main features** of each one.

Independent advisers also need to consider the **choice of product provider**, and this is also discussed in this chapter.

1.2 Requirements

There are various requirements which recommendations need to meet, and advisers need to consider in particular:

- **Relationship between need and solution**. Whatever the need which has been identified, the solution chosen must be **adequate** to meet it. Sometimes this will require a **combination** of products, or may mean that it must be accepted there will still be a **gap** between the recommended provision and that which the client might ideally want.

For example, providers of personal IPI (PHI) arrangements will not generally provide cover in excess of **60-65% of pre-disability income**, and at higher income levels, the maximum is often lower. This is not a legislative or taxation requirement, but reflects the **insurers' wish** to ensure that there remains a **motivation** to return to work on recovery. The client may ideally want **more extensive** cover, but in reality will almost certainly have to accept that the gap exists.

The adviser should consider how the **gap** between the required income and the income provided by the IPI arrangement **would be met** in the event of incapacity, and this may mean **drawing on other assets**. This might be one reason why an element of **cash** on deposit should be included within the portfolio.

- **Degree of risk**. The solutions put forward should be **consistent with the attitude to risk** agreed with the client in relation to the need area concerned. Remember that the level of risk which will be acceptable will **vary from need to need**, as well as according to the client's attitude, as discussed in Chapter 3. This is likely to mean that **different aspects** of the adviser's recommendations will involve **different degrees of risk**, with longer term arrangements involving the greatest risk and potential reward.

- **Tax position**. Recommendations should be as **tax efficient** as possible taking account of the tax advantages available for various types of provision. The evaluation of any product needs to take account of the **tax position** of the client, and where appropriate of any **likely changes** to that tax position in future.

  This may also involve a consideration of the **ownership of assets** where advice is being given to a couple. Sharing the assets between the partners may improve the overall tax efficiency of the arrangements, by utilising the allowances and tax bands of both.

- **Affordability**. The arrangements must be **affordable** by the client and in particular any ongoing commitment, for example to pay regular premiums to a protection arrangement, must be **realistic** in terms of the amount of money the client has available.

  In many cases, this may also mean that the adviser's recommendations must acknowledge that **some needs cannot be met immediately** but must be deferred for later consideration.

The process of advice must follow **regulatory requirements**, and in particular the advice given must be **suitable**. Meeting the requirements listed above, together with an **appropriate choice of provider**, should ensure that the suitability requirement is met.

The regulatory requirements also underpin the need for advisers to ensure that **communication** with clients is **full, comprehensible and accurate**. This will include disclosure of product details, and where applicable, commission details. As with many regulatory requirements, this would be necessary in terms of **good practice** in any event.

There may be areas where **no solutions** , or only partial solutions can be put forward, perhaps because of **product limitations** (as in the case of the IPI limitation mentioned above) or **legislative limits** (such as those applying to ISAs) or **lack of product availability**. In some cases, the client's particular circumstances may make it impossible to find a suitable solution, for example in the case of someone in **ill-health** who wishes to establish a protection contract.

In these cases, the problems must be admitted and **explained**, and consideration must be given to **alternatives**, such as the utilisation of existing assets in the most appropriate way. For example, in the case of an individual who is suffering ill-health, it may be appropriate to **reposition certain assets** to ensure availability when they are likely to be required by the individual's heirs. In addition, in these circumstances, consideration should be given to **transferring ownership** of some assets, perhaps the creation of suitable **trusts** and ensuring that the client's **will** is up to date.

2 Life insurance protection

2.1 Types of policy

Life insurance (or assurance – the terms are interchangeable these days) is perhaps the most basic, and the most widely recognised form of **financial protection**, and will therefore often figure in recommendations.

There are **three basic forms of life insurance**, namely **term**, **whole of life** (sometimes referred to simply as 'whole life') and **endowment** insurance. The endowment policy is a combination of savings and protection, with the emphasis towards savings, so for protection purposes, we will concentrate on term and whole life.

Term insurance can take a number of forms, but essentially provides **purely for protection** needs and will pay benefits only if the life assured dies during the term of the policy. It is the most **basic** form of life insurance protection and is also the **cheapest**. Because it is designed to provide cover for a **defined term**, it is suitable only for needs which are temporary in nature. For example, dealing with the need to protect a loan which will be repaid over a specified period of time is a natural use of term insurance.

2.2 Types of term insurance

There are **various types** of term insurance which are designed with specific **additional features**, intended to meet the needs of particular situations, and these can **extend the application** of term policies considerably. For example, **increasing (or sometimes index-linked) term insurance** is designed to help the policyholder maintain cover at a level which increases to make an allowance for inflation. The **premium** for such a policy is **higher** than would be the case for a level (ie non-increasing) term insurance policy because the insurer agrees to allow the increases **without further medical evidence**, and therefore is taking on a higher level of risk.

Use of increasing term insurance

Peter wants a term insurance policy to cover him for the period during which his children are likely to remain financially dependent. The intention is that if he were to die, the lump sum will be invested to provide an income for his family.

He chooses an index-linked policy, so that he can be sure that the cover will increase each year to counteract the effect of inflation, and that even if he suffered ill-health, those increases would still apply without any special terms. It is also convenient for him to see the increases occurring automatically, rather than there being a need for him to take specific action each year.

However, he still needs to review his cover, and may need to adjust it from time to time. For example, if his income increases faster than inflation, his need for cover is likely to increase faster too, because the cover is designed to replace part of his income. The adviser should stimulate this re-evaluation of cover as part of the normal review process (discussed in Chapter 8).

Some policies apply the increases **automatically**, whilst others include an **increase option**. In the latter case, future options will usually fall away if an option is declined (or sometimes if two such increases are declined). This is to reduce the degree of selection against the insurer which could occur if the choice was entirely unrestricted.

Renewable term insurance allows the policy to be renewed at the end of the term, so for example, at the expiry of an original ten year term policy, **instead of the cover simply lapsing**, the policyholder can opt to take out a **further policy** of the same sort, to extend the cover for a further ten years. The new policy will generally include a **further renewability** option, so this process can be repeated several times, though insurers will impose a maximum age of perhaps 70 or 75 for the final expiry of cover.

The renewal takes place **without medical evidence**, so this option helps to reduce or remove a major disadvantage of ordinary term insurance policies, namely the possibility that cover will lapse and the individual will not be able to obtain further cover because of a worsening of health. Because of the increased risk for the insurer, the **premium** for renewable term insurance is **greater** than for policies with no renewability option.

Convertible term insurance will allow the cover to be **converted** to a whole of life policy or endowment policy at a future date and can therefore be a cost effective way in the short term of providing cover which will be needed over the long term. Once again the advantage is that the conversion can be made **without any further evidence of health** being required.

The premium for the new policy taken out under a renewability or conversion option will reflect the individual's **age** at the time the new policy is issued. This means that where cover is provided over a long period by means of a series of (for example) renewable term insurance policies, the premium will generally **increase at each renewal point**.

Note that policies often **combine a number of features**, for example an increasing term insurance policy which is both renewable and convertible. (Where a policy is renewable and/or convertible, the option generally allows the **original level of sum insured** to be provided under the new policy. However, where the cover is **increasing**, the option will apply to sum assured at the **level it has reached at the time**, including the increases which have been applied to date. Some policies allow a **further increase** option at the date of renewal so there is no interruption to the pattern of increases.)

These policies **widen the application** of term insurance and a renewable policy allows for the fact that, particularly with needs such as family protection, it is often **difficult** to know **exactly the period** for which the cover will be needed. A new born child is likely to be dependent until he leaves school at a minimum age of 16, but might then become self-sufficient. On the other hand, he could continue at school or college to study for and take A levels, then have a gap year, then take on a university degree, perhaps followed by a Master's degree. He could therefore be dependent into his mid-twenties or beyond. **Renewability** allows the cover to be **continued** through the **required period**.

A **convertible policy** can take the place of a whole life policy, and so may initially be intended to cover family protection, but later be converted and used for **longer term needs** as discussed in the next section.

Decreasing term insurance covers needs which themselves decrease, for example a loan which is being repaid over a period of time. A mortgage protection policy is a variety of decreasing term, since the sum payable on death **decreases in line with a formula** reflecting the reduction in the outstanding loan.

There are also decreasing term policies known as **inter vivos policies**, specifically designed to cover the **inheritance tax liability** that can arise on **potentially exempt transfers**. The cover in this case reduces according to the **taper relief** scale under inheritance tax rules.

Another variation on the decreasing term insurance product is the **family income benefit policy** where an income is payable for the remainder of the term following the death of the life assured. If death occurs early in the term, the income will be payable for a long period whereas if death occurs towards the end of the term, it will only be payable for a short time. This kind of arrangement is very useful for protecting the **needs of a family** over the period during which they are likely to be dependent, and is one of the cheapest forms of cover available.

The **advantages and disadvantages** of this form of insurance were discussed in Chapter 1.

2.3 Whole of life policies

Not all protection needs exist only during a defined term. Some will be present indefinitely and these are best covered by a **whole of life policy** which will provide benefits irrespective of when death occurs.

Examples of the need for whole of life policies are the need to protect the **financial position of a dependent spouse or partner** and the need to protect an estate against the possible impact of **inheritance tax**.

As with term insurance, there are many types of **whole of life policies**. This in part reflects the fact that there will always be an **element of investment** within a whole of life policy, and this can be treated in a number of different ways.

Non-profit policies guarantee a known death benefit for a fixed premium, but the amount of cover will not increase at any time. A **with-profits policy** on the other hand will increase the sum assured through bonus additions and may thus help to increase cover generally and protect it at least to some extent from inflation. As with increasing term insurance policies, the adviser will need to **prompt** the client to **review** cover from time to time rather than relying solely on these increases to maintain cover in line with needs.

Over recent years **unit-linked arrangements**, often known as **flexible whole of life plans**, have started to dominate this market. Their popularity arises largely from the greater **flexibility** and greater **choice** these allow the client. Generally for any given premium level, the range of possible sums assured will be very wide, in some cases designed so as to be capable of being maintained throughout life on the same premium level, whilst in other cases designed to give maximum cover in the short term, on the understanding that maintenance of cover will require increases in premium at a later stage. Premiums are **reviewed** at fixed intervals, often ten years, though **shorter review periods** are often introduced at older ages, when cover costs increase more rapidly.

Advisers need to ensure that clients understand the basis of the plan they adopt. If the plan is arranged to give maximum cover for a given premium (often known simply as the **maxi-cover** basis), the premium will **increase** when the policy comes to its first **review**. The initial cover is therefore cheap, with a premium similar to that which would apply under a term insurance policy, but the increases which occur later can be **substantial**. This basis would be suitable for someone with a need for substantial cover, and limited spendable income, but with the expectation that income will increase in the future.

The profile of premiums under a **maxi-cover** whole of life policy is therefore similar to that under a series of **renewable term insurance policies**, as discussed above. However, under a whole of life policy, there is no **maximum age** by which the cover must expire.

If the premium is calculated to remain the same throughout life (often known as standard cover), this calculation is based on various assumptions, including the growth rate to be achieved on the investment part of the policy. If the assumed growth rate is not achieved, the premiums will increase (or the sum assured must be reduced). Conversely, if the assumed growth rate is exceeded, the premiums could be reduced or the cover increased.

A number of other factors could influence the premiums required following the review, and these are listed in the table below.

Factors affecting premiums under a flexible whole of life policy

There are many factors which could affect the premium levels determined at each policy review. The most important of these are:

- Investment growth achieved
- Any changes to risk rates generally
- The increasing age of the insured
- Changes to policy charges
- Changes to the taxation treatment of the fund
- Changes to the level of cover required

Whole of life contracts will normally develop a **surrender value** over a period of time, although this is likely to be modest in the early years. However the main emphasis of whole of life plans is on the provision of protection. For savings needs, other products are likely to be more efficient, both in terms of their **charge structure** and often their **tax treatment**.

They are also in general more expensive than term policies, because the level of cover provided is more extensive in the sense that it is **available indefinitely** rather than being restricted to a particular period.

3 Health insurance

3.1 Background

The majority of people have at least some life insurance arrangements, even if these only cover major liabilities such as a mortgage. Far fewer have **protection against health problems**, yet an individual is more likely to suffer an illness or injury which prevents him working for an extended period than to die before the age of 65.

The impact on an individual or a family budget which will result from an inability to work can be extremely dramatic. In many cases it will be **more severe** than the impact which would result from death. This reflects the fact that not only is the individual unable to work to produce an income, but in addition, **normal living expenses** are likely to continue. Often **further expenses** will result from the disability itself.

The provision of suitable protection to cope with this situation is therefore particularly important. There is a range of different products available and each of the main types is dealt with in turn.

3.2 Income Protection Insurance

Income Protection Insurance (IPI), or Permanent Health Insurance as it is often called, is central to the protection of income against incapacity. IPI provides for the **continuation of income for an individual who is unable to work through sickness or injury,** and benefits are paid after a deferred period which can range from a few weeks up to a year, or occasionally more. Clearly the longer the deferred period, **the lower the incidence of claims** and the lower the premium.

In addition, different **definitions of incapacity** apply which may also affect premium levels. For example under some policies, in order to claim, it is necessary only that the individual is unable to follow his **own occupation**. On the other hand, other policies require that the claimant be unable to follow **any occupation**. The latter is a significantly more difficult definition to satisfy, and would be expected to result in fewer claims, and premiums are therefore lower.

The policy will have a **termination date**, which is when cover ends, or, if a claim is in force, benefit payments will cease. This should usually be chosen to correspond with expected retirement date, so the cover matches the timescale of the need to replace income. The earlier the termination date, the lower the premium, because the claim payment period is less.

Although **maximum benefits** are not controlled by law, **insurance company practice** is that benefits provided should be limited, so as to encourage individuals to return to work as soon as they are able to do so. The maximum level of cover available from most insurers is **60 – 65% of pre-disability income**, and this maximum is further reduced by **State benefits** and any other benefits paid as a result of the incapacity.

For those on high levels of income, a **lower limit** may apply. This reflects the fact that not all of the income is regarded as necessary to support a reasonable lifestyle, and the lower limit is therefore consistent with the intention of ensuring the motivation to return to work.

Generally only **earned income** is taken into account in determining the limit, because other income, such as income from investments will not be affected by incapacity. However, sometimes where an individual is a shareholding director of a private company, and draws most of his income in dividends, these may be taken into account at least to an extent. This reflects the fact that the company's ability to pay dividends may be dependent on the contribution to profit made by the individual's ability to work.

IPI is also available from some insurers to cover **'housepersons'** who are not in paid employment, but whose incapacity could nevertheless create financial problems because their **responsibilities** would need to be taken on by others, probably on a **paid basis**. Benefit levels are usually restricted to the likely cost of providing for this.

Some employers provide **group IPI** arrangements, which pay a continuation of salary at a known level, perhaps 50% of pre-disability income in the event of incapacity. Unlike the position with personal IPI arrangements, the benefits from these schemes take the form of a continuation of salary and are subject to **tax and NI contribution liability**.

The amount and availability of State benefits has decreased over the years, partly as a result of the replacement of Invalidity Benefit by **Incapacity Benefit**, with effect from April 1995. This increased the importance of Income Protection Insurance still further.

Protection against incapacity is important for anyone who **relies on income** produced by working, as opposed to income from other sources such as investment or pensions. The need is greatest for those with **limited liquid assets**, who would therefore find it hardest to provide for their everyday living expenses from other sources.

The **self-employed** often have a greater need that the employed, because there is no employer to provide benefits, and State benefits are slightly less generous.

Where there are **dependants** relying on the income of an earner, the **responsibility** of the earner to arrange suitable protection is that much greater.

3.3 Waiver of premium benefit

A related benefit is **waiver of premium** (also called **'waiver of contribution'**). This provides for the maintenance of premiums to a life insurance policy or pension arrangement if the policyholder is **incapacitated** for a given period, often six months. The advantage is that the **benefits**, which may be even more important as a result of the incapacity, can be **continued**, without imposing additional pressure on an already **restricted budget**.

Under Personal Pensions and Stakeholder Pensions, the rules regarding waiver changed for new arrangements in 2001. Until **5 April 2001**, waiver could be included within the arrangement, with tax relief on the cost, but no relief on contributions funded by the waiver in the event of incapacity. This reflected the fact that strictly the contributions were waived rather than paid, so no relief could arise. This approach also had the advantage that contributions could be credited to the arrangement irrespective of the individual's level of earnings, or even if he had none at all, which is often the case if the individual is unable to work. At that time, contributions were not allowed for people with no earnings.

The basis applicable from 6 April 2001 requires that the waiver can only be provided **outside the personal pension or stakeholder pension**. No relief is available on the cost, but contributions funded by the waiver qualify for relief in the normal way. However, tax relief is also limited by normal rules. Often the individual has no earnings, because he is incapacitated, so relief is only available on contributions up to £3,600 pa, even if the amount paid whilst the individual was working was much higher.

Also, **relief** is available at the **rate applicable** to the individual at the **time they are paid**, so if as a result of the incapacity, the individual becomes a basic rate taxpayer, he will obtain only basic rate relief, even if he was a higher rate taxpayer at the time he was working and paid the cost of the waiver.

IPI policies themselves generally include waiver of premium **automatically**, in the sense that they provide that premiums are not payable during any period when income benefits are in payment.

3.4 Personal accident and sickness insurance

Personal accident and sickness insurance policies are considerably cheaper than IPI, and provide benefits largely in lump sum form, in certain specified circumstances such as if the insured loses his sight, or a limb as a result of sickness or injury.

Limited **income benefits** are usually included, but are payable for a short period of perhaps one or two years if the insured is totally disabled. In addition, it is important to realise that these policies are not permanent – that is, **renewal can be refused** by the insurance company at any annual renewal. The cover is therefore substantially less extensive than that offered by an IPI policy, although the premiums are also much lower.

Cover is also available under some policies to provide similar benefits in the event of **redundancy** or **unemployment**. Benefits are often linked to the insured's mortgage payments in this event, and these policies are sometime known as **ASU policies** (Accident, Sickness and Unemployment). Cover for redundancy starts after an **initial period** of perhaps three or six months to avoid those who anticipate redundancy taking out cover at the last minute and benefiting **unfairly**. **Voluntary redundancy** would not be covered at any time however.

3.5 Critical illness benefit

Critical illness benefit or **critical illness cover (CIC)** is a relatively recent innovation to the UK insurance market. It provides for a benefit, usually in **lump sum** form, if the insured suffers from any one of a number of specified illnesses, which are invariably serious and often life threatening. Benefits are **paid on diagnosis** and do not require the individual to be incapacitated in any way (except if the claim is in respect of total permanent disability). Because the benefits are paid in lump sum form, subsequent recovery, even if total, would not prejudice the claim in any way.

Critical illness benefit is often written **as a rider to a life insurance policy** and the benefit is payable in the form of an acceleration of the sum assured which would have been payable on death. Once the critical illness benefit has been paid therefore, the policy **lapses**. This means that there will be no benefits payable on subsequent death, and this may leave an **important need unprotected**.

Freestanding critical illness benefit policies therefore provide a more effective type of cover. These do not include any life insurance in the conventional sense, and provide simply the critical illness cover.

This benefit is sometimes seen as an alternative to IPI. It should really not be viewed in this way, but is better used to **supplement** IPI cover. Whereas IPI seeks to replace income which is lost as a result of incapacity, critical illness benefit can provide a lump sum which may assist with necessary modifications to lifestyle or could provide for the repayment of a mortgage in order to lessen the financial pressure resulting from the situation. In some cases the benefit can be used to obtain faster treatment of the diagnosed condition.

CIC: conditions typically covered

The range of conditions covered depends on the policy, and the adviser should ensure that the client understands the conditions concerned. Typically, the policy will cover:

- Most forms of cancer
- Heart attack
- Coronary bypass surgery
- Stroke
- Kidney failure
- Major organ transplant
- Multiple sclerosis
- Alzheimer's disease
- Blindness
- Paralysis
- Total permanent disability

Note that AIDS is usually excluded from the conditions covered.

3.6 Private medical insurance

Private medical insurance (PMI) provides for payment of medical expenses and is particularly useful for those who wish to be able to use private medical facilities rather than the NHS.

Various levels of cover are available, and the premium level will reflect the cover provided. In some cases cover is restricted to situations where the **waiting time** for NHS treatment exceeds a **specified period**, whilst in other cases the provision is much wider.

It could be argued that PMI is not usually a pressing need, because **NHS care** is in place and will always deal with **emergency needs**. However, the **substantial waiting lists** which can arise may mean that treatment for conditions which are debilitating, but not immediately life threatening, may take a **long time** to arrange. Also, **referrals** to specialists take longer under the NHS than they commonly do on a private basis.

These factors can mean that PMI is a **high priority** for **some clients**, particularly those such as the **self-employed** and **business owners** who are dependent on their own activities to generate income, and for whom any lengthy interruption to this ability can be difficult to cope with.

3.7 Universal life plans

A further development in recent years has been the introduction of **universal life plans**. As well as life insurance cover, generally on a whole of life basis, these plans include a number of **additional benefits** such as waiver of premium, disability benefit, critical illness benefit and so on, all provided under one arrangement. The range and amount of benefit can be altered from time to time, subject to whatever adjustment to premiums may be necessary and further medical evidence may be required.

These policies are **convenient** and **flexible**, and can focus attention on the range of protection arrangements which should be considered. However, the **cost** may be **relatively high** if the provider's rates for some types of cover are not particularly keen.

3.8 Long term care insurance (LTCI)

LTCI is intended to **provide for care** needed by the elderly in cases where their ability to perform everyday activities of living may diminish. It is likely to become increasingly important over the next few years as **life expectancy** continues to increase. **Activities of daily living (ADLs)** used for this purpose include such things as washing, dressing and going to the toilet. It is the extent to which an individual is unable to carry out these tasks unaided that determines eligibility for long term care benefits, and often the amount which is payable.

Benefits arising from long-term care insurance policies will be paid **free of tax** in all cases. These insurance based arrangements are sometimes known as pre-funded arrangements, where premiums are paid either as a lump sum or on a regular basis, to purchase insurance against needing care in the future.

Immediate care arrangements, designed for those who are already in care, or are about to go into care, provide an immediate benefit to meet fees. Rather than being a type of insurance, these arrangements are usually based on an **annuity**, with the terms taking account of the medical position (in particular, life expectancy) of the individual at the time the arrangement starts. They are therefore in effect impaired life annuities.

Where an immediate care arrangement is based on an annuity, the instalments of the annuity are also tax free, as long as they are paid to the care provider (eg the nursing home in which the individual lives). Otherwise the **normal taxation provisions** applicable to purchased life annuities (PLAs) apply, with part of each instalment regarded as a return of capital, and being tax free, with the balance treated as taxable savings income.

One of the reasons that Long Term Care fees planning is so important is that the extent to which **help is available from Local Authorities** (whose responsibility this is) depends upon the individual's assets. This is a very complex area, but in principle, if an individual has assets valued in excess of £21,000 (2006/07), there will usually be **no assistance** from the Local Authority, though **other State benefits** such as Attendance Allowance, which is not means tested may still be available. Care fees will therefore have to be provided largely by the individual, from his accumulated assets. The result can be a severe **erosion** of the individual's **estate**, and therefore of any **potential inheritance** which can be passed on to later generations. This can be a great worry for the usually elderly people involved.

It also remains a concern for those receiving care that their **financial resources might run out**, leaving them wholly **reliant** on the **Local Authority** and/or their own **family**.

4 Making choices – protection

With a large number of different forms of insurance available and with a number of options available within each product type, the **choice for the consumer** can be difficult.

For life insurance, much depends on the need being covered, and whether it is **temporary** or **permanent**. Also, likely changes in the level of cover required will determine whether an increasing or decreasing arrangement would be preferred.

Cost is often a primary concern. Given that most people cannot afford to provide as much cover as they would ideally have, the lower premiums associated with term insurance can be attractive, and convertible term insurance gives the option to move to whole of life later.

For **health insurance**, IPI should be seen as central, where this cover is not already provided by the employer. The **self-employed** particularly should see this as a priority. However, **cost considerations** could point towards the limited cover provided by sickness and accident insurance policies, at least as a **temporary stop gap** measure until the fuller cover offered by IPI arrangements can be afforded.

Private medical insurance is important for many people, but perhaps less so than IPI, since NHS treatment is available as an alternative, except for those for whom any treatment delay would be unacceptable.

Long-term care is also growing in popularity as the likelihood of a long life beyond retirement increases, and a greater proportion of people are likely to need care at some time in their lives.

5 Savings

5.1 Background

One of the most important aspects of financial planning is to deal with the requirement of many people to **build up capital on a regular basis from income**. There are many types of product which are designed to assist **saving** in this way and the main types are now considered.

Important aspects in the choice of product are **accessibility**, **tax treatment** and **risk profile**. Because these factors will differ significantly from client to client, there can be no 'right answer' to the question of which savings product is the best, although some products will be more suitable for particular clients than others, and **some may be unsuitable**.

5.2 Deposit arrangements

Deposit accounts of various sorts are available from banks and building societies, with interest rates generally increasing where the deposit is made for a **specified term** or where **notice** is required for withdrawals.

Although the **return** on deposit accounts is likely to be significantly less in the longer term than on asset-backed investments, the security and accessibility of deposit accounts generally make them attractive.

In terms of saving from income, deposit accounts could be used to build up an **emergency fund** or alternatively may be used **as a holding account** to accumulate sums which can then be diverted to asset-backed investments.

As a general rule, an emergency fund of **between three and six months' income** is desirable, and it is usually best for this to be held in an account offering immediate access. If dealing with the investment of a lump sum, holding between 10% and 15% of the total in this way would be considered usual.

The extent to which more funds should be held on deposit will depend upon the **immediate needs of the client** and his **risk profile**. However, attention should be given to increasing the interest rate achieved by **grouping funds** to allow larger deposits which may qualify for a higher rate, as well as opting for **notice accounts** for that part which is not likely to be required for immediate access.

5.3 TOISAs

The TESSA (Tax-Exempt Special Savings Account) is no longer a current product, but there was a **reinvestment option** which allowed the capital (but not the interest) at maturity, or within 6 months afterwards, to be reinvested in the **cash component of an ISA**, without affecting normal ISA investment limits. (ISAs generally are covered in more detail below.)

TESSAs were five year accounts offering **tax free interest**, provided the account was not closed early. The last date on which a TESSA could be started was 5 April 1999, so the last possible maturity date was 5 April 2004, and the last possible reinvestment date was 5 October 2004.

Although this reinvestment could be made into the cash component of a maxi-ISA, or into a cash mini-ISA, it was **most common** to use a **TESSA-only ISA (TOISA)**, which is a freestanding account designed specifically for this purpose. If a TOISA was used, not only did the amount invested not count towards normal limits, but in addition, the individual could still choose freely between the mini- and maxi-ISA routes for his 'normal' ISA investment. The TOISA **only offers a cash component**.

The TOISA has **no fixed term**, and there are **no restrictions on withdrawals**, so this is a flexible way of maintaining the advantage of **tax free** interest **indefinitely** (under current legislation).

5.4 Cash mini-ISAs

Individual Savings Accounts (ISAs) replaced TESSAs (and Personal Equity Plans or PEPs) from 6 April 1999, and provide **tax free growth**, but without any minimum term, nor any restriction on withdrawals.

ISA **investments are limited**, and full details are given later in this Chapter, when the subject of ISAs generally is covered. The cash mini-ISA is a type of ISA that may appeal to the same clients that found TESSAs attractive.

Investment into a **cash mini-ISA** is limited to £3,000 per year. Interest is **credited gross** and there is **no tax** to pay, irrespective of the tax position of the investor.

Withdrawals are available at any time, and are **unlimited** in amount, so one of these accounts can be used as a very tax efficient and accessible instant access account. Note however that there are some **constraints**. In particular, taking a withdrawal from an ISA does not affect how much further investment is allowed.

For example, if an investment of £1,000 is made to a cash mini-ISA in May 2006, up to a further £2,000 can be invested later in the year. If £500 is withdrawn in June, this does not change the position, in other words still only £2,000 can be added – this **cannot be increased** by reinvesting the amount withdrawn. This means that although the money deposited is **accessible**, it will usually be **unsuitable** as an instant access account where **significant numbers of payments in and out** are expected.

However, if the investor takes out a **cash mini-ISA**, he cannot take out a maxi-ISA in the same tax year, and will consequently find his ability to invest in **stocks and shares** through ISAs is **restricted**. If stocks and shares investment is important, it may be more suitable to use the cash component of a maxi-ISA (see below) or to maximise stocks and shares investment through ISAs and accept less tax efficient deposit investment as a result, outside ISAs.

Since 6 April 2001, **16 and 17 year olds** have been able to contribute to **cash ISAs** (though not to any other component) with a maximum investment of £3,000 per year. However, if the investment is made with money gifted by a parent, the income will be aggregated with other income arising from gifts from that parent, and will be taxed as the parent's income if the total is in excess of £100 pa.

Remember that although tax free interest is attractive in principle, it remains **important** that the **asset allocation** across the portfolio as a whole is suitable for the client's needs. It may be better in some cases to have some **equity investment**, even if not entirely within a tax advantaged wrapper such as an ISA than to have all investments held on deposit, even if all interest is free of tax.

5.5 Offshore deposits

Deposit accounts can be held **offshore**, and interest on these accounts is credited **without deduction of tax**. Attractive interest rates are available at times, but **interest is taxable** in the tax year it is credited to the account.

If the offshore account is denominated in a foreign currency, then potential **exchange rate fluctuations** will add an element of risk to the investment.

5.6 National Savings & Investments (NS&I)

Various arrangements are available from **National Savings & Investments**, matched to various specific needs. Latest information can be readily obtained either direct from National Savings & Investments via the internet or from major post offices.

Security is always a feature of National Savings & Investments products and, since they are backed by the Government, the degree of security offered is difficult to beat. Many of the products also enjoy **tax advantages**, and in a number of cases offer tax free interest. This is particularly useful for **higher rate taxpayers** who benefit from the same net return as everyone else, whereas with most alternative investments their tax position will reduce the net yield.

The terms of National Savings & Investments products need to be considered carefully. For example, **NS&I Savings Certificates** accrue interest tax-free, and this is rolled up within the certificate through the term. This is a good, secure and tax efficient investment, but would not be suitable if the investor required income.

In addition, although capital is always guaranteed, early withdrawal can lead to a loss of part, or in some cases all, of the interest earned. This means that products such as NS&I Savings Certificates are **not ideal for emergency fund money**, which is best held in an instant access account.

National Savings & Investments products in general are geared to **lump sum investment** although those with relatively low minimum investments can be used to save from income. There is also a **monthly investment option** for Premium Bonds. **Fixed Rate Savings Bonds** offer the investor the choice of various investment terms (which vary from time to time) with a guaranteed interest rate (which varies according to the term) and a choice of whether interest is paid out or accumulated. The table below gives brief details of the main NS&I products currently available. Further details are available from the NS&I website (www.nsandi.com).

National Savings & Investments products			
Product	**Interest rate**	**Tax position**	**Comments**
Fixed Rate Savings Certificates	Fixed	Tax free	Attractive for higher rate taxpayers and for those requiring absolute security. Those who are not higher rate taxpayers can usually find better interest rates elsewhere. Two and five year terms available.
Index-linked Savings Certificates	Fixed addition to RPI increase	Tax free	Again attractive for higher rate taxpayers, and those who want certainty that the value of their investment will outpace price inflation. Three and five year terms available.
Income Bond	Variable	Taxable, paid gross	Income is paid monthly and this can appeal to those for whom income is a high priority. There is risk however because of the variable nature of the income.
Capital Bond	Fixed	Taxable, credited gross	A fixed five year term applies, but this product offers complete security of capital, plus a guaranteed interest rate. Interest is taxable when credited, so for taxpayers, the tax liability must be met from other resources.

Product	Interest rate	Tax position	Comments
Children's Bonus Bond	Fixed for 5 years	Tax free	Available for children aged under 16, with interest usually competitive and fixed for 5 year periods. Matures at age 21. Tax efficient and a straight-forward way of saving for children, within modest limits.
Premium Bond	Variable	Tax free	Prizes are awarded according to a monthly draw, and take the place of interest, so an unlucky bond holder may receive no interest if he wins no prizes. The gamble in relation to the interest, with complete security of capital appeals to many, and the tax free nature of the prizes is attractive for higher rate taxpayers.
Fixed Rate Savings Bond	Fixed	Taxable, 20% tax deducted at source	Various terms are offered and these can vary from time to time. Interest can be paid out or accumulated, and rates vary according to the choice made and the term. The fixed rate of interest appeals to many investors.
Pensioners' Bond	Fixed	Taxable, paid gross	Available to those over 60 (whether pensioners or not). Various terms are offered which can vary from time to time. The fixed rate is attractive to those requiring income, with total security of capital.
Guaranteed Equity Bond	Linked to stock market	Taxable	Terms vary according to each issue, but generally capital is protected and the investor benefits from a fixed percentage of any increase in the FTSE 100 index. There are no dividends, and the index growth is not adjusted for dividends. This product appeals to those who want to share in stock market growth, but without the risk of loss. However, growth is taxable as income, so no use can be made of CGT exemptions and reliefs. These Bonds are not always available, but a new issue is made from time to time, and is available for a limited period.
Easy Access Savings Account	Variable	Taxable, credited gross	This account replaced the Ordinary Account in 2004, and is intended to compete with bank and building society accounts. The interest rate is better than on the old Ordinary Account and increases according to the amount invested. Interest is fully taxable however.
Investment Account	Variable	Taxable, credited gross	This is a one month notice account, which offers higher interest rates at some (but not all) levels of investment than the Easy Access Account. Generally, better rates can be obtained on the high street.
Cash ISA	Variable	Tax free	Can be competitive with other cash ISAs from banks and building societies and offers the usual tax advantages with no fixed term.

5.7 Endowment policies

Endowment policies are intended specifically as **regular savings vehicles** and are almost always designed to meet the **qualifying rules** for life insurance policies. This allows the proceeds to be taken at maturity without any personal tax liability, although the investment fund will have been liable to tax throughout the term on both income and gains.

These arrangements provide a **disciplined approach** to regular savings and can be particularly attractive for higher rate taxpayers for whom the **freedom from personal taxation** on the proceeds is of considerable value.

The **inclusion of life insurance** is a useful feature too, and endowments are, of course, commonly used in conjunction with mortgages, because of their ability to pay off the loan on death or on maturity, though it is recognised that there are now more tax efficient approaches available.

Endowment policies can be non-profit, where both premium and benefits on death and maturity are fixed from outset, although this is relatively uncommon these days. More usually they are arranged on either a **with-profit or unit-linked basis**. The former is more secure, because of the guarantee that bonuses once added will not be taken away, but the unit-linked arrangements give greater investment flexibility and control.

Remember also that any **terminal bonus on a with-profits policy** is not guaranteed until it attaches to the benefits on encashment.

The existence of a **managed fund** for **unit-linked arrangements** reduces risk by utilising the skills of professional investment managers, and there will usually be a deposit fund, into which the accumulated investment can be switched as maturity approaches, or at any time the investor feels nervous about market prospects.

Endowment policies have served many investors well in the past, but the fact that the **investment fund is taxed** will usually mean that an ISA offers a more tax efficient savings vehicle. However, for higher rate taxpayers who have used their ISA allowances, the qualifying endowment policy still has a place. For those who are not higher rate taxpayers, there is **little advantage**, because the tax paid by the life fund broadly equates to the liability of a basic rate taxpayer. Indeed, because many basic rate taxpayers do not utilise their **CGT annual exemption**, and the life fund has no exemption, there can be a **disadvantage** from a tax point of view in relation to capital gains.

In addition, the **minimum term** for a qualifying endowment policy is **ten years**, though a policy can be surrendered without adverse tax consequences if premiums have been paid for ten years or, if less, three-quarters of the original term (ie seven and a half years if the original term was ten years). The **commitment** to regular premiums is therefore **extensive** and early surrender usually carries **penalties**. This can be disadvantageous to many potential investors, who will require greater flexibility.

5.8 Unit trusts and investment trusts

Regular savings arrangements are available from a number of unit trust and investment trust houses. These products provide the smaller investor with the opportunity to benefit from a **spread of investment** and from **professional management**.

In general they offer considerable **growth potential**, **low charges** and are very **flexible**, but at the same time carry a **higher degree of risk** than an endowment policy.

Because the prices of **unit trusts** and **investment trusts** will fluctuate with investment conditions generally, there is almost always an element of risk with these arrangements. However the potential for growth is greater than with deposit-based products in particular, especially if the plan is operated over the medium to long term.

The principle of **pound cost averaging** can also enhance the returns available from arrangements of this sort. This principle is based upon the fact that if regular payments are made to purchase units or shares at prices which fluctuate, the effect of purchasing a large number of units when prices fall, tends to outweigh the impact of the reduced number of units purchased when prices are high. This process can make investment into a volatile fund on a regular contribution basis very attractive and certainly reduces the risk associated with such investment, as discussed in Chapter 3.

Clearly however as the size of the investment builds up, relative to the regular monthly input, the effect of pound cost averaging tends to become **outweighed** by the fluctuations in value in the **existing investment** from a risk point of view.

Pound cost averaging applies equally to **unit linked endowment policies**, and because of the availability of managed funds (which are less common with unit and investment trust based vehicles) and deposit funds, the endowment based products would normally be regarded as lower risk than unit or investment trust products.

There are important **differences** between the structure of **unit trusts** and **investment trusts**. Unit trusts are perhaps simplest, with the unit price representing an equal division of the total value of the unit trust. Assets are valued periodically, usually daily, and (in simple terms) the unit price is found by **dividing the total value by the number of units in issue**.

Where new investors want to buy units, or existing investors wish to encash, the number of units is **adjusted accordingly**, so there is always a precise **balance** between supply and demand. The term '**open-ended**' is used to describe this situation where the number of units fluctuates to maintain this balance.

Investment trusts on the other hand are '**closed-ended**', because they have a fixed number of shares in issue at any time. As a result, supply and demand influences the price as well as the value of the underlying assets within the investment trust, and shares often trade at a discount to the net asset value (NAV), or at a premium to it. This can affect the return to the investor significantly.

Effect of changing levels of discount

Suppose an investor buys shares in an investment trust. At the time of purchase, the NAV is £5 per share, but the shares are trading at a 15% discount, so the share price is £4.25.

The investor sells some time later, when the NAV has increased by 5%, to £5.25 per share. However, the discount has widened to 20%, so the share price is £4.20. Even though the NAV has increased, the investor has made a loss because the price of the investment trust shares has decreased.

Conversely, the effect of a narrowing of the discount is beneficial to the investor. Suppose in the example above, all the details are unchanged except that, at the time of sale, the discount has narrowed to 10%. The share price is therefore £4.73 and the investor's gain is around 11%, even though the increase in NAV has been only 5%.

The closed-ended nature of investment trusts therefore adds a further unknown in the form of the influence of supply and demand, and this can increase **volatility** and **risk** compared to a **similarly invested unit trust**, but **potential return** is also greater.

A further **risk/reward factor** with investment trusts is their ability to gear. **Gearing** is simply borrowing to invest, and the manager of an investment trust might decide to do so if they believe investment prospects are rosy.

Effect of gearing

Suppose an investment trust manager believes that markets are to experience very positive performance in the next year. The value of the trust is currently £100m. He decides to gear, by borrowing £40m, at a rate of interest of 10%, so he must repay £44m at the end of the borrowing period. He now has £140m invested.

Suppose markets are positive and the assets within the trust increase by 30%. The £140m therefore increases to £182m, from which the £44m loan repayment is made, leaving £138m. The effect is that a 30% increase in investment values has increased the NAV of the investment trust by 38%. This should be reflected (though not precisely) in good share price performance.

On the other hand, the effect is disadvantageous if the market moves down. Suppose now that asset values reduce by 30%, so the £140m becomes £98m. Again the loan repayment of £44m must be made, leaving £54m. The 30% reduction in the investment values has resulted in a 46% decrease in the NAV of the trust.

Investment trusts **publish their policy** as regards gearing, and this allows investors and their advisers to evaluate the risk involved. Some investment trusts are considerably more aggressive than others in this way.

5.9 Open-Ended Investment Companies (OEICs)

A further choice is now widely available for investors, this being an investment through an **Open Ended Investment Company (OEIC)**.

The intention of introducing OEICs was to provide a product which was more closely in line with those available through the rest of Europe, and so to provide greater opportunities for UK institutions to market their products. OEICs combine arguably the **best features** of unit trusts and investment trusts, though all three products remain available.

The investor purchases **shares** in the OEIC, but unlike investment trusts, the number of shares in issue from time to time can vary (hence the expression 'open-ended'). This means that the **share price will reflect the underlying asset value** at all times and will not be subject to additional fluctuations as a result of market forces. There is **no bid/offer spread** on OEICs, which are bought and sold at the same price, though there will usually be an explicit **initial charge** instead.

In addition, like unit trusts, OEICs are not generally permitted to gear – ie borrow for investment purposes – except to a limited extent. This means that the **risk** associated with OEICs is **in line with unit trusts**, rather than investment trusts.

Because the price of shares in an OEIC will fluctuate in line with the value of the underlying asset value, **pound cost averaging** is still relevant.

In most cases, it will not be appropriate to recommend investment in unit trusts or OEICS outside an ISA unless the ISA allowance has already been taken up.

5.10 Personal Equity Plans (PEPs)

No further investments in **PEPs** are permitted after 5 April 1999, but **existing funds** can remain invested and enjoy the **same tax advantages as ISAs**. The existence of PEP investments does not affect the client's ISA limits or choices in any way.

Investment choices are limited within a PEP, with investment generally being in **equities** or related investments such as unit trusts, investment trusts and OEICs. It is also possible to invest in certain corporate bonds. From April 2001 the range of investments has been brought into line with the **stocks and shares component** of ISAs (see below) and so now includes certain gilts.

5.11 Individual Savings Accounts (ISAs)

ISAs were introduced from 6 April 1999, and provide a form of tax free investment in place of PEPs and TESSAs. The **main features** are as follows:

- A **Maxi-ISA** allows the investor to place the whole of his ISA allowance into one account. The investment limit is £7,000 per tax year (it has now been announced that this limit will remain in place until (at least) April 2010).

- The Maxi-ISA can be made up of two components:

  - **Stocks and shares component** (for which the range of permitted investments includes equities, gilts, unit trusts, investment trusts and OEICs)

  - **Cash component** (which can invest in deposits and similar investments)

- The stocks and shares component must always be present, but the inclusion of the cash component is optional.

- If included, the **maximum investment** allowed to the cash component is £3,000 per tax year.

- A **Mini-ISA** allows investment in only **one of the two components** discussed above, and the investor can take out two Mini-ISAs in any tax year, if he wishes, so as to place each component with a **different manager**. Limits are as for the Maxi-ISA, except that a limit of £4,000 per tax year applies to a stocks and shares Mini-ISA. Under a Maxi-ISA, any part of the total allowance not allocated to the other components can be invested in the stocks and shares component, giving a maximum of £7,000 pa.

ISAs will be **attractive for investors generally**, and should be seriously considered as part of any investment portfolio. In principle, there is **no reason** why an investment which could be held in an ISA should be held **outside**, unless ISA limits have been **fully used** already.

Particularly important is the fact that there is **no minimum term** for an ISA, **nor any restriction on withdrawals**. As always however, equity linked investment will only be suitable where the client expects to be able to leave the investment undisturbed for a **reasonable period** – say five years at least.

Although there is no tax liability on income or gains within the ISA, **dividend tax credits cannot be reclaimed** after 5 April 2004. This has reduced the tax advantages, particularly for basic rate taxpayers if the investment is in stocks and shares.

An investor with a balanced portfolio may therefore be best advised to hold the **fixed interest** part of his portfolio in an ISA rather than shares, unit trusts and so on, since this will maximise the **income tax efficiency**. However, he must also consider the CGT implications, because direct fixed interest holdings (though not fixed interest unit trusts and similar vehicles) held outside an ISA are generally exempt from CGT, whilst gains on shares etc are not. As always therefore, the decision must be based on the **individual circumstances** of the investor.

There are a number of 'catches' with ISAs, which must be taken into account when using them in a portfolio.

- It is **not permitted** for an investor to contribute to **both** a maxi-ISA and a mini-ISA in the same tax year. Nor can he contribute to **more than one maxi-ISA**, or **more than one mini-ISA of the same type** in the same tax year. This means that investing £1 in a cash mini-ISA restricts an individual to using a mini-ISA for stocks and shares investment, and so limits the amount available for such investment to £4,000.

- Also, it is **not permitted to transfer money between components** once it has been invested, so it is not possible to use the cash component as a temporary investment shelter, while awaiting more favourable stockmarket conditions.

- **Interest** arising under the cash component is tax free, but if it arises under the **stocks and shares component**, it is **taxed** at 20%. (There is no further liability for higher rate taxpayers, nor any ability for non-taxpayers to reclaim.)

Changes were made to the ISA rules from April 2005, and these allow inclusion of the new stakeholder cash and medium term investment products (but not stakeholder pensions) within the **cash** or **stocks and shares** component respectively. The CAT standards which related to Charges, Access and Terms and could be adopted on a voluntary basis by ISA providers are no longer applicable to new investments (because the stakeholder conditions take their place). CAT standard products taken out before 6 April 2005 must continue to apply the standards however.

5.12 Pensions

Although often considered as an entirely different area, **pension arrangements** are really just **part of an individual's overall approach to savings**.

Because of the **tax advantages** associated with pensions, they provide a particularly effective means of saving towards retirement. The benefits however generally need to be taken wholly or partially in the form of **pension**, which is **taxed as earned income**. This can reduce the attractiveness of pensions in some situations and further consideration is given to this point later in this Chapter.

6 Making choices – savings

Choice may be limited by **available money** for savings, because different products have different **minimum requirements**. Offshore arrangements, for example, generally require a higher minimum input than equivalent onshore products.

Many clients will want to avoid products which require a high level of **regular commitment**, unless they are sure of the regularity of their own income in the long term.

Major factors in considering recommendations are the **degree of risk** that the client is prepared to take, and the **period of time** over which the savings are expected to accumulate. The longer the period, the more likely it is that asset-backed investments (ie those where values fluctuate in line with the values of the underlying investments) will be suitable, since there is more chance that overall returns will ride out any short term reduction in values.

Bear in mind too that some savings plans have **minimum terms** under governing legislation. For example, a **higher rate tax liability** may arise if a qualifying life policy is surrendered early (and **penalties** levied by the insurance company are likely too).

Potential **need for access** generally is a further important consideration. Money which is likely to be required in the short term should generally be held in a **secure** investment vehicle where **capital values** are protected, and where there are **no tax or product penalties** on early surrender.

Access to pensions can be most **restrictive** of all (depending on the age of the investor) with benefits not usually available until the investor reaches the **age of 50 at the earliest**. This minimum age will **increase to 55** from 2010.

Taxation is also a factor, with the tax advantages of ISAs being particularly attractive to **higher rate taxpayers**, but of virtually no relevance to non-taxpayers.

For most savers, a **spread of investments** will be appropriate, both to avoid having 'all the eggs in one basket' and to allow a **range of levels of risk**. High potential return is likely to be allied to high potential risk, and most people will therefore seek a reasonable degree of security, spiced with a moderate level of higher risk/higher return savings vehicles.

7 Lump sum investment

7.1 Background

Lump sum investment will need to take account of many of the same considerations which apply to savings from income. However some products are more usually associated, and in some cases are only available, for lump sum rather than for regular contribution investment. The main features of lump sum investments are covered in this section.

7.2 Unit trusts, investment trusts and OEICs

Lump sum investments into **unit trusts** and **investment trusts** often provide a good alternative to direct equity investment because of the **diversification** and **professional management** involved. Only larger investors who can achieve a reasonable diversification of their portfolio should consider direct equity investment.

Although for convenience we have dealt with **unit trusts**, **investment trusts** and **OEICs** all together, remember that there are significant **differences** between them. For example, the unit price under a unit trust and the share price of an OEIC will always exactly reflect the value of the underlying assets. On the other hand an investment trust, which is constituted as a limited company and has a fixed number of shares in issue at any time, will have a **share price** which fluctuates not only according to the value of the underlying assets, but also to reflect market sentiment in the sense of supply and demand for the shares.

In addition, investment trusts have wider powers, particularly in the sense that they can **borrow money to invest**. This tends to **amplify performance** (for good or ill) and therefore tends to make investment trust prices more volatile.

These issues were discussed in more detail in the savings section of this chapter.

7.3 Direct equity investment

Many investors have **shareholdings**, often as the result of **privatisation or demutualisation issues**. In some cases, the shareholdings arise through tax advantaged **share schemes** offered to employees of (usually) quoted companies. The problem for the smaller investor, as mentioned above, is ensuring that he has sufficient **diversification** of his of investment to provide reasonable security. There is a particularly high degree of risk in holding a significant proportion of an individual's investments in **shares in his employer**, because the failure of the company could result in a loss of income, and **simultaneously** a large reduction in the value of his investments.

For small investors it will usually be more appropriate to use a **collective investment vehicle** such as a unit trust, OEIC or investment trust.

7.4 Investment bonds

An **investment bond** (sometimes called a **single premium bond**) is a life insurance policy designed to take in a lump sum (or a series of lump sums). Generally the arrangement is written as a **non-qualifying whole of life policy** and does not therefore have a fixed maturity date.

These arrangements are often unit-linked and offer a wide range of different investment funds, again with the advantage of professional management. **Switching** between funds is usually available at no charge or at a small charge, significantly less than the cost of moving from one share to another or from one unit trust or investment trust to another.

The **taxation** of bonds reflects their status as life insurance policies and growth, although taxed within the life office fund, will not lead to a personal tax liability until the bond is encashed or withdrawals over a certain limit are made. This limit on withdrawals is 5% of the **amount initially invested** each year for up to 20 years, with any **unused balance** carried forward **indefinitely**.

For higher rate taxpayers, a tax liability at higher rate, but not basic rate arises if a gain on surrender, or a withdrawal in excess of the cumulative 5% allowances takes place. Top-slicing relief is available to reduce (or even eliminate) the extent to which a gain or excess withdrawal falls into higher rate tax. The credit given for the tax paid by the life fund is 20%, so where a **higher rate liability** arises, the **rate is 20%**.

Because of their tax treatment, there can be useful applications of bonds, particularly for **higher rate taxpayers** who expect their tax position to alter in the future.

For example, suppose an investor is **currently a higher rate taxpayer**, but expects to be subject only to **basic rate tax in retirement**. Investing in a bond allows him to shelter the investment return from higher rate tax whist he is working. By timing the encashment of the bond to occur when he is only a basic rate taxpayer, and assuming the gain itself does not take him back into higher rate, the gain will then be crystallised, with **no higher rate liability** at all.

In the meantime, he would have **access to withdrawals** within the 5% allowances, again with no higher rate liability. Remember that these withdrawals are taken into account when the bond is encashed, and will increase the chargeable gain taken into account at that time. For this reason, they are often described as '**tax deferred**' and should not be described as tax free.

Investment bonds are **not generally suitable for non-taxpayers**, because there is no provision for tax paid by the life fund to be reclaimed.

7.5 Offshore bonds

A **bond which is issued by a company based offshore** may offer further tax advantages in some situations. It is possible for investment growth to be rolled up within the fund without any UK tax liability at all, although the potential tax liability when funds are withdrawn is higher as a result.

These arrangements can be attractive but often a **higher minimum investment** applies than would be the case for an onshore single premium bond. **Charges** also tend to be **higher**.

7.6 Annuities

An **annuity** is often not thought of as a **lump sum investment** but, in reality, it is. An annuity is a mechanism by which a lump sum is paid to an insurance company and provides a return in the form of a **stream of regular payments**, either over an agreed fixed period, or for life. It is not usually possible to surrender the annuity subsequently, so a disadvantage is that access to the capital is not available.

Where **income** rather than preservation of capital is a **major consideration**, an annuity may be an attractive option, particularly as under current legislation, tax is payable on only part of the regular payment stream, the rest being regarded as a return of capital.

Like income from many other types of savings such as bank or building society deposits, the **taxable element** has tax deducted only at 20%, with no further tax liability for basic rate taxpayers. Higher rate tax payers will be liable for further tax, to bring the rate paid up to 40% in total. Non-taxpayers can reclaim, or arrange gross payment, and starting rate taxpayers can make a partial reclaim. (This tax treatment applies to **non-pensions annuities.** Annuities arising directly from pension arrangements are **compulsory purchase annuities,** often abbreviated to **CPAs** which are fully taxable as **earned income**.)

A particularly good application of annuities may be for an **elderly individual** who wishes to have **security of income** and for whom the maintenance of access to capital is of little or no concern.

Annuity rates are sensitive to interest rates, so the timing of the purchase of an annuity will be an important consideration.

Different types of annuities are available to meet different needs. For example, increasing annuities are available, and annuities can be paid for life or for fixed periods.

Arrangements can be made so that, on the **death of the annuitant**, any shortfall between the original purchase price and the annuity instalments so far provided, is made up by a single lump sum payment. This is known as **capital protection**. Alternatively, annuities can be established on a **joint life** rather than a **single life** basis. These decisions must be made at outset and will affect the amount of income available for any given lump sum purchase price.

As mentioned above, one feature common to the various types of annuity is however a **lack of access to capital**, so an annuity will only be suitable where such access is not required.

Although annuities are often criticised these days, because **annuity rates are expensive**, this is a reflection of the economic situation, with **low interest rates**, and, in the case of lifetime annuities, **increased longevity**. **Low inflation** means that annuity payments **hold their value**, and the **certainty** of income meets a **major requirement** of many elderly people.

If the required income can be provided by an annuity, this also **frees up other assets**, for spending, or perhaps for gifting to assist with estate planning.

BPP)))
PROFESSIONAL EDUCATION

8 Making choices – lump sum investment

Similar considerations apply to **lump sum investment** as to savings, and a spread of investment will usually be appropriate. The **construction of portfolios** to meet specific objectives is dealt with separately in Chapter 6. There we also consider risk in more detail.

It is worth mentioning here that **risk** is **amplified** in some ways when investment is made by lump sum rather than by regular savings. Clearly the moderating influence of **pound cost averaging** does not apply; a large investment on the Stock Market made just before a significant fall in share prices generally could have serious consequences for the investor, particularly if he has not been sufficiently cautious in his overall approach to building a **balanced investment portfolio**.

There can therefore be an advantage in **spreading the timing of entry** to an asset-linked situation, perhaps by investing in three or four tranches spread over a one or two year period. Some products are available where an automatic facility is available to do exactly this.

9 Retirement planning

9.1 Background

One of the major areas of concern for most people is **saving for retirement**. With **increasing life expectancies**, the need to provide at a realistic level for a time when earned income may reduce or stop is considerable. There are however a number of factors to consider and we look at some of these in this section.

Pension arrangements of various types will be important in this area, but **other lump sum investments** will also contribute to retirement planning needs.

9.2 Personal pensions

1988
2001
PP non occupational schemes
any body can contribute to PP

Personal Pensions (PPs) were introduced in 1988, and were initially aimed exclusively at those who had **earned income**, but were not members of an occupational pension scheme (see below). They have provided this group with an **effective means of providing for retirement for many years**.

In April 2001, and again in April 2006, eligibility was extended and now anyone (whether in an occupational scheme or not, and including **non-earners**) can contribute, with **tax relief,** provided they are **under 75 years of age**.

PPs enjoy the usual **tax advantages** associated with pension arrangements. In particular:

- **Contributions** (within allowances) qualify for **tax relief** at the highest rate or rates of tax paid by the individual
- The investment fund grows **free of all tax on income**, except that **tax credits** associated with dividends **cannot be reclaimed**
  no tax on fund – CGT. Interest income.
- The investment fund is **free of tax on capital gains**
- **Death benefits** can usually be provided **free of inheritance tax** *No IHT on death except Dividend tax.*
- Part of the fund at **retirement** can be taken in the form of a **tax free pension commencement lump sum** (with the remainder providing an **income taxed as earned income**)

The proportion of the fund which can be taken in the form of **tax free cash** at retirement is **25%**. In the past, no cash was available from any part of the fund which was **Protected Rights** (see below), but this restriction has now been removed.

The maximum contribution by an individual which can qualify for tax relief in any tax year is 100% of earnings, or if greater (for example, in the case of a non-earner), £3,600. If an employer contributes, the employer contribution is unlimited in theory, but must be accepted by the local Inspector as being wholly and exclusively for business purposes.

If the total contribution (individual and employer, if applicable) exceeds the annual allowance (£215,000 in 2006/07), the excess is taxed on the individual at a rate of 40%, effectively reversing the tax advantages.

All contributions paid by **individuals** (whether employed or self-employed) are paid **net of basic rate tax relief**, and higher rate relief can be claimed from the Inspector of Taxes where appropriate. There is **no clawback** of relief from starting rate or non-taxpayers. Note however that the contribution allowances are always based on the gross contribution.

Total benefits are controlled by means of an **lifetime allowance** (£1.5m) in 2006/07. This covers **all benefits** under all **registered pension schemes**. If benefits in excess of this are provided, the lifetime allowance **tax charge** applies. This is 25% if the excess is taken as **taxable income**, or 55% if taken as a **lump sum**. These charges are intended to make it **unattractive** to build up benefits in excess of the lifetime allowance.

9.3 Life insurance

Life insurance policies can also be arranged **under PP rules**. In the past, contribution limits have applied, but from 6 April 2006, contributions are **only limited** as part of the normal **overall allowances** described above. Lump sum benefits paid on death are tested against the **lifetime allowance** and if in excess of that level, can result in a **lifetime allowance tax charge**. However, if the benefits are provided by means of **income** for a spouse, civil partner or dependant, there is no lifetime allowance test, though the income would be taxable as **earned income**.

Life insurance on this basis is attractive because the cost attracts **tax relief** in the same way as a PP contribution for retirement benefits. However, the market has **not been as competitive** as the ordinary term insurance market in the past (though there are signs of this **changing**). Costs should be **compared** by the adviser, taking into account the effect of tax relief. In some cases, the fact that the contributions reduce the amount that can be paid for retirement benefits with tax relief will be a disadvantage.

In addition, where an individual has claimed **enhanced protection** under the transitional rules available when the new simplified regime was introduced in April 2006, entry to a new life policy under PP rules would result in this protection being **lost**. This could prove **very costly** and is **unlikely to be desirable**.

9.4 Stakeholder Pensions

Stakeholder Pensions (SHPs) are a **variation of Personal Pensions**, and were introduced from 6 April 2001. The intention was to make pension provision more **accessible** to moderate earners in particular.

SHPs are subject to the **same eligibility and tax rules as PPs**, but are required to conform to **CAT (Charges, Access and Terms) standards** set by the government. These include a restriction on charges to a maximum of 1.5% pa of the fund for the first ten years, and 1% pa thereafter. (The cap on charges for Stakeholder Pensions started before 6 April 2005 was set at 1% pa throughout the life of the product, and this still applies to such arrangements.) Also, there must be no entry or exit charges, and there is a requirement for product providers to accept contributions of £20 or more, whether regular or not.

Most employers are required to provide employees with access to a **designated** SHP arrangement. This means allowing the provider to give **information to employees**, collecting **contributions** from pay if the employees so wish, and passing them on to the provider by the 19th of the month following that of the deduction. There is **no requirement for employers to contribute**, though they can if they wish.

Some employers are exempt, in particular, those with fewer than five employees, and those whose employees are **all** eligible for a group PP arrangement with an employer contribution of at least **3% of basic pay**, and no exit penalties. There is no requirement to provide access to a designated Stakeholder scheme in certain circumstances, in particular for those belonging to, or eligible for an occupational scheme.

9.5 State Pensions and contracting out

The availability of **State pensions** will also be important in considering retirement planning needs. State pensions are **modest in amount**, and are intended to provide for **basic living standards** only.

However, **employees** are eligible for the **State Second Pension (S2P)**, subject to certain conditions, in particular that they earn more than the **Lower Earnings Limit** (£84 per week in 2006/07). The **self-employed do not qualify for S2P**, and so receive only the basic pension (£84.25 per week for a single person and £134.75 for a married couple). This means that the **self-employed** have a **more pressing need** to make their own plans for retirement than employees.

It is possible for employees to **contract out** of S2P through a PP, assuming they are not already contracted out as a result of belonging to a contracted out occupational scheme (see below). A **risk** is involved, since contracting out means **giving up S2P benefits** in return for a partial **rebate of national insurance (NI) contributions**. The rebate can then be invested to provide alternative benefits in place of those given up.

These alternative benefits are known as **protected rights**, and where an **annuity** is purchased with the fund at retirement, this must be on **unisex rates** and must include provision for a **50% spouse's pension** if the individual was married at the time of annuity purchase. A similar provision applies where the individual has a **registered civil partner**. There is no longer a prohibition on taking benefits in cash, so a **tax free pension commencement lump sum** of 25% of the fund is available, and benefits can be taken from **age 50** (55 from April 2010) in the same way as other PP benefits.

Up to April 1997, the **rebate of NI contributions** available to those who contracted out was a **flat rate** percentage, independent of age and sex. Because younger employees had longer to invest this rebate, and assuming investment returns in excess of inflation, this meant that contracting out was **attractive** for the young, although **unattractive** for older employees.

From April 1997, the rebates available under PPs switched to an **age-related basis**. The thinking behind the age-related rebates is to make contracting out an attractive option for more people and over a longer period, so **reducing the strain** on State Pensions generally.

The level of age-related rebates has generally been regarded as **low** compared to the value of the **S2P benefits given up**, and as a result, **few advisers recommend contracting out** in practice.

9.6 Occupational schemes

Occupational schemes are funded at least in part by an **employer** and will therefore almost invariably represent **good value for money**. There will be **minor exceptions** where individuals are sure that they will leave the service of the particular employer within a short period of perhaps a couple of years, and do not benefit from the scheme beyond a **return of their own contributions**. However, from 6 April 2006, schemes must make a **transfer value** (though not necessarily a preserved pension) available for members who complete a minimum of **3 months' qualifying** service (generally this means scheme membership).

It would therefore be **very unusual** for it to be appropriate to suggest to an individual that he should either **leave** or **forego potential membership** of an employer-sponsored scheme. To do so is known as **opting-out**, and this has been an area scrutinised by the regulatory authorities over recent years.

It will more often be advisable for the individual to consider **topping up** his benefits on a personal basis, so that he enhances his retirement benefits without losing the benefit of the employer's contributions.

Contribution and benefit **allowances** are essentially the **same as for PPs**, as described above. However, for defined benefit schemes, it is the notional value of the **increase in benefits** each year that is tested against the **annual allowance**. The entitlement is calculated at the start and end of the year and the increase is converted to value using a **10:1 conversion factor**.

In testing the **lifetime allowance** when benefits are taken, a **20:1 conversion factor** is used.

9.7 Contracting out

Occupational schemes can also contract out, though the basis is different depending on whether the scheme is on a **defined benefit** or **defined contribution** basis.

A defined benefit scheme must meet a quality based test, known as the **Reference Scheme Test**. This requires benefits to be at least **broadly equal** to those provided by a hypothetical Reference Scheme defined by legislation. The structure of this scheme is:

- **Pension of 1/80th** of final earnings for each year of membership (maximum of 40 years to count)
- Retirement age **65**
- Qualifying earnings taken into account are **90% of those between the Lower and Upper Earnings Limits**
- Final earnings are based on the **average of qualifying earnings in the last three years** before retirement
- 50% spouse's pension on **death in service**, based on service completed
- 50% spouse's pension on **death in retirement**
- Escalation in line with **Limited Price Indexation (LPI)** requirements

Up to 5 April 1997, contracted out defined benefit schemes had to guarantee that the benefits provided would at least equal those given up under SERPS (the predecessor of S2P). This guaranteed benefit is known as the **Guaranteed Minimum Pension (GMP)**. Although the GMP test no longer applies for current service, it must be honoured for service up until its abolishment in 1997. No part of the GMP benefit can be taken in cash at retirement.

Although there is now **no guarantee** that the occupational scheme benefits will at least match the SERPS/S2P benefits given up, the benefits under the Reference Scheme are far **superior** to SERPS/S2P, so it is **unlikely** that a member would be **disadvantaged** by being contracted out.

Under **defined contribution** schemes, the position is similar to that under PPs, in that **protected rights** are built up to replace the SERPS/S2P benefits given up. The reduction in NI contributions is handled differently, with part given as a **reduction** in the NI contribution collected through **payroll**, and an **age-related addition** paid direct to the scheme by HMRC after the end of the tax year concerned.

An amount equal to the saving through payroll must be used to provide **Protected Rights**, and it is the **employer's responsibility** to ensure this is done. In most cases, this means that part of both the employer's and employees' contributions are used in this way. Sometimes, the scheme may be **non-contributory**, in which case the employer would meet the **whole** of this cost.

The age-related rebate paid by HMRC must also used to provide **Protected Rights**.

The **requirements** for Protected Rights under a DC occupational scheme are the same as those which apply under PPs, as discussed earlier in this Chapter.

9.8 Additional contributions

If an individual chooses to top up pension benefits, he may choose to do so through in-house **additional voluntary contributions** (AVCs), through a **free-standing AVC scheme** (FSAVCS) or through a personal pension (PP). Total benefits from **all sources** are tested against the **lifetime allowance** on crystallisation (ie when taken). Total **contributions by the individual** are subject to the limit of the greater of 100% of earnings or £3,600 on the maximum that can qualify for **tax relief**. The **annual allowance test** is based on the total of any **increase in benefits** under defined benefits arrangements (including added years AVCs), plus **contributions** to defined contribution (money purchase) arrangements.

The **in-house** AVC arrangement often benefits from a **lower level of charges** because of a degree of subsidy by the employer. It may also have relatively **low minimum contribution levels** for essentially the same reason. On the other hand, the investment is the responsibility of the trustees of the scheme and it will be the trustees therefore who determine the types of arrangement which are available to members. As a result the **choices are sometimes restricted** and may encompass only deposit-based and perhaps with profit arrangements.

An **FSAVCS or a PP** on the other hand is entirely outside of the main scheme and the **choice of provider**, and the **specific investment area chosen**, is the responsibility of the **member**. They also provide an increased degree of **privacy** for the member.

Note that the introduction of the new simplified tax regime for PP and SHP arrangements from 6 April 2006 has allowed all members of occupational schemes to contribute to PPs and this may mean the end of the market for FSAVCS in practice.

9.9 Alternatives to pensions

Although pension plans represent the most obvious method of providing for retirement, there are valid **alternatives**. In essence, **any investment or savings arrangement** which will provide either **income** or **lump sum benefits at the appropriate age** could be used for **retirement planning**.

In general, **deposit based vehicles** are less likely to be suitable than **asset backed arrangements**, because of the lower potential return involved. However for those close to retirement they may be suitable, and investments made in an asset backed situation may reasonably be transferred to a deposit basis close to retirement.

Asset backed investments generally are the best approach to retirement planning and ISAs in particular, with their considerable **tax advantages**, are a real **alternative to pension plans**. Although there is no relief on the contributions made to ISAs or, in the past, to PEPs, equally there is no taxation on benefits when the proceeds are withdrawn.

Pension arrangements benefit from the availability of a tax free pension commencement lump sum and, to the extent that benefits are taken in this form, are highly attractive. However the restrictions on the timing and form of benefit make pension plans less flexible than PEPs and ISAs and some clients would regard the flexibility as being at least as important.

Other asset backed arrangements which do not enjoy such great tax advantages would be less appropriate, although they could be considered as an additional method of building up benefits in the form of cash once the ISA allowance has been used. These would include **qualifying endowment policies**, and **unit trust** and **investment trust savings plans**.

10 Mortgages

10.1 Background

There are many types of **mortgage arrangement** both from the point of view of different interest rate options and different repayment methods.

We also consider in this section the question of whether a mortgage should be paid off if there is capital available.

10.2 Repayment methods

Many of the same considerations apply to the effectiveness of **repayment vehicles** as apply to savings. There is however likely to be a greater emphasis towards **security** in many cases, given the importance of ensuring that a client's mortgage obligations are fulfilled.

The **capital and interest repayment method** is perhaps the most secure approach of all, since, provided payments are made on time, repayment of the loan at the end of the term is guaranteed.

The only other type of arrangement which guarantees repayment is a **full endowment** which has a guaranteed sum assured equal to the loan. Such an arrangement is likely to be very expensive in cash flow terms, although the further benefits which would result from the addition of bonuses could be extremely desirable.

Other repayment methods, including **low cost endowment policies**, **ISAs** and **pension plans**, rely on the achievement of certain rates of growth, and so necessarily carry a degree of risk.

Changing the repayment basis of a mortgage is possible and may be desirable. It is important however that any increase in risk is taken into account and that any costs involved, particularly if the loan is switched from one lender to another, are identified and evaluated.

Whichever basis of repayment is chosen, care should be taken to ensure that the mortgage is protected against the **death or incapacity of the borrower**. This means arranging life insurance if the repayment method does not automatically provide it, as an endowment policy would.

Also, **IPI** would provide **continuation of income** to deal with ongoing mortgage interest payments if incapacity occurred, but should also be supplemented with waiver of premium on the repayment vehicle where possible, to protect the borrower's ability to discharge the mortgage at the end of the term.

10.3 Interest rate basis

In recent years, lenders have offered an increasing number of options as to the **interest rate basis** too. The most straightforward is the variable rate, where the interest rate varies according to market conditions generally.

Fixed rate loans can be attractive if the borrower expects interest rates generally to rise, and therefore seeks to tie his loan to rates before any rise takes effect.

Deferred interest loans allow lower initial repayments of interest, with amounts unpaid being added to the outstanding capital. Through the term, monthly repayments increase, usually annually, so as to eventually repay the increased amount outstanding.

These loans can be useful to allow those in **progressive jobs** to borrow more than would otherwise be possible, in the expectation that a rising income will enable them to service the repayments as they increase through the term. Clearly however there is a **risk** that income may not rise as expected, and a loan of this type should only be countenanced by the relatively **sophisticated borrower**. They are much less commonly available now than in past years when inflation and pay rises tended to be at higher levels.

Other types of loan are also available, including those with maximum and/or minimum interest rates, or a reduced interest rate for the initial period of the loan. Matching the type of loan to a particular client's circumstances can be complex, but attitude to risk is an important factor, as is the nature and security of his income.

Where a change is made to the terms of the loan rather than, or as well as the repayment vehicle, there may be costs or redemption penalties. This will particularly be the case if the change is from a fixed rate to a variable rate, since such a change is only likely to be desirable if the variable rate is below the fixed rate, and this would involve the lender in loss. Recouping all or part of this loss (or discouraging the borrower from changing lender) is the function of a redemption penalty.

10.4 Flexible mortgages

The idea behind flexible mortgages is to provide a more **modern approach** to mortgage lending generally, with **various options** open to borrowers, and often, an additional element of tax efficiency.

The borrower can **vary monthly repayments**, generally in either direction. If he pays more than the 'normal' repayment, the capital outstanding reduces accordingly. Over the mortgage term, **significant savings** can be made by overpaying to even a modest extent each month, because the higher repayments will lead to early repayment of the mortgage and resultant **interest savings**. (Generally, there will not be any early redemption penalties under flexible mortgages.)

If the borrower **pays less**, the capital outstanding increases, and repayments will have to be **increased later** to redress the balance. The lender will usually put **constraints** on the extent of underpayment permitted, both to ensure that the debt does not become unmanageable, and to keep the **loan to value ratio** at an acceptable level. Nevertheless this flexibility is attractive to many borrowers.

It is also possible to make **lump sum payments**, for example from bonuses, to reduce the debt. Similarly, the borrower can choose to have a **repayment holiday** (usually for a limited period), which can be useful in terms of unusually high expenditure.

To accommodate these options, **interest** is calculated on a **daily basis**, to reflect the exact amount outstanding at any time.

There is often a facility under flexible mortgages to **draw down** further loan amounts. The maximum is calculated at outset, based on the property valuation at that time. For example, if a borrower obtains a mortgage of 50% of the property value in order to purchase it, he might be given a facility whereby he can draw up to an additional 20% of the property value as determined at outset, **without having to go through the formality of a further loan application**. (If he wanted to increase the loan by more than this, he could still re-apply, but a further property valuation would probably be required.)

A further feature of some of these loans is **'offsetting'**, where the borrower has a current account and/or a deposit account with the lending institution. Instead of receiving interest on this, and paying full mortgage interest, the amount in the current account is offset from the mortgage loan **before interest is calculated**.

This is attractive because the interest rate on the mortgage is likely to be **higher** than the interest that could be obtained on the current or deposit account. Also, if interest is paid on a current or deposit account, it is **taxable**, but there is **no tax relief on the mortgage interest**. Where offsetting operates, there is no tax liability, so it is a very tax-efficient approach, particularly for higher rate taxpayers.

Mortgages of this type can be very attractive to those with fluctuating incomes, perhaps with bonuses which might be used to accelerate repayment.

10.5 Repaying a mortgage from capital

Where an individual has capital, but also has a mortgage, an important consideration is whether to use some of the capital to **repay the mortgage** loan.

Fundamentally, it is more attractive to invest rather than repay all or part of the loan if the **return** (after tax) which is likely to be generated is in excess of the **cost of interest** if the loan remains outstanding.

It is clearly more likely that the return under a **PEP** or an **ISA** will exceed the interest paid than would be the case with an **endowment policy**, because of the **tax advantaged** nature of the investment. It is also true that moving money into deposit is unlikely to be appropriate for a long period because the return is likely to be **relatively low**, and the cost of maintaining the loan is likely to exceed the interest earned.

Tax relief on residential mortgage interest was withdrawn entirely from April 2000. In the past, when mortgage relief was available, repayment has not always been an attractive option, at least from a purely theoretical point of view. The withdrawal of relief has made the interest payments more expensive, so paying off the loan has become more attractive.

Against these considerations needs to be balanced the **security** and **risk** aspects, and the **emotional appeal** of security in relation to an individual's own home. These are personal issues, and may lead to an individual wanting to pay off a mortgage, irrespective of the possible financial benefits of maintaining it.

This consideration is not just important in relation to large sums of capital. If an individual chooses a **repayment mortgage**, he is paying off some capital each month. Conversely, if an **interest only** mortgage is used, with an **investment vehicle** building up to repay the capital at maturity, the monthly contribution is being invested rather than used to repay the loan immediately. The **relative advantage** must be considered in the same way.

11 Education costs

Planning for **school fees and other education costs** will be important to some clients and perhaps irrelevant to others even if they are parents. Much depends on the **attitude of the parents** and the perceived need for education outside of the State system, or continuing beyond secondary school.

There are many approaches, and this is really only a **particular application of savings and investment** generally, rather than something entirely different. Nevertheless there are some **particular considerations** which should be borne in mind.

First of all, certain arrangements based on educational trusts exist which enjoy **favourable tax treatment** and which are geared to the **provision of school fees**. It may be appropriate to make use of these arrangements where they are available.

Also, in many situations it will **not be practicable** for the parents to **save** sufficient money to provide for the **necessary school fees**. In these cases it may be necessary to use a combination of methods. These could include **saving in advance for part of the school fees** and allowing the balance to be met from **normal income**, or even through **borrowing**. It may then be appropriate to consider the best method by which such a loan could be repaid.

In any of these circumstances, there will be a **protection need** as well as a **savings and investment need**. Clearly if death or disability strikes, the ability of the family to provide for education fees will be placed under severe pressure and specific arrangements could be made in this area. It might be appropriate to protect the provision of fees against disability by providing **IPI** cover or **waiver of premium** where an arrangement such as an endowment policy is in use.

In addition, **life insurance**, probably on a **term insurance** or **family income benefit** basis, would be necessary to protect against the risk of death.

One important consideration is that the need for education fees often stretches considerably **beyond secondary school**. Full grants are generally no longer available so parental contributions need to be higher. Even where a full loan is available to the student, this may not provide sufficient money to support a student at university to the extent that the parents might wish. Suitable advance provision may therefore be vital.

Importantly also, many parents who might not wish to make private provision for primary or secondary education because they are content to rely on the State system will nevertheless need to do so if there is a significant chance of **further education** being required.

12 Estate planning

The protection of an estate from **inheritance tax** will often be an important issue. The **use of trusts** is an important part of this, as discussed in Chapter 1 and care should be taken to ensure that the provision of **life insurance arrangements** is made in a way that does not itself increase inheritance tax liability.

The provision of cash to pay an inheritance tax liability is usually most suitably arranged through a **whole of life policy**, or alternatively a **convertible term policy** with the option to convert to a permanent insurance at some future date. Clearly this reflects the fact that the liability will definitely arise at some future stage, but that the timing is uncertain.

Another aspect of estate planning which needs to be taken into account is the ability to use lifetime gifts constituting **Potentially Exempt Transfers (PETs)** to pass assets on to succeeding generations. Because PETs made more than seven years before death are ignored for inheritance tax purposes, this can be a very effective way of minimising tax.

However it is important to bear in mind that the needs of the current owners of the capital must be met as a prime consideration. Because the making of a gift 'with strings attached' is likely to constitute a **gift with reservation**, which is ineffective from an inheritance tax point of view, any gift made would need to be non-recoverable. It follows that gifts should only be made to the extent that they can be afforded without endangering the living standards of the donor.

13 Choosing product providers

13.1 Background

Choosing a product provider will come **after choosing an appropriate product**, and in the case of investments, both will come after deciding the **appropriate asset allocation**. However the choice of a suitable product provider remains an **important issue**, and in this section we consider some of the factors which need to be taken into account.

13.2 Protection products

At first sight, it may seem that a protection product either does the job for which it has been selected or not. However, in reality, there are many **differentiating features** between products which superficially seem the same. The differences must be considered by the adviser in choosing a suitable provider. The factors include:

- **Premium rates**. The cost of cover can vary considerably between different providers, particularly where some **specialise** in a particular marketplace or in **clients of a particular type**. In principal, the cheaper a premium rate is, the better, but only subject to all other differentiating factors being at least equal.

- **Premium basis**. With protection products, sometimes rates are quoted on a basis which is **guaranteed**, whilst in other cases the rates are **reviewable**. Where they are reviewable, there is a risk that adverse experience on the part of the insurer will result in an increase in rates which could be applied to **existing policies**, so increasing the cost of the cover concerned.

  In some cases a reviewable rate will (at least initially) be **less expensive** than a guaranteed rate, and may therefore be **attractive** if the client feels able to **take the risk** that rates will be reviewed upwards. However if **affordability** is tight, there may be **insufficient margin** to accommodate this risk. (It is also true that reviewable rates may be adjusted downwards, which would be to the client's advantage, but this possibility may still not make it acceptable for the client to bear the risk of an increase).

- **Underwriting**. Underwriting limits vary considerably from insurer to insurer, and this may mean that a client will need to provide more **extensive medical evidence**, or perhaps attend a **medical examination** with one insurer, but would be underwritten from the application form with another. Meeting more detailed underwriting requirements may be **inconvenient**, and many clients **dislike** having to undergo a medical examination, so this may be an important consideration for some clients.

  Bear in mind that more **lenient underwriting requirements** should not be taken as inviting the client **not to declare** a relevant condition because, irrespective of the approach taken by the insurer to the underwriting process, **failure to disclose** can **invalidate a claim and is fraudulent**.

- **Service**. Administrative performance should be taken into account, including the speed and efficiency of dealing with **applications** and putting a policy **on risk**. Once the client has decided to proceed with a selected cover it is clearly a good idea to put it into effect as soon as possible so that the need is dealt with.

- **Increase options**. There is a considerable advantage in cover which builds in increase options **without medical evidence**, since it allows the client to go some way towards maintaining his need for cover (which in most cases tends to increase over the years as income and commitments increase) without the **inconvenience** of having to complete further applications and provide **further medical evidence** on too regular a basis.

  The inclusion of increase options generally means paying a hig**her initial premium rate**, but in many cases this is a **reasonable price** to pay for the convenience, in addition to which a proportion of clients will become **uninsurable**, or at least subject to **special terms**, after the initial cover has been put into effect. Where increase options apply cover will be available on standard terms, but if there are no such options, it may be difficult for the client to increase the cover to the extent he would wish in later years.

- **Claims criteria**. In the case of a life insurance policy, a claim may only be payable in the event of death. However for other policies, such as **income protection insurance**, there are other issues, and in particular the definition of **incapacity** written into the contract. In some cases, an IPI policy will only provide benefit if the individual concerned is **unable to perform any work**, and this would require a very **severe** degree of incapacity indeed. The premium for such cover is likely to be cheap because the incidence of claims will not be great, whereas a more lenient definition of incapacity is likely to result in a higher premium, but will provide more **realistic cover**.

  Other terms under the policy, for example the **deferment period** under an IPI arrangement, the **range of conditions** covered under a critical illness benefit policy and the **qualification** for benefits under a private medical insurance policy will all influence cost. Once again, this explains why it is **not appropriate** to rely solely on selecting the **cheapest** possible premium.

- **Financial strength**. This may affect the provider's ability to **remain in business** throughout the term of the arrangement and is always important for **protection business**. Although it is generally perceived that the chance of major problems at a substantial insurance company is modest, there have been examples in recent years where difficulties have arisen which have caused considerable problems for clients.

13.3 Pension products

Many aspects of pension products **do not differ** between providers, for example, tax treatment, eligibility, maximum contribution allowances and minimum access age. However, there are **many important aspects** which **do differ** and which must be considered by adviser and client in choosing the provider. These include:

- **Investment choice and performance**. The **range of choice** can be important, and the range of fund types (UK equity, property, managed etc) needs to be considered. It is useful to have a **choice of managers** too, rather than just having a range of funds managed internally by the product provider. Increasing numbers of providers offer funds managed by **external investment houses**.

  Performance is often more **difficult to judge**, because the future is unpredictable and past performance does not give a reliable indicator for the future. Advisers will therefore need to consider **factors** which contribute to an **expectation** of future performance, such as **investment strategy**, **research capability** and so on. In considering **past performance**, any change of manager or investment strategy should also be taken into account.

  Terms for **switching** between funds should also be considered.

- **Service**. Administrative performance should be taken into account. Applications and top-up contributions need to be **processed promptly**, benefit statements should be **reliable** and retirement benefit illustrations must be **comprehensive and accurate**.

  The provider's record of dealing with **death claims** may be a further consideration.

- **Financial strength**. As with protection products, this may affect the provider's ability to remain in business **throughout the term** of the arrangement. If it does not, the position after a takeover (for example) is **entirely unpredictable**, and may not be satisfactory.

  If a **with profits** investment is involved, financial strength also influences the provider's investment options and the likelihood of **strong future bonuses**.

- **Waiver of contribution**. Not all providers offer this, and terms, including **cost**, **underwriting** and extent of **cover** all vary. This will be an important consideration where the client wishes to take up this option.

- **Charges**. The level of charges does **vary** considerably from provider to provider, and it is important that the product chosen represents **good value**. This **may not be the cheapest option**, because sometimes a low cost plan may be **less flexible**, or have **less options**, than a slightly more expensive one.

- **Minimum contributions**. Maximum contribution allowances are set within the **legislation**, but **providers** set their own **minimum contribution levels** (subject where applicable to stakeholder CAT standards). This will be most relevant to clients intending to pay modest contributions.

- **Benefit options**. Some providers do not offer **income withdrawals**, or may be restrictive in their approach to **phasing retirement**. Although transfers are possible to improve the position at retirement, it can be useful to have a **flexible arrangement** from outset.

13.4 Investments

The relevant aspects of investment products will **vary according to the product** concerned in some cases, but the **major issues** are as follows.

- **Investment choice and performance**. Just as with pension products, this is a major consideration. However, whereas pension products are generally established for a known term, other products are sometimes used to provide greater **accessibility**, and this may place greater emphasis on factors such as **volatility** as well as long term performance. It is important to understand that past performance alone is **not a reliable basis for judgement** of the potential for good performance in future. Other factors come into play, for example whether the fund manager is new, or has been in place for some time. The **size of the fund** may have increased in recent years too, and if strong past performance was achieved when the fund was small, and could change strategy quickly, this may not give any indication at all as to the potential with a large, **less easily manoeuvrable** fund. **Investment strategy** and **research facilities** are further factors to take into account in assessing performance.

- **Investment profile**. Some clients invest for **income**, some for **capital growth**, and some require both. The product chosen must meet the client's particular needs.

- **Service**. The particular features of the product concerned will dictate what particular aspects are important. For example, **underwriting attitude** and turn-round time will be important for endowment policies.

- **Financial strength**. Again this is important just as for pension products.

- **Charges**. Because of the possibility of the investment being **encashed early**, any extra charges in these circumstances should be carefully considered, as well as charges more generally.

Choosing a provider is not easy, and an adviser can never be sure that the provider chosen will turn out to be the **best** in the long term. However, taking account of **all relevant features** will ensure that recommendations are **suitable**, and should serve the client well.

Remember that within a **portfolio of recommendations**, some will turn out better than others. It is the **overall result**, rather than the outcome of individual selections that is important.

Key chapter points

- Solutions must be adequate to meet the need they address, or any gap must be recognised and consideration given to how it would be dealt with in practice.

- The degree of risk involved should be consistent with the client's attitude to risk for each objective.

- The tax position and the effects of the solution must be considered.

- In addition, affordability must also be taken into account if the solution is to have any chance of succeeding.

- These aspects contribute to certainty that the regulatory requirement to give suitable advice is met, though it is also important to observe the various disclosure requirements.

- Life insurance is a basic protection solution and there are three main types – term insurance, whole of life and endowment.

- Term insurance is the most basic type of life insurance, but various options such as renewability, convertibility, and increases can be built in at an additional cost.

- Decreasing term insurance policies can be useful for dealing with specific needs, such as the protection of a mortgage arranged on a repayment basis.

- Whole of life policies are useful for inheritance tax provision and for dealing with needs which may persist beyond a defined term.

- Unit linked whole of life plans are particularly flexible and have wide application, but advisers need to ensure that clients understand the basis of the plan they are considering.

- Health insurance is important, but often is considered as a lower priority by clients than it should be.

- IPI provides for income replacement in the event of incapacity, and is particularly important for the self-employed and those with limited other resources to fall back on.

- Care is needed in the selection of IPI policies, which can have different definitions of incapacity.

- Other factors such as deferred period and termination date also affect cost.

- IPI provides more complete cover than is available under Personal Accident and Sickness policies, but the later can provide a cheap, temporary solution in some cases.

- Waiver of premium is a useful additional benefit to add to life policies and personal pension arrangements, and is in effect a type of IPI arrangement.

- Critical Illness benefit pays out on diagnosis of a specified range of conditions, without there being any requirement for the individual to be incapacitated.

- This cover can provide for necessary alterations to the home, or mortgage repayment, or could meet special treatment costs.

- Private medical insurance (PMI) is useful for those who cannot afford to wait for NHS treatment to be available if they contract an illness for which there is a long waiting list under the NHS.

- Long term care arrangements can be insured or investment based, and are designed to meet an increasingly important need.

- Deposits will be an important part of savings for most people.

- Existing TOISAs provide a tax efficient method of keeping invested the capital from a matured TESSA and continue the availability of tax free interest, with no fixed term and no restriction on withdrawals.

- The cash component of ISAs also provides tax free interest, though the use of ISAs for cash reduces the scope for stocks and shares investment within the ISA wrapper.

- NS&I offer a range of products which are secure, and which have features designed to appeal to a range of different investors.

- Endowment policies provide a disciplined form of regular savings, but the qualifying rules are restrictive and the tax advantages modest for investors other than higher rate taxpayers.

- Regular savings arrangements linked to unit trusts, investment trusts and OEICs are available, and offer good growth potential, though they involve risk.

- Investment trusts are generally higher risk than unit trusts invested in the same way, because the value of the investment is affected by supply and demand, and because investment trusts are permitted to gear.

- Open-ended Investment Companies (OEICs) are similar in risk profile to unit trusts and are not generally permitted to gear.

- PEPs can no longer accept contributions, but enjoy the same tax advantaged treatment of investment returns as ISAs.

- The range of permitted investments for PEPs is the same as for the stocks and shares ISA component.

- ISAs and PEPs are free from tax on income although dividend tax credits cannot be reclaimed, and are free of tax on gains. They have no fixed term, nor any restrictions on withdrawals.

- Investment bonds are life insurance policies, designed for lump sum investment, and are generally written as whole of life plans. They allow higher rate taxpayers to defer higher rate tax on gains until encashment.

- Withdrawals within limits are also permitted without immediate personal tax liability, although such withdrawals are taken into account in calculating the gain on encashment.

- Annuities provide a secure income, but at the cost of the loss of access to capital.

- Pensions are important in retirement planning because of their tax advantages.

- Personal pensions are available to those with earnings, to non-earners and to members of occupational schemes.

- Life insurance can also be arranged under PP rules, with tax relief on the cost.

- Stakeholder pensions are subject to the same tax rules as PPs, but must also conform to CAT standards on Charges, Access and Terms.

- State pensions contribute to retirement planning but are much less generous for the self-employed, who qualify only for the basic pension.

- Employees can contract out of the State Second Pension (S2P) using a PP, but the rebate of NI contributions may not be good value for the benefits given up.

- Occupational pension schemes are usually good value for employees who are eligible because of the employer contribution involved.

- Members of occupational schemes may be contracted out of S2P.

- Under contracted out DB schemes, benefits must at least broadly match those under the Reference Scheme.

- Under DC schemes, an amount equal to the total NI saving (which is given partly by a reduction in NI contributions paid through payroll, and partly by a rebate direct to the scheme) must be used to provide Protected Rights.

- Benefits can be topped up using in-house or freestanding AVC arrangements, or a PP.

- The complex rules governing pension arrangements were simplified in 2006, with a single regime now covering all arrangements.

- **Mortgages can be important in financial planning, both in the terms obtained, and in the method and timing of repayment.**

- **There are many remortgage opportunities currently available, offering attractive terms.**

- **Flexible mortgages allow payment variations and are attractive to many borrowers.**

- **Repayment of a mortgage is attractive unless the investor believes a better return after tax can be obtained by investing money than from the reduction in interest resulting from partial or full loan repayment.**

- **School and education fees provision is largely a question of applying normal savings arrangements to a particular purpose.**

- **Choosing providers is an important exercise and needs to take account of a wide range of factors, which often vary between different products.**

Chapter Quiz

1   If a term insurance policy is renewable, what does this mean? .... (see para 2.2)

2   What is an inter vivos policy? ....(2.2)

3   What is meant by standard cover under a unit-linked whole of life plan? ....(2.3)

4   From a taxation point of view, what is difference between the treatment of benefits under personal and group IPI (PHI) schemes?..(3.2)

5   List the main conditions likely to be covered by a critical illness benefit policy. ....(3.5)

6   For what cover would a claim revolve around Activities of Daily Living? ....(3.8)

7   What limit applies to investment in a cash mini-ISA in the current tax year?....................................(5.4)

8   How is the interest under the NS&I Capital Bond taxed? ....(5.6)

9   Which collective investment product(s) can use gearing? ....(5.8)

10 What is meant by describing an investment trust as closed-ended and what impact does this have on risk?...(5.8)

11 What restriction applies to OEICs as regards the bid/offer spread? ....(5.9)

12 Is it possible to transfer money from the cash to the stocks and shares component of an ISA?.................. (5.11)

13 What rate of tax applies in 2006/07 to a chargeable gain made under an investment bond, assuming the investor is a higher rate taxpayer? ....(7.4)

14 How is the taxable element of an instalment of a non-pensions annuity taxed?...............................(7.6)

15 How are benefits under pension arrangements limited under the simplified pensions tax regime introduced in April 2006? ....(9.2)

16 What is 'offsetting' in connection with a flexible mortgage? ....(10.4)

Chapter topic list

Creating an investment portfolio

1 Background

In Chapter 5, we considered various products and needs in some detail, looking at the **advantages and disadvantages** of using those products as part of a solution for a client. In this chapter, we look specifically at some of the issues involved in the design of an investment portfolio, based on a **substantial lump sum** investment.

The particular considerations we will look at are:

- The need for accessibility
- Dealing with expected expenditure
- Income and capital growth
- Taxation
- Existing arrangements
- Costs
- Revising an existing portfolio

Many of the matters covered elsewhere in this Study Text, in particular the consideration of risk, are also relevant.

2 Accessibility

2.1 Immediate needs

We have discussed the importance of identifying and dealing with immediate needs in a number of different contexts. When dealing with lump sums, an extremely important consideration is the extent to which the individual is likely to **need access** to the amounts invested in the short term. This will necessarily affect the freedom with which investment decisions can be made, both in terms of the choice of asset classes and choice of products.

The greater the sum available, the more flexibility there will be to invest in assets which are not immediately accessible but which are geared to provide the **best possible return** in the longer term, subject to the attitude to risk of the client.

However a first priority in virtually all cases will be the establishment of an adequate **emergency fund** which should be available immediately and thus be accessible to cover the unexpected. As previously mentioned, a figure of **between three and six months' income** would usually be regarded as appropriate for an emergency fund. This may however vary from case to case according to the circumstances and indeed, the wishes of the client.

Even after establishing the emergency fund, further consideration needs to be given to **accessibility**. It may well be acceptable for part of the investment portfolio to be inaccessible for long periods, in order to qualify for tax benefits. For example, a pension related investment enjoys considerable tax advantages, but is not usually available until age 50 or later under current rules, and this minimum age will become 55 from April 2010.

In the case of a **young investor** however, even if the objective is to start saving towards retirement, it is likely that a mix of investments, with varying degrees of accessibility, will be desirable. So for example, an investment in an ISA enjoys tax advantages, which although different to those enjoyed by a pension arrangement, may be just as attractive. The ISA should certainly be viewed as a medium to long term arrangement, but nevertheless can be encashed at any time if required. It is this accessibility that can be a vital factor for a younger investor, because of the potential for changes to occur in his circumstances and needs.

As always, it is **balance** and **spread** which are important and which will enable a client to achieve good returns without undue risk or inconvenience.

2.2 Expected expenditure

Provision should certainly be built into the portfolio to deal with any **specific expected expenditures**. These might include provision for a daughter's wedding, for a special holiday or for the purchase of a new car. The range is almost limitless and factfinding will enable you to pinpoint any likely need for large expenditures of this type.

The adviser may need to prompt the client in this area, based on the factfind details obtained and it is generally wise to ensure there is a margin to allow for additional, unpredicted items.

As well as specific expectations, most people will recognise that other items inevitably arise, such as repairs to property, replacement of household appliances, and extra holidays. It is natural to want to draw on capital for some of these expenditures, and if no allowance is made, the client may become dissatisfied with the portfolio as a whole.

3 Income and capital growth

Where required, the need to draw regular amounts by way of **income** from the investment will also be an important factor in determining the portfolio construction overall. Sometimes the balance between **income** and **capital growth** required by the investor will be largely influenced by **tax considerations**, whilst in other cases it will simply be that the reason for investing is to generate one or the other.

The requirement can also be influenced by attitude, with some investors feeling more comfortable if an income can be seen to be derived from their portfolio.

Be aware that where the client's requirement is for **regular amounts to supplement day to day expenditure**, it may be possible to provide some of this using investments which do not generate income as such from a tax point of view, by **crystallising capital gains** on a regular basis. In some circumstances this may be more **tax effective** than generating income in the normal sense and certainly this is a reasonable way of meeting everyday expenditure, provided the client accepts the risk involved if asset values decline. This risk may make it unwise to rely entirely on this approach.

If possible, withdrawals should not be made from arrangements which offer **tax advantages for continued investment**, such as PEPs and ISAs. Clearly it is preferable to continue to make use of the **tax shelter offered by** these products for as long as possible. Once money is withdrawn from the tax advantaged environment however, it cannot be put back, except within the **normal limits**.

If money is withdrawn from products which are no longer available such as PEPs, it will **not be possible to re-invest** the money back into the same contracts at all, though there may be scope within a currently available and similar contract such as an ISA.

4 Taxation

4.1 Personal tax position

The **tax position** of the investor will also be important, just as it is when considering savings and pension arrangements. It will often, for example, influence the **relative value** to a client of investments aimed at producing **income** as against those aimed at producing **capital growth**.

In particular, relatively few people find themselves liable to pay **capital gains tax** on a regular basis, because of the availability of **taper relief** and sometimes **indexation allowance** to reduce gains, and because the **CGT annual exemption** can be used. If investment vehicles which are aimed at producing capital gains rather than (or as well as) taxable income are used, this can therefore be extremely **effective**.

Investments producing a **tax free return** will be even more attractive to higher rate taxpayers than to basic rate taxpayers, or indeed to non-taxpayers, and the higher rate taxpayer will therefore be more inclined to accept any accompanying **limitations** on **accessibility** or **flexibility** in return for those tax advantages.

In other cases where the client's taxation position is likely to **change** in the foreseeable future, an arrangement such as an **investment bond**, which has the effect of deferring taxation liability might be extremely attractive. An individual who is a higher rate taxpayer now can **defer** higher rate liability, and may **avoid it entirely** if his income is relatively low when the bond is encashed.

4.2 Ownership of assets

As part of the consideration of taxation, the adviser should give thought to the **ownership** of assets in the case of **couples**. For example, it is not unusual for one partner to be paying **higher rate tax** whilst the other has not fully used the **basic rate tax band**. Sometimes the difference may be even more marked, with one partner a higher rate taxpayer, and the other being a non-taxpayer.

If some investments are made in the name of the **partner with the lower tax liability**, the income generated can utilise any **unused portions** of the personal allowance, and the starting and basic rate bands. This can significantly improve the **net return** achieved for the client.

Similarly, one partner may be using the **CGT annual exemption** in full, whilst the other is not, and again, a **division** of assets between the two will allow the so far **unused exemption** to be applied.

There may also be advantages, particularly from an **inheritance tax** point of view, in passing assets to **children** (or grandchildren), perhaps using a **trust**, especially if the children are young.

Advisers need to consider aspects beyond the simple use of tax allowances and bands however, for example:

- If the couple are not legally married spouses or registered civil partners, a gift from one to the other constitutes a **disposal for CGT purposes.**

- Similarly, such a gift is a **transfer for inheritance tax purposes**, unless covered by an exemption (such as the annual exemption or small gifts exemption)

- Some clients will want to **retain ownership** of the portfolio entirely themselves for **personal reasons**, irrespective of the tax implications, particularly if they feel their relationship is foundering

- In some cases, there may be a reluctance to pass assets to children if they have shown themselves (in their parents' eyes) not to be sufficiently **responsible** with money

It is important to be **sensitive** to these points, and, for example, to ensure that the factfinding process establishes whether the couple are legally married or, for same sex couples, are in a registered civil partnership under the Civil Partnership Act 2004.

4.3 Taxation changes

Changes in taxation will influence the relative merits of different investments from time to time.

For example, the increase from April 2004 in the amount of **higher rate tax** payable on chargeable gains on **investment bonds** has affected the attractions of these arrangements for some investors, even though the change was relatively slight.

The removal of the ability of ISAs to reclaim **tax credits** on dividends has also reduced the attractions of these products, particularly for basic rate taxpayers.

5 Existing arrangements

5.1 Balance

Any **existing investments** must be taken into account in designing a portfolio since they will affect the overall balance achieved by the client. If a client who already had a **substantial emergency fund** were to receive an inheritance, there might be no further need for emergency fund provision from the inheritance, which could therefore be used in a **more adventurous** manner.

Similarly if existing investments are predominantly **UK-based**, then the availability of further monies could usefully create a **wider geographical diversification** within the portfolio as a whole.

Existing arrangements may also have used some of the **allowances**, such as ISA allowances, which otherwise would figure as an **important part** of the adviser's recommendations.

5.2 Costs

Different investments incorporate different levels of **cost** and inevitably this will be a factor which influences overall portfolio design.

Particularly if investment is intended only for the **short term**, any significant **initial costs** would seriously erode or could even eliminate any potential return. On the other hand longer term investments should have time to **recoup** initial charges and the level of ongoing charges will be more important.

It will be the **net return after tax and charges** which is of concern to the investor since this is the measure of the extent to which he will profit. This therefore must always be taken into account in any recommendations.

6 Revising a portfolio

6.1 Cost of revision

Costs are also an important factor in deciding whether or not a portfolio should be **reorganised**. Although for example, the XYZ UK equity unit trust might be **preferred** to the ABC UK equity trust for new money, the extent of this preference might not be **sufficient** to **justify** any **cost** in changing an existing investment in the ABC trust to one in the XYZ trust.

Similarly, suppose that the **current investment recommendation** for new money was that 75% of unit trust holdings should be in the UK with 25% in Japan (for example). If a client had an **existing investment portfolio** where the current split was 72% in the UK and 28% in Japan, the cost of readjusting the portfolio would probably be too great to justify a **realignment**.

Because different investments do not perform identically, any portfolio once established is likely to move away from the exact spread recommended. It is then a **matter of judgement** as to when an adjustment should be made.

Bear in mind that if the investment recommendation itself has not altered, but the **spread in the portfolio has moved out of line**, this will be because one holding or group of holdings has outperformed the other and has therefore become a **greater proportion** of the total portfolio. To bring the portfolio back into line would necessitate selling some of the more successful elements and retaining the less successful. This can be a difficult judgement and one which must be **carefully timed**.

6.2 Effect of capital gains tax

Whenever a portfolio is revised, care must be taken to ensure that any **tax liability** is fully taken into account. This does not just mean the taxation of the investments themselves, and any income they produce, but also includes the **effect of capital gains tax (CGT)** at the time of the revision.

If assets such as **shares** or **unit trusts** are sold, then a CGT liability can occur as a result. Any potential gain from **improved investment performance** can be completely **negated** by any CGT liability that arises and which could have been deferred or even avoided had the sale of some of the assets been at least **delayed**.

So, for example, a move from **direct shareholdings to unit trusts**, in order to improve the spread of investments and to benefit from professional management, could be achieved in stages to make use of the **annual CGT exemption** over a number of years.

The introduction in 1998 of **taper relief to replace indexation allowance** for CGT purposes means that it has become attractive from a tax point of view to hold investments for **longer periods**. This may affect the choice of assets to be sold in order to utilise annual exemptions, and may also encourage investment into **pooled investments** such as unit trusts. The point about pooled investments is that the managers can buy and sell **within the portfolio** without immediate liability to tax on capital gains, whilst the individual continues to hold the unit trust, so benefiting from taper relief for the **whole period of ownership**.

6.3 The effect of income tax

Similarly, on encashment of an investment bond under current rules, a **liability to higher rate tax** could arise, which again needs careful handling. If the bond is **segmented** (ie consists of a number of constituent policies) it may be best to **stagger** encashment over a number of years, to avoid large gains falling in one year and creating a substantial higher rate tax liability.

If there is only one bond, it will be necessary to consider the effect of full or partial encashment, since the calculation of any **gain for tax purposes** is different in each case.

Key chapter points

- There are particular issues which need to be addressed in designing a portfolio for a substantial lump sum investment.

- The need for accessibility is an important aspect which can affect both the choice of asset classes and the choice of products. Provision for an emergency fund is always a prime concern.

- Accessibility should be allowed for in respect of anticipated expenditure, but an allowance should also be made for the unexpected.

- The needs of the client may be towards income, or capital growth, or a combination of the two, and the portfolio should be designed with this in mind.

- A need for 'income' can sometimes be discharged through a series of crystallised gains rather than directly through the provision of income.

- Ideally, withdrawals should not be made from products such as ISAs, in order to maximise the use made of the tax advantages.

- Many people do not have any liability to CGT, and making effective use of the available CGT reliefs and exemptions can improve the overall net performance of the portfolio significantly.

- Investments which produce a tax free or tax advantaged return are likely to be most appealing to higher rate taxpayers.

- Ownership of assets is an important issue for couples, and consideration should be given to ensuring that use is made of the tax allowances and bands of both partners.

- Care is required in dealing with both the technical taxation impact of transferring ownership and the emotional aspects of doing so.

- Existing arrangements will affect recommendations in various ways, particularly in relation to the balance of investment, and because allowances such as ISA allowances may already have been used.

- Costs involved in different investment products will also influence choice, and will have the greatest impact if the products are to be held for only a short time.

- In revising a portfolio, the costs of changes, including the taxation consequences, may influence whether a change is worthwhile.

Chapter Quiz

1   Why might it be tax effective to provide for an 'income' need by means of a series of capital gains? ... (see para 3)

2   Why might an investment bond be particularly attractive to a higher rate taxpayer who expected his income to fall in the future? ....(4.1)

3   What difficulties arise in discussing changes to the ownership of assets between unmarried partners? ....(4.2)

4   If a portfolio of existing investments is not in line with current recommendations, what factors should be considered in deciding whether to realign it?...(6.1)

5   Why might it be wise to spread a move from direct equity holdings to collective investments over a period of time?...(6.2)

Putting recommendations into effect

1 Presenting the recommendations

1.1 Background

It is possible to **communicate recommendations to clients** in a number of ways, and the style of communication will reflect the preferences of the adviser and the client. Nevertheless, given the complicated and, for many clients, unfamiliar information which needs to be imparted, there will usually be a great advantage in a formal written report.

Increasingly, the use of products in financial planning is required to be accompanied by **literature in a format which is prescribed** to a greater or lesser extent by the regulatory authorities. These documents are intended to ensure that the client has sufficient information available to him to understand the products being recommended.

What these documents do not do, and cannot do, is to put those products into the context of the client's financial circumstances and objectives and this will then be the function of the **financial planning report**.

There is **no single correct way** to construct a report. It must however cover certain areas if it is going to be effective and must also be understandable from the client's point of view. In any field requiring expertise, it is easy to slide into **jargon** and abbreviation which can disguise or even obliterate meaning from the reader's point of view.

However, this section gives **guidance** as to the **likely content** of such a report.

1.2 Report content

The **introduction** will explain the structure of the report and will relate it to the service which the adviser offers.

It may therefore mention that the report has been prepared following an **initial meeting**, and that a **further meeting** will take place during which the **recommendations** can be explained in more detail and any questions or concerns the client may have can be answered.

1.3 Current position

The **current position** will be based upon the information provided by the client as part of the factfinding process. It is not necessary within the report to provide details of all the information collected, but instead a summary should be given.

Certainly the **most important aspects** will be covered, including the client's income and outgoings, with a statement of the **amount agreed to be available** for financial planning purposes, on a regular basis, as a lump sum, or a combination of the two.

A **summary of current investment and protection arrangements**, together with their value would also be necessary together with a note of any liabilities. Where existing arrangements, for example life insurance policies, have been established for a **particular purpose**, it is important that this purpose be specified in the report.

1.4 Objectives and priorities

A summary of the current position naturally leads on to a consideration of the position in which the client would wish to find himself. It is the difference between the **desired position** and the **current position** which determines **needs**.

These needs should therefore be identified from a consideration of the objectives and the report should contain confirmation of the priorities specified by the client, as guided by the adviser.

Because the report is a **document for consideration** rather than a **final statement**, it may be that the client will have reconsidered some of the matters covered in it. It is important that the client should feel **comfortable** in telling the adviser if he has **changed his mind**, or if he has anything to add or to correct in relation to the information given during the factfinding process.

It is therefore a good idea to include an **invitation** to do so. If the client does not feel comfortable, he may not give the adviser the necessary information to amend his recommendations to meet the client's real requirements.

1.5 Recommendations

The **recommendations** should be linked to the **priorities** specified in the previous section. They can then be seen as addressing the needs the client considers most pressing.

Recommendations need to be explained, not in technical terms, but in understandable terms so that the client is fully aware of the way in which any particular product or arrangement being recommended will meet his needs.

It will also be appropriate to include an **explanation of the choice of provider** and this can be done either **in the body of the report** or **as an appendix**.

The documents such as **Key Features**, giving details of the products as required from a regulatory point of view, may also be referred to and are likely to **accompany the report**. They should **reinforce the recommendations**, because they will set out the nature and objective of the product concerned, the client's commitment and the risk factors involved. Because the adviser's recommendations are based on the same considerations, there should be a **clear correspondence** between the report contents and the product details.

1.6 Considerations deferred

There is little point going into detail regarding recommendations which would be made in order to cover those of the client's needs which are **too far down the list of priorities** for them to be addressed immediately.

You should however include a **brief summary** of those needs where you have agreed that consideration should be **deferred**.

This will serve **two functions**. Firstly, mentioning these areas in your report will give your client a chance to reconsider whether the priorities he has specified are in fact correct.

Secondly, during subsequent meetings, it will provide a **framework** within which to start the discussion of further recommendations.

In addition, the inclusion of this section of the report underlines that the recommendations do not necessarily provide solutions to all aspects of the client's financial planning needs, because of the need to **prioritise**. This avoids any potential misunderstanding on the part of the client and protects the adviser should any future query arise.

In some cases, the client may even reconsider his priority decisions, once they are set out in 'black and white'.

1.7 Tax implications

The client's **tax position** should be summarised, and the **taxation implications of the recommendations** made in the report should also be covered.

Where there is a change to tax liability, for example through the payment of personal pension contributions upon which relief can be claimed, the method by which relief will be granted should be specified with details of any action which the client must undertake.

The tax implications should be **related to the client's position** and any **potential pitfalls** (for example, the existence of a deadline) should be commented upon.

1.8 Action required

Finally, the **action required** to implement the recommendations should be documented. This may include reference to any **medical requirements** where life insurance policies are involved and will also detail the role which the adviser will take in assisting the client towards implementation.

1.9 Communicating verbally

Although a written report will usually be desirable, and indeed necessary from a regulatory point of view, this does not mean that there is no place for **verbal communication**. Indeed quite the opposite is true in that a face to face discussion of the recommendations, preceded by confirmation that the adviser's understanding of the client's needs and priorities is correct, can **add greatly** to the written word.

A face-to-face discussion will also allow the client to **ask questions** and discuss any thoughts which have occurred to him since the meeting at which it was agreed that the recommendations would be prepared. It is unusual for recommendations to be put into effect without such a meeting.

2 The holistic view

When presenting recommendations, the adviser should be careful to present an **holistic view** of the client's situation, in other words a view which takes account of **all of the relevant factors** and their **interaction**.

For example, there could be a recommendation in the report to use part of a capital sum to **repay an outstanding loan** rather than to make an additional investment. The advantages and disadvantages of doing this will have been included as part of the **justification** for the recommendation and the proposition will also have been evaluated in the light of the client's **attitude to risk**. (Not paying off a loan when the opportunity arises is usually only valid if the client believes that the likely return net of tax on the investment that he makes instead is likely to exceed the interest that is paid on the loan, and to give himself the potential to achieve this return, a relatively **high degree of risk** is likely to be necessary.)

However, there will be other aspects of the client situation which will also be affected. For example, it may be that there is a **life insurance policy** currently covering the mortgage and assigned to the lender. It could be that this life cover is **no longer required** because the need to repay the loan on the individual's death is no longer present. Alternatively it may be considered that the life cover should be kept in force to provide for **other needs** which could arise on his death, but it might then be appropriate to **write the policy in trust** to improve its inheritance tax efficiency.

Financial planning arrangements do inevitably **interact**, and advisers should always be alert for the **impact of one recommendation on another**. Even at a very basic level, the allocation of money to deal with one need will reduce the amounts available to deal with other needs. At a higher level, actions such as **placing assets into trust** may **reduce the access** to income and capital of the settlor. With any set of recommendations, therefore, the adviser should look at this particular aspect with care.

3 Taking account of change

The adviser will already have collected a significant volume of information relating to the client during the factfind process, and will have **checked** the information for apparent gaps, errors or inconsistencies which may have led to **additional information** being required or **amendments** being made. At the time when recommendations are being made, it is appropriate to confirm that the position really is as the adviser believes.

Part of this is covered by the setting out of the **current position** in the report and perhaps, subject to the practice of the firm, giving the client a copy of the factfind document for his own records. However **changes** can and do occur in the client situation between the time of the initial collection of data and the time when recommendations are presented, even if this is only a relatively short period.

The adviser should therefore check whether there have been any changes, for example:

- Salary increase or promotion
- Redundancy
- Change in health
- New needs, for example a decision to save for a particular event
- Consideration of moving house

This list gives some **examples** of changes which can occur, but does not cover all possibilities. The adviser will want to **prompt the client**, for example by asking if there have been any changes at work, or perhaps by reminding the client of the **objectives** discussed at the previous meeting and checking that these remained valid.

Where changes have occurred, it may be necessary to **adjust** the recommendations to fit the **new circumstances**. Sometimes this will be a minor adjustment, but in other cases it will require the recommendations to be **reworked from scratch**. This might, for example, arise where there has been a significant change in the individual's priorities, or where a major change has occurred such as the receipt of a substantial inheritance.

4 The insistent client

In an ideal world, the adviser would collect all the relevant information from the client, including his priorities and objectives, and would then prepare **recommendations** which the client would then **willingly take up**. In the real world, although this can often happen, it certainly does not always happen.

For various reasons, the client may **disagree** with the recommendations made by the adviser, or not be fully convinced by them. It may be that, although the adviser has suggested that **protection** arrangements for a dependent family should be a **priority**, the client intends instead to use all of the available financial resource for **savings**. Perhaps less dramatically, the client may wish to make investment selections which contain a **higher degree of risk** than the adviser would recommend, taking into account the client's experience and circumstances.

These and many other situations can arise, and inevitably the **final decision** as to what is and what is not done must **rest with the client**. The adviser must therefore be able to deal with these **'insistent client'** situations where the client is not prepared to follow the adviser's recommendations but would rather follow his own inclinations.

The adviser will need to ensure that the client **understands** the recommendations which he is making, and the **reasons** for them, and will also need to check that the **information** on which he made those recommendations is **still valid** (this may already have been done as part of the advice process anyway, but it may be appropriate to re-confirm at this stage.) The adviser would need to consider the client's **intended action** and the areas where those intentions meet the client's needs **less well**. In some cases, the difference may be very small, perhaps particularly if the client has a particular aversion to a chosen product provider, and where the adviser would still consider the client's choice to be suitable. In other situations the disagreement may be far greater.

It is important that the adviser ensures that the client fully understands what he is doing, and in particular any risk aspects of his intended actions. The adviser cannot escape the obligation to give full and suitable advice to the client, including explaining the consequences of what the client wants to do.

The adviser is still able to **arrange** the investments which the client has chosen, but he will need to **protect his own position** by setting out the fact that the client is not following his recommendations and that the adviser is **not responsible** for the **choices** which the client makes.

5 Reaching agreement

When agreement has been reached on the actions which will be taken and the products which will be established, the adviser will need to ensure that the **appropriate forms** are completed to allow these arrangements to be progressed. Application forms will often require details such as **medical information** which can only be provided by the client, though sometimes, for the sake of simplicity, the adviser will complete the forms on the client's behalf. The client must always be asked to **read through** the details completed by the adviser with care, to ensure that the information completed is **accurate** and that **nothing has been excluded**.

With protection orientated products such as **life insurance** and **income protection insurance**, the principle of **utmost good faith** means that the client is under an obligation to disclose all relevant matters, even if there is no specific question on the proposal form. Even though in practice, a court might well interpret this provision in favour of the client in the sense that his knowledge of what is relevant is likely to be less acute than the understanding of the person who designed the application form, it is only through **full disclosure** of relevant facts that there can be **certainty** that the cover (when accepted by the insurance company) is in place as expected. If there has been a **failure to disclose**, this could allow the insurance company to **void** the policy and avoid paying out at the time when the protection is needed. The adviser must ensure that the client fully **understands** this position and should be sure to pick up on any **apparent inaccuracies** such as a smoker claiming to be a non-smoker on the application form.

It is also likely to be necessary for the client to complete one or more **means of** payment, for example a cheque for a lump sum investment or a direct debit for a regular contribution arrangement.

The adviser will also need to explain **what happens next**, for example in relation to the underwriting procedures for a risk contract, or the investment allocation arrangements for a lump sum.

6 Regulatory matters

6.1 Right to cancel

An important feature of many financial services products is the right of the client to change his mind and **cancel or withdraw** from the arrangement **without meeting charges**. The right to withdraw is a pre-sale right in the sense that no investment is made until the end of the period, which is between 7 and 14 days depending on the product. More frequently there is a post-sale right to cancel, which means that money is invested through a period of reflection (between 7 and 30 days depending on the product) and in this situation, if a client cancels, there may be a loss of money as a result of **market movements** (though no charges will be made).

Although some might regard this possibility of a loss of capital as being unfair, if this provision were not in place, it would allow an individual who made an investment and then found that the market fell to withdraw not because the contract was unsuitable or he did not understand its terms, but merely to **avoid an investment loss**. This would **not be fair** in relation to the rights of other investors.

At the time the recommendations are agreed, the adviser will need to run through the **withdrawal and/or cancellation rights** for the various products selected with the client and ensure that he fully understands his rights, and understands the related paperwork that he will receive.

6.2 Access to Medical Reports Acts 1988 and 1990

These two Acts are in place to give an individual rights over information held in relation to them by their **medical advisers**, including their GP. Under the legislation, clients have the right to **refuse** to allow information to be released, for example to an insurance company, and also have the right to see a **copy of any report** before it is sent to the insurance company. Application forms will give the insurance company **permission** to obtain the information and will give **permission for their GP to release** the information.

It is important that the adviser explains these rights to the client, though without the release of the relevant information, the insurer is extremely unlikely to take on the risk concerned.

6.3 Money laundering

The adviser will need also to make sure that any required actions under the **Money Laundering Regulations** are met, and this will include the requirement for new clients to **prove their identity**. Although there are monetary limits where the regulations allow this provision to be avoided, in practice most firms will always seek the **appropriate evidence**.

The identification requirements may well require the adviser to have sight of, and copy, documents such as a **passport or driving licence**, and verify address details from items such as a **utility bill**.

It is crucial to the operation of the money laundering requirements that this process is **properly documented**, and that records are retained by the firm for the **appropriate period**, which is usually **five years** from the **termination of the relationship** with the client.

Once again, the adviser needs to explain the process to the client and put this into its legislative context, otherwise clients may find the process of the provision of identity information extremely irksome.

It follows that the adviser needs to fully understand the provisions of his firm's **money laundering procedures**, which will specify what kinds of identification and address verification are suitable, and the way in which the firm requires its records to be kept.

6.4 Suitability letter

A suitability letter is **required** in many cases and is **good practice** in most cases. The suitability letter sets out **why** the recommendations made are **suitable** for the client in his particular circumstances. It is possible to rely on the report to the client as described above to fulfil this function, because it does explain the recommendations, but many firms treat the suitability letter as a **separate exercise**, to reflect the fact that the position may have changed since the report was prepared.

It is important that the suitability letter relates the recommendations to the **client's circumstances** rather than merely going over the features of the product itself. This issue has been one which the regulatory authorities have **highlighted** in the past as being a major cause for concern and an area in which many suitability letters they have seen during inspection visits fail to reach the necessary standard.

Key chapter points

- **A formal written report will usually be necessary as part of the advice process.**

- **There is no single correct approach, though reports generally have a similar construction and content.**

- **The report should include details of the client's current position, including existing investment and protection arrangements.**

- **Objectives and priorities should be detailed, because the recommendations will address these.**

- **The report should allow scope for the client to change his objectives and priorities if necessary.**

- **Recommendations must be explained in the client's context rather than in highly technical terms, though the information must be complete and accurate.**

- **Similarly the choice of product provider needs to be explained.**

- **The tax position of the client should be stated, together with details of the effect of the recommendations from a tax point of view.**

- **The actions necessary to put the recommendations into effect should also be spelt out.**

- **It is important that the recommendations are based on an holistic view of the client's situation, and can be seen to be so.**

- **The adviser should be prepared to check that there have been no changes in the circumstances of the client since the factfinding stage was completed, and should react to such changes as appropriate.**

- **Clients may not always take up recommendations as made, but may be insistent that other arrangements are made.**

- **Many products give the client cancellation or withdrawal rights, and these need to be fully explained by the adviser. These rights allow the client to require his money back without deduction of charges, but the amount returned can be adjusted to reflect losses in investment values.**

- **The rights of the client under the Access to Medical Reports legislation must also be explained.**

- **Money laundering procedures must also be followed in accordance with the firm's procedures, for example, regarding verification of identity.**

Chapter Quiz

1   Why should a report contain details of the client's current position in financial planning terms?....... (see para 1.3)

2   What are the advantages of including details of considerations which are deferred in a report?.....................(1.6)

3   What is meant by an 'holistic view' in financial planning? ....(2)

4   List some of the changes in information which could occur between an initial factfinding meeting and the adviser presenting his recommendations...(3)

5   What is the difference between cancellation and withdrawal rights? ....(6.1)

chapter

8

The review

1 The nature of the review

1.1 Background

Change is **inevitable** in all aspects of life, and financial planning cannot stand aloof from this. **Reviewing** the position of clients is therefore **part of the service** that financial advisers should provide.

The review process should be **explained** by the adviser at the outset of the relationship with the client, so that the client fully **appreciates** that financial planning is an **ongoing process**, rather than a single event. This should also encourage the client to contact the adviser if significant changes occur to his circumstances before a review would normally be due.

In this section we consider the **nature of the review**, and look at more specific aspects in the remainder of the chapter.

1.2 Topics to review

The review needs to consider how the client's needs have **changed**, and the way in which the approach **implemented** has performed. There will therefore be many aspects to consider, including the following.

- **Client circumstances**. There may have been major changes in the client's circumstances which will result in a need to **review** his financial planning arrangements and **modify them** accordingly. For example, his health may have changed, perhaps creating pressure on his earning ability and therefore his spendable income. There could be an increase in the **number of dependants** for whom he needs to provide, for example, following the birth of a child, or an elderly relative becoming dependant as the result of a need for long term care. Sometimes the changes are **less dramatic**, but still important, such as an increase in salary, or a new long term objective such as a major holiday in an exotic location.

- **Change in attitude**. The attitude of the client to various financial planning issues can change over a period of time. It is common for **attitude to risk** to become more cautious as time goes on, as the ability to leave an investment to **recover** following a fall in market values declines. This is not universal however, and for some, **increased investment experience** results in an increased tolerance of risk. **Priorities** might also change. For example, the client might have had a minor accident at work, from which he has recovered, but nevertheless, as a result, he may feel that protecting himself and his family from the **potential effect of incapacity** should be a higher priority than he previously thought.

- **External events**. Sometimes external events have a major impact on the client's objectives, for example, publicity relating to **positive stock market performance** might encourage him to want to invest in equity related products. Alternatively the debate on **pensions provision** in the UK might stimulate him to take further action to secure his own retirement.

- **Employment benefits**. The benefits provided to the individual as part of his remuneration package at work may have changed, for example, with modifications to the **pension scheme**, or the introduction of a tax advantaged **share option scheme**. Such events are likely to change the **balance** of the arrangements he needs to make personally and sometimes could affect the **suitability** of existing protection and investment arrangements.

- **Legislative and tax changes**. There may have been changes to the legal or tax position affecting products, or the client personally. An example of this has been the introduction of a **simplified regime for the tax treatment of pension arrangements** from 6 April 2006. The effect on the client and his existing financial arrangements should be considered as part of the review.

- **Performance of existing arrangements**. The recommendations put forward previously need to be evaluated, so that their performance **relative to the objectives** they were designed to meet can be considered. Where those objectives have now changed, the nature of the change must also be considered as part of the review, because it is the **current suitability** of the existing arrangements which is important. (The comments made in Chapter 6 about the advantages and disadvantages of reorganising a portfolio are relevant here. There may be **costs** and **tax implications** in changing products, or encashing early, and these need to be weighed against the **desirability** of any change.)

- **Predictable changes**. Often the recommendations previously taken up will have made **allowance** for changes or events expected in the short to medium term, such as a need to buy a new car, or finance a special holiday. At the time of the review, the adviser will need to establish whether such changes have **taken place**, and if so, whether the costs or effects were **as expected**. If they have not taken place, are they still anticipated for the future, and are there any changes to their **expected timing** or **financial implications**?

- **Tax efficiency**. Recommendations will often have made use of tax efficient investments, such as ISAs and pension arrangements, and there may at a review be the opportunity to make further investments in these products if a new year's allowance has become available. There may be new issues of NS&I Savings Certificates to consider, because they give the opportunity for additional investments producing tax free returns. If the CGT annual exemption has not been used and it is towards the end of the tax year, it may be appropriate to consider selling an investment to utilise the exemption, followed by reinvesting the proceeds in a different investment. These are only some of the possibilities, but note that many will be triggered simply by the passage of time rather than by any specific change in the circumstances of the client(s).

The list of possible areas requiring review is virtually endless, and the list above simply gives examples. The adviser will need to consider **all changes** which could impact on the client's **financial planning needs** and this will involve a significant factfinding exercise.

In addition to changes, remember that there will usually have been some needs which were **deferred** in the past, because of **priority considerations** in the light of affordability. These should also be **reconsidered**, to determine if they remain relevant, and whether there is now scope, perhaps because of an increase in spendable income, to **take action** in relation to at least some of them.

1.3 The review in context

The way in which the review fits into the **process of financial advice** generally will have been introduced to the client initially and will be **reinforced** at each review. It should be part of the client's expectation that the plan be reviewed to take account of changes.

The **frequency** of the review will need to be agreed between client and adviser. Most advisers aim to see clients at least **once each year**, but in some cases **more frequent** reviews will be desirable, particularly if an individual is going through a period of rapid change. For example, a client who is thinking about changing jobs, or who is faced with the threat of redundancy, may need to adjust existing plans to take account of these events, should they arise.

Similarly, there could be some **likely occurrence** which is anticipated, and which will also need to be built into the overall approach to financial planning. For example, paying off a mortgage will have a number of effects. It may reduce the need for both life assurance and income protection insurance and create a possibly considerable **increase in disposable income** which could be used in other ways. There could also be a lump sum surplus, perhaps from the maturity of an endowment linked to the mortgage, where the proceeds exceed the debt. Alternatively, any action necessary to deal with a shortfall might have to be discussed.

Prior to the mortgage being paid off, the client and adviser might **discuss and agree** the likely impact that these changes will have on the financial plan, but final decisions can only be made at the time, on the basis of **facts** rather than expectations.

The agreement of a **regular pattern** of review meetings should not prevent **additional reviews** taking place as necessary. Some of the events mentioned above may occur unexpectedly, for example, an individual losing his job is not usually predictable. It is therefore important that the client should always feel in a position to **contact the adviser** to discuss developments, and indeed should realise the necessity to do so.

When the review takes place, changes in the **information** which the adviser has collected in relation to the client and his circumstances will need to be **updated**. The process then effectively starts again, with a further consideration of the updated facts by the adviser, the agreement of priorities, presentation of recommendations and agreement on their implementation.

2 Ongoing financial needs

As well as considering changes, it is important to review aspects of the client's ongoing needs which have not changed. For example, there may already be and should continue to be an emergency fund in place,

Protection arrangements will also have a continuing role to play in the financial planning of most clients. It is useful to **remind** the client of the **purpose** of existing arrangements, and (where applicable) the continuing need for them.

Sometimes a client will have **suggestions** of his own, which can be discussed at the time of the review. These may be valid and useful, in which case they can be built into the overall plan. Sometimes however, the client's ideas might not be as beneficial as he believes, and the adviser will then need to **explain** why this is.

An example might be a client intending to purchase an **investment property** on a 'buy to let' basis. Such investments can work very well, but the client needs to understand the possible **disadvantages** as well as the **advantages**. An attraction of this form of investment is often the expectation that rental income will meet the interest cost of the loan used to purchase the property, leaving the client with a capital gain on eventual disposal of the property.

This is a valid point, but there are risks, for example as follows.

- The property may have **void periods** when it is not let and there is no rental income, so that the interest costs have to be met from other resources.

- A tenant **might not pay** the rent due.

- Interest rates might **increase** to a level above the amount of rent being received.

- The level of rent which can be achieved might **reduce** to less than the interest costs.

- There might be a need for **unbudgeted expenditure** (for example repairs or improvements) which would add to expected costs.

- Property prices might **fall**, wiping out any potential gain.

Virtually all investments carry some **risk**, so these points alone do not make the property purchase **unsuitable**. However, for some people, the risk will be **excessive**, particularly if they have limited other resources which they could use if problems did arise in connection with the property. The question of **diversification** is also important, and if their investments are predominantly in property, the **concentration** increases risk.

3 The effect of external change

3.1 Background

The impact of external change has already been briefly discussed in section 1 above, but it is worth considering this in more detail. Remember that the client may not be aware that a change has, or is about to occur, and often will not be in a position to evaluate its potential effect.

The financial planning position is affected by change in many ways, often with no control on the part of the client or the adviser, and often the change is both rapid and unexpected. Some aspects which should be considered at the review are discussed in this section.

3.2 Economic factors

The economic situation affects clients in many ways, including the following:

- **Interest rates** will affect the return he can achieve through secure investments such as deposits, and if he relies on this to an extent to provide income, this will impact on the **surplus income** available for financial planning purposes.

- In the longer term, interest rates will affect the cost of **buying an annuity**, and as a result may affect the amount he needs to devote to retirement planning.

- The level of **taxation** levied by government will also affect **spendable income** and may affect the relative attractions of tax advantaged products such as ISAs and pension arrangements.

- **Stock market performance** will affect the **value of investments**, and therefore progress towards any relevant objectives.

- **Price inflation** affects the value of assets and the spending power that could be generated on disposal.

- **Earnings inflation** affects the likelihood of substantial pay increases, which will in turn affect the **relative impact of costs** such as mortgage repayments on the client's budget.

3.3 Regulatory issues

Regulation may impact on the client in a number of ways, for example through requirements under **money laundering rules** to prove identity, and often to create a need to show the **provenance** of cash and other assets.

Over time, one of the roles of regulation is to increase the **awareness** of the public of financial matters generally, and this should gradually create a **more sophisticated market place**.

3.4 Social factors

Social factors affect people's expectations in various ways, but particularly their **lifestyle** expectations.

Although it is common to focus on the effects of inflation as measured by prices when considering the need to protect assets from inflation, this may not in reality be enough to maintain an **individual's standing** in society. Living standards tend to increase over the years, largely because earnings increase (on average) faster than prices, but also because of the gradual accumulation of capital and the passing down of inheritances.

This means that people expect to be able to **live better** and afford **more luxuries** as time goes on. For example, en suite bathrooms in the home are now quite common, but even twenty years ago, were much less so, and fifty years ago were rare. Similarly, foreign holidays are now the norm, but were once the province of the rich or the highly adventurous.

These changes in expectation should be built into the financial planning process. It is not enough to aim to maintain the status quo.

4 Interaction of financial planning areas

In some ways, this chapter has highlighted the difficulties faced by advisers in attempting to do a complete job for their clients. The **range of aspects** which need to be taken into account, including existing arrangements, objectives, priorities, expected change, possible unexpected change, and external factors, is extremely wide. The role is therefore a **demanding** one.

A further aspect which should always be at the **forefront** of the adviser's mind is the interaction of the various components of the financial plan, and the need to take an **holistic view** as discussed in Chapter 7.

The client needs to be aware of this. It sometimes happens that clients change arrangements **without consulting** the adviser beforehand, and **without understanding** fully the impact that removing one piece of what is a complex jigsaw puzzle can have. For example, because of cashflow constraints, a client might cancel a life insurance policy which had been written in **trust** to ensure inheritance tax efficiency.

The consequences could be **disastrous** if the individual died whilst the cover was not in force. However, suppose this does not happen, but instead, cashflow later improves and he takes out a **new policy**, similar to the one he cancelled. However, he might not think about writing the policy in **trust**.

If he does not, and the policy proceeds on death would form part of his estate and would be liable to **inheritance tax**, he is in effect **wasting 40% of his premiums**.

The adviser would have **advised** him on this point, but might also have been able to suggest **other ways** of improving his cashflow, without having to cancel a potentially valuable protection policy.

If the client is aware of the **interaction** between the various parts of his financial planning arrangements, the result should be:

- Greater awareness of the **importance of the adviser's role**, and his skill
- Increased willingness to **involve the adviser** as early as possible when changes must be dealt with
- **Improved** financial planning

Although the adviser's job is a **challenging** one, the better it is done, the greater the client's awareness and the easier it will be to build on and improve the long term relationship with the client.

Key chapter points

- Reviews are a natural and necessary part of the financial planning process and this should be explained to clients from the outset. There are many potential areas of change to consider, including client circumstances and attitudes.

- External events, including publicity relating to financial matters, can affect the client's objectives and attitudes.

- There may be aspects of the client's employment situation which need to be taken into account, particularly the provision of benefits such as a pension arrangement, or a share option scheme.

- Changes in the law or tax provisions may also impact on the client or on existing products, or indeed those which might be recommended at the time of the review.

- The existing arrangements should be reviewed in relation to the objectives they addressed, though any changes in those objectives must also be taken into account.

- If changes are made to existing arrangements, such as early encashment, any costs or tax consequences need to be considered in comparison with the expected advantage of the change.

- Future predictable changes need to be considered, particularly those for which arrangements were made in the past – they may have already happened, or the expectation may have changed.

- The frequency of regular reviews should be agreed between adviser and client, but is unlikely to be less frequent than annually.

- Clients should be encouraged to contact the adviser between reviews if important changes occur, which might require immediate action.

- It is important to ensure that the client fully understands the purpose of existing arrangements, even if they are not affected by any change.

- Dealing with external change is a major issue at the time of the review, as the client might not be aware of the potential change or its effect.

- Economic factors will often have a significant impact because they can affect spendable income, asset values and progress towards objectives.

- Regulatory and social factors can also be important, including changes to the individual's desired lifestyle as expectations amongst the population generally change.

- Clients should also be aware of the importance of taking account of the interaction between different parts of the financial planning arrangements. This should increase his understanding of the importance of the adviser, and the value he places on the advice given.

Chapter Quiz

1   Is it likely that a client's attitude to risk might change over time?.. (see para 1.2)

2   Outline some examples of legislative or taxation changes that have occurred recently and could affect recommendations or advice. ....(1.2)

3   If a client suggests an investment which the adviser feels is not suitable, what should the adviser do? ....(2)

chapter

9

Dealing with written case studies

1 Introduction

Although the content of the syllabus for the CII's CF5, the SII's IFA Paper 4 and the *ifs* CeFA® Module 4 are essentially the same, the style of the exams are different.

- The **SII's IFA 4** is based on case studies, provided in advance by the Securities & Investment Institute. In the exam itself, vignettes are given which extend the case study information, and questions are then set in relation to the vignettes. The questions are in multiple choice format, and some of the questions require candidates to choose from a number of combinations of statements, rather than just choosing a single statement as correct.

- The *ifs* **CeFA® Module 4** paper is also tested by multiple choice. You may well be becoming familiar with multiple choice questions from other papers you have been or are taking. The Module 4 exam includes six different case studies. For each case, details of approximately 200 words in length are given, and then there are 10 multiple choice questions about the case.

- The **CII's CF5** is a written paper, based on two case studies with a number of related questions. Candidates need to respond to these in writing and this requires specific examination skills. Like its predecessor, FP3, the CF5 examination therefore requires **technique** as much as it requires **knowledge**. This means that **practice** as well as knowledge is vital in your preparation – a failure to apply proper technique is likely to end in disaster. The broad nature of the questions is quite well defined and it is possible to pinpoint certain areas of technique which avoid the most likely pitfalls. Applying technique within the context of the exam will often be the difference between passing and failing. This Chapter will help CF5 candidates master the required technique.

This Chapter is provided mainly for students studying for the CII's CF5 paper, which requires some special attention to the exam techniques involved in answering written case study questions.

2 The CF5 exam

In the CF5 exam, there are two Questions. A different approach is required to each, and the examiner is looking for different things.

There are also four full practice exam papers modelled on the style of CF5, with model answers, which will give you the opportunity to practice further under exam timing constraints.

2.1 Answering questions

When you answer questions in CF5, you do not need to write essays. Use a bullet point style to highlight your points succinctly. Bullet points are grammatically correct sentences which generally make a single point.

Take note of the words used in the question, and do what you are asked to do. The question often guides you as to the type of answer required by using words such as the following.

- **LIST** – which requires no more than a list of the items requested

- **STATE or IDENTIFY** – a brief statement rather than a full explanation

- **NOTE** – short answers are required

- **EXPLAIN** – the candidate is expected to show the examiner that he understands the issues behind his answer

- **CALCULATE** – this is self-explanatory, but always show your workings, whether the question prompts you to do so or not

- **COMPARE** – make sure the points you make in your answer relate to the comparison concerned rather than being more general

- **RECOMMEND** – You should come to a definite conclusion, rather than hedging your bets, and state what that conclusion is

One problem with writing answers in bullet point style is that it is easy to over-abbreviate and for the answers to become ambiguous as a result. You need to avoid this. For example, a candidate might write 'Short term for asset backed investments.'

Try to put yourself in the shoes of the marker. What does this mean? It could mean that a short term is appropriate for asset backed investment, which would be incorrect. Although it is likely that the writer meant the opposite, the marker does not know.

A better alternative might be: 'The term is too short for asset backed investments'. This version is slightly longer, but it is unambiguous and would earn good marks.

It might be better still to be more comprehensive. You could extend your answer by stating:

- Minimum 5 years time horizon recommended for asset backed investments
- Because of volatility of market value and income levels

2.2 Planning

Time is very tight in this exam. Because of this, there is a temptation to start writing without thinking or **planning**. Do not fall into this trap, particularly with question parts that require analysis, or a list of factors or features. If you do, you are likely to not answer the question set and to produce confused and inefficient answers.

Instead, for such question parts, plan your approach carefully. Read the questions you must answer before you read the case study details, so that you consider the details in a focused way. Then begin tackling the questions.

For each part, prepare yourself by brainstorming the points you want to include in your answer, writing very brief notes of them. Allow only a minute or so for this process. Then re-read the question to make sure you have kept to the points being examined.

Only then are you ready to commit your answer to paper. You should deal with the points you have brainstormed in priority order.

Not all question parts need to be dealt with in this way. Some might just require a calculation, for example. However, planning for more complex questions is extremely important.

2.3 Use of time

The examination lasts for two hours and is marked out of 100 marks. As a broad guide therefore, this works out at roughly **one mark per minute**, with a little time over for reading and checking.

The exam paper will also give you a guide as to how much time it is expected you would spend on each question. This suggests allowing one hour for each of the two Questions. You should avoid going over time on Question 1 at all costs. Question 2 involves recommending a portfolio, and this requires a clear head, without the stress of feeling you are 'behind the clock'. Indeed, it may help some candidates to do Question 2 before Question 1 (which is allowed).

2.4 Justification of recommendations

You are normally expected to justify recommendations, and even if you are not specifically asked to do so, it is still worthwhile giving brief justifications. The reason for this is straightforward, in that the examiner will have a marking scheme which incorporates a certain amount of flexibility, but he will want to be sure that your recommendations are soundly based.

2.5 The examination paper

Questions follow a prescribed pattern.

Q1   Factfinding, technical and recommendations

Q2   Portfolio planning

The detail of each question in each exam will vary. We provide guidance in the following sections to help you prepare for the style of questions you can reasonably expect.

3 Question 1

Question 1 of the CF5 paper tests your ability to **factfind** and to **apply** technical knowledge. You will also be asked to make and justify recommendations. The Question will normally explore several different areas of financial planning, so you should not feel put off if some parts concentrate on areas which you find difficult. Other parts will focus on other areas which you know better.

Normally, there are several parts to Question 1, and you should ensure that you attempt each part. Marks are available for quite basic information, so you should be able to score a few marks even in your weaker areas.

3.1 Question sequence

The first part of Question 1 will often involve you constructing a question sequence which will elicit more information on specific subjects. Commonly, the subject will be retirement planning, but other information areas could arise. The question sequence can attract high marks, so this can be an important part of the Question and of the exam as a whole.

The two main types of question you ask in practical situations are **closed** questions and **open** questions.

Closed questions are those which are designed to elicit a specific piece of information, such as a date of birth, or an income figure. Closed questions can gather accurate information in a short time, although on their own, they do not give a complete picture of the client's circumstances. Most of the questions you should include in your question sequence for CF5 will be closed questions.

Open questions give the client the opportunity to express his views, or his feelings, and invite a longer response.

Examples might be:

- 'What are the schools like in this area?' or
- 'How do you feel about investments which can go down as well as up in value?'

You may need to include some questions of this type in your sequence. The answers give you information which can help you identify the considerations which are important to your client, and can give clues as to how he would react to different recommendations. Refer back to **Chapter 1** for a more detailed consideration of questioning technique.

Note you must always **write the question** as though you are addressing the client. This means writing 'John, what is your take home pay?' rather than 'I would ask John what his take home pay is'. The first would score a mark, but the second would not.

You must also ask questions in a way which would be **understood by your client**. This means that you should avoid jargon, and abbreviations which are unlikely to be familiar. For example, asking 'Are you a member of a PPS?' is not likely to be a productive question. A better question would be 'Are you paying contributions to a personal pension of your own?'

Always aim to make your questions understandable, taking into account your client's level of knowledge and awareness of financial matters. The examiner will consider whether the client is likely to be able to answer the question. If not, it will not score. This also underlines the importance of asking factfinding questions rather than unsettling questions.

The **order and progression** of questions is important too. For example, if you ask 'Have you got enough life cover?' or 'Are you happy with your investments?' the answer is likely to be 'Yes'. Otherwise, the client would presumably have done something about it. You need to plan the question sequence to show the examiner that you know how to deal with this aspect of the client meeting.

Questions should be succinct and direct, but unambiguous. You should practice writing question sequences, bearing these points in mind.

The following are examples of questions to ask in various scenarios and are typical of the style employed in the examination guides, so give a good indication of what is required.

Pensions

- How much income will you need in retirement?
- At what age would you like to retire?
- Do you have a pension arrangement at the moment?
- Have you ever had any private pension provision?
- Does your pension arrangement provide a widows or dependant's pension?
- Are you entitled to full state pension?
- Are there any early retirement reductions or penalties if you take your pension at 60?
- What is the current value of your pension fund?
- May I see your pension scheme booklet?
- Do you pay any extra contributions to the pension scheme?

Protection

- Other than the endowment policy, is there any life assurance on your life?
- How much income would you need if you were unable to work due to ill health?
- Mary, how much income would you need if John were to die?
- May I see the protection/insurance scheme document?
- Do you have any health problems?

Investments

- What investments and savings do you have?
- How much of your capital would you need to keep accessible?
- With regard to investing, would you describe yourself as cautious or adventurous?
- Do you need to draw an income from your investments?
- Would you prefer the investments to be in single or joint names?
- Are you concerned about the effects of inflation on your investments?

Savings for specific needs, eg education

- How much do you expect the school fees will be?
- When will your son start private education?
- How long will Joanna's university course last?
- How much can you afford to save each month?

Mortgage

- How much do you wish to borrow?
- Are you repaying part of the capital on your mortgage each month, or just the interest?
- Can I see the information you have received from your lender describing the mortgage details?
- How much is your outstanding mortgage?
- When will the mortgage be repaid?
- Are you concerned about rises in interest rates?
- Are there any penalties if you repay the mortgage early?
- Have you asked the building society if you can reduce your payments or extend the term?

Capital/income tax

- How much income do you receive from your savings/investments?
- What income does your husband/wife have?
- Would you be willing to put investments in your spouse's name?
- Are you willing to tie up your capital for 5 years?

Inheritance tax

- Have you made a will?
- What is the total value of your estate, by which I mean all your assets?
- Are there any significant liabilities, such as a mortgage or any other loans?
- Who are the beneficiaries under your will?

- Are all your assets jointly owned?
- Is the life policy/whole of life policy written in trust?
- Have you made use of the inheritance tax nil rate band to make gifts?

It can be effective to use the clients' names in your questions, both to help you focus and to show the examiner you are relating your answer to the case study. Sometimes you will want to ask different questions of each person, and you can then save time by using the name as a sub-heading. When a question could be asked of, and answered by, either, you can use 'Either' as a sub-heading.

It can also be helpful to use sub-headings if you are dealing with more than one area in your question sequence. You will not score any marks for questions which do not relate to the area you are asked to deal with, however well worded, and irrespective of their relevance to the broader context of the client(s). You can waste a lot of time unproductively if you do not ensure that your questions are focused on the right areas of information. The sub-headings help to ensure you concentrate in the relevant areas.

3.2 Errors and inconsistencies

It is possible that part of Question 1 could require you to identify **errors and inconsistencies** in the case details. Your ability to identify these will depend on your technical knowledge and reading skills.

Errors and inconsistencies arise for many reasons, and you need to be alert in your reading of the case study. Generally the error will be a straightforward mistake in technical information given, for example, the client says he does not receive tax relief on his contributions to an occupational pension scheme.

Inconsistencies can be more subtle, and may be in the form of conflicting views between husband and wife, for example, one stating that their main priority is to move house, the other stating that it is to save up to send their children to a private school.

Sometimes there will be information that does not fit together. For example, a couple state that their attitude to risk is cautious, but they have investments in highly volatile overseas unit trusts.

To gain full marks you must:

- Identify the error/inconsistency
- Separately explain why it is an error/inconsistency

You generally do not need to guess how the error or inconsistency might have arisen.

Note that you do not need to distinguish between an error/inconsistency. If you think something is wrong, put it down. However, do not go fishing for 'subjective' inconsistencies, for example, aspects of their financial situation that you would not have recommended. The examiner is primarily testing your technical knowledge.

Generally in this sort of question, there will be one mark available for identifying the problem area, and one for explaining it. You should not spend longer on each one than these marks warrant, so around two minutes per error/inconsistency is reasonable.

You may want to look again at Chapter 4, in which we considered the errors and inconsistencies that can arise during factfinding.

3.3 Dealing with technical questions

The technical aspects of CF5 Question 1 may cover any area of the knowledge you built up in studying for the other units of the Cert FP. You should make sure this knowledge is refreshed and updating in your preparation for CF5.

When dealing with these aspects in the exam, use bullet points in your answer, and be aware that questions usually require you to relate their answers to the question scenario, rather than just list everything you know.

For example, the case study might concern Alan, and might tell you that he has £100 per month available to invest. One of the tasks might be to list the factors that Alan should consider in deciding whether make invest his £100 per month in a personal pension or a maxi-ISA.

- A **poor answer** would simply give the technicalities.
- A **good answer** would analyse the main points in the context of the cashflow and tax position of the individual in the scenario.

So, the fact that the limits on contributions to personal pensions and ISAs are different is not relevant – he could contribute his £100 per month to either.

Explain your answer fully. It is easy to fall into the trap of using expressions such as 'in the relevant tax year' or 'in the normal way'. The examiner will want you to demonstrate that you know which is the 'relevant' year, or what is the 'normal' way.

Remember that even if the main focus of Question 1 is on an area in which you feel your knowledge is weak, then still attempt each part. The first few marks are always the easiest to achieve.

Question 1 (and Question 2, which is dealt with later) will involve giving financial advice. You must consider all the factors which are relevant to the case study, which are likely to include:

- Affordability
- Priorities
- Attitude to risk
- Inflation
- Impact of taxation
- Potential for change
- Existing arrangements

3.4 Affordability

However much a client may need a particular financial solution, unless he can **afford** the outlay it entails, it cannot form part of a realistic recommendation. Arrangements beyond a client's spending power are unlikely to achieve the client's objectives, and early termination is likely to lead to loss in many cases.

You should therefore ensure that your recommendations are always within the client's capacity. This may mean that you have to prioritise when making your recommendations. Sometimes, the Question will be specifically geared to this and will ask you first to list all the products that might be relevant to their needs, and then decide which is likely to be the highest priority. For example, their may be a situation where the client is about to take out a new mortgage, and you might be asked to list the protection policies that should be considered alongside.

Your answer might include life assurance. Income Protection Insurance (IPI, also commonly known as Permanent Health Insurance or PHI), Critical Illness cover, and Accident, Sickness and Unemployment (ASU) Insurance, all of which are relevant to mortgage borrowers.

The question will often then ask which one or two you consider to be the highest priority, if the borrower has limited affordability. The most obvious response is probably life assurance and IPI, but consider this in the light of the case study details. For example, the borrower might already have some IPI cover at work and this might negate the need for this cover to be provided personally.

3.5 Priorities

Priorities may be examined in a wider context rather than just in relation to a specific circumstance such as arranging a mortgage. As it is unlikely that a client would be able to afford all the financial planning arrangements that would be useful to him, the question of prioritisation is almost always central to recommendations.

A **priority list** for an employed young married man could be:

- Life insurance
- Income protection
- Pension planning
- Savings and investments

A priority list for a self employed single man could be:

- Income protection
- Pension planning
- Savings and investments

These lists follow the generally accepted rule that **protection is a higher priority than investment**. However, remember that although these lists may be useful as a general guide, you will need to consider the circumstances of the case study you are dealing with, rather than give a general answer.

3.6 Attitude to risk

Risk relates to security of capital **and** variability of income. Where you are given details of the client's attitude to risk, you will need to take this into account in your answer, and the question may require you to include a description of the degree of risk involved in each investment under consideration.

Attitude to risk is generally of more importance in Question 2 however, which we will deal with later in this Chapter.

3.7 Inflation

The effect of **inflation** is a very real issue in actual financial planning, and may be relevant in Question 1.

You should consider:

(a) Whether there is a need to increase protection arrangements automatically in future, for example, by recommending an increasing term policy rather than a level term policy

(b) Whether contributions should increase in future, for example, linking pension contributions to earnings.

These issues may be specifically pointed to in the case study scenario, for example by indicating that the clients are concerned about the effects of inflation. If so, you should ensure that that your answer deals with the issue. If not mentioned in the case study, it is less likely to be a mark scoring issue. However, if you are, for example, recommending cover to protect **school fees**, it would be foolish not to take account of the fact that they are likely to increase in the future.

3.8 Impact of taxation

The usefulness of different investments will vary from client to client depending on their **tax situation**. You should always remember that the attractiveness of a portfolio from the client's point of view will be largely judged according to the return he achieves after taxation, not before.

You should be ready to give details of the features of tax advantaged products, such as pension arrangements and ISAs, which often figure prominently in Question 1.

3.9 Potential for change

The portfolio and recommendations you make must allow some flexibility for **changes in circumstances**, where relevant from the case details.

The following events are amongst those which will generate potential changes.

- Death
- Illness
- Divorce
- Birth of children

Consequently you should consider the **flexibility of products** while giving advice. Products which may tend to reduce flexibility include:

- Fixed term insurance-related investment contracts
- NS&I Savings Certificates
- Annuities
- Guaranteed products
- Pensions

3.10 Existing arrangements

A client's **existing arrangements** will inevitably affect recommendations because they will impact upon the extent to which his needs in various areas are **already met**. It is also important to take into account whether or not those existing arrangements **remain relevant** to the client's needs.

In most circumstances, it is inappropriate to terminate existing arrangements, particularly where this would entail a loss from the client's point of view. You must simply identify the weaknesses and the benefits (there will be some) of the current arrangements.

With existing investments, such as shares and unit trusts, there are also costs involved in sale and replacement. The effect of taxation on restructuring should also be considered, particularly if it could lead to a liability to income tax or capital gains tax which would not otherwise have arisen or would have been deferred.

3.11 Occupational pension and other benefits

In framing recommendations, you should also be aware of benefits associated with the individual's **employment**. Very often this will include pension and life assurance arrangements but there may also be other benefits including income protection insurance and private medical insurance.

To the extent that these are funded by the employer, they will certainly be an extremely attractive benefit from the point of view of the employee. It would therefore be very unusual for it to constitute good advice to opt out of an employer based scheme in favour of private provision which the employee would normally have to fund entirely himself.

In preparing your recommendations, you would therefore seek to build on top of the benefits provided by the employer.

An example would be where the question asked you to calculate how much extra life cover a client would need in order to provide an income at a certain level. Such questions could arise, and are quite simple to deal with. The case study will state the income requirement, and the rate of return the client feels comfortable to assume. You simply calculate the lump sum which, if invested at the assumed rate of return, would provide the required income.

For example, if the income required is £10,000 pa, and the assumed rate of return is 4% pa, the lump sum required is £10,000/0.04 = £250,000.

However, if you are told that the client already has life cover of £120,000 under his employer's occupational scheme, the **extra** cover required is only £130,000.

Note that, in these questions, it will be made clear whether the requirement and the return assumption are before or after tax (generally both will be expressed in the same way) and you will probably be told to ignore State benefits, or that the amount required is additional to State benefits. You will also not be expected to factor in a gradual drawing of the capital sum, but rather will only need to take account of the interest generated. The calculations required would be too complex otherwise.

Be aware that employers do change the basis of benefits provided for employees from time to time so, as part of your ongoing review of your client's affairs, you would necessarily need to keep up to date with any such changes. In addition, the provision of benefits will almost certainly be dependent upon the continuation of employment and this therefore should also be kept under review.

4 Question 1 Example

The following is an example of a typical Question 1 case study. Attempt it under exam conditions, allowing yourself one hour. Then compare your answer with the model answer which follows, and mark your answer according to the marking scheme.

Gordon and Hannah are in their mid-thirties, and are shortly to get married. This has prompted them to feel that they should review their financial planning arrangements and so they have decided to seek your advice.

They have no children and at the moment are not planning a family. Both work for local companies, though Hannah is about to leave her job, to take up a better paid and more senior role with a new business starting up in the area. Her current salary is £31,000 and she will earn around £38,000 in her new job.

She has been a member of the occupational pension scheme of her current employer, and will have completed four years membership by the time she leaves. She is not sure of her position regarding the pension benefits when she leaves.

Her new employer does not have a pension scheme at the moment, but has told her during the interview process that they are actively considering introducing one. Hannah feels that retirement provision is important and she wants to try to make some provision herself until she knows what her new employer will eventually offer.

Gordon and Hannah already live together in a house which they jointly own, and which was bought three years ago, using a low cost with profits endowment mortgage. The value of the house is around £140,000, and the mortgage is £75,000. They find the repayments manageable, but they are concerned about the adequacy of their policy after reading some articles in the press regarding mortgage related endowments generally.

Gordon is also employed, and is also a member of an occupational scheme. He is content with this aspect of his finances, but he has asked you for advice on ISAs. He contributed £1,500 to a cash mini-ISA with a local building society in the last tax year, but otherwise has not made use of ISAs at all. He is a higher rate taxpayer, and is a very cautious investor, who likes his investments to be both accessible and secure. He currently has about £20,000 on deposit in an ordinary building society account.

Questions

(a)   List the questions you would want to ask Hannah so that you would have all the information you need to advise her on her retirement planning needs.

(10 marks)

(b)   State the options that would be available to her regarding her pension rights when she leaves her current employment.

(4 marks)

(c)   (i)   What would be the tax advantages of Hannah contributing to a Personal Pension (PP) once she starts her new job?

(5 marks)

(ii)   How much could Hannah contribute to a PP in the current tax year with the full benefit of the available tax advantages?

(5 marks)

(d)   (i)   Under a traditional with profits endowment policy, state and describe the two main types of bonus that arise.

(9 marks)

(ii)   Explain how the low cost endowment policy operates in conjunction with the mortgage, and comment on what they should do to deal with their concerns about their own policy.

(9 marks)

(e)   (i)   State the maximum that can be invested in a cash mini-ISA in 2006/07.

(1 mark)

(ii)   Explain how the interest on the existing deposit account with the building society will be taxed.   **(3 marks)**

BPP
PROFESSIONAL EDUCATION

(iii) Would you recommend that Gordon should invest in a cash mini-ISA? Give the reasons for your conclusion.

(4 marks)

(Total marks for question: 50)

Model answer

(a) Marks are awarded for soundly structured factfinding questions, expressed in an understandable manner from the client's point of view. Your questions do not need to exactly match those below.

- Do you have a booklet or a benefit statement giving details of your pension benefits?
- Has your new employer given you any indication of when the decision will be made on whether they will introduce a scheme?
- When do you plan to retire?
- What benefits will be available from Gordon's scheme at that time?
- What level of income do you think you would require in today's terms?
- Will you want to have access to a lump sum in addition to the pension income when you retire?
- Do you have any other savings that could contribute towards your financial position in retirement?
- How much are you thinking of committing to your own retirement planning?
- Will you need to be able to access some or all of these savings before retirement?
- Are you willing to accept some risk that investment values could fall as well as rise in order to improve the long term growth prospects of your savings for retirement?

(b)
- A preserved pension under the scheme
- A transfer of the value of the pension rights to a personal pension
- A transfer to a section 32 buy-out policy
- A transfer to her new employer's occupational scheme (when and if established)

(c) (i)
- Contributions attract tax relief at the highest rate of tax Hannah pays
- The fund grows free of tax on income
- Except that dividend tax credits cannot be reclaimed
- And free of all tax on capital gains.
- Up to 25% of the fund can be taken as a tax free lump sum at retirement.

(ii)
- Maximum contribution is 100% of earnings to all registered pension schemes
- If she contributes to a PP, she would therefore need to take account of anything already paid to her current employer's occupational scheme
- A contribution of £3,600 (gross) can be paid irrespective of earnings
- Also, if total pension input exceeds the annual allowance (£215,000 in 2006/07), there would be a tax charge on Hannah at 40%
- Pension input includes her PP contributions plus either the increase in value of he benefits under the occupational scheme if on a defined contribution basis or the contributions by Hannah and her employer if on a defined contribution basis.

(d) (i)
- The two main types are reversionary bonus
- And terminal bonus
- Reversionary bonuses are added through the life of the policy, usually annually
- They increase the guaranteed sum assured payable on death or maturity

- The rate of bonus is not guaranteed in advance

- Once added, they cannot be taken away

- The terminal bonus is added at maturity

- In the light of investment conditions at the time

- Neither its existence nor amount is guaranteed until it is added

(ii)
- The policy combines investment and protection benefits

- The amount payable on death before the date the policy matures is generally guaranteed to be at least equal to the amount of the loan

- The term of the policy is geared to the time when the loan is repayable

- The maturity value is not guaranteed

- It will be sufficient to repay the loan if growth is achieved at or above an assumed level.

- Although growth assumptions are set at what is believed to be a conservative level when the policy is established, in practice this may not turn out to be so, as economic conditions may change substantially over time.

- They should check with their insurer whether their policy is on target to repay the borrowing.

- If it is, they need take no further action, beyond continuing to monitor its progress.

- If not, they should consider either increasing the payments they make to the endowment, if permitted, or contributing to an alternative investment vehicle to provide additional funds for repayment of the loan.

(e)   (i)   £3,000

(ii)
- 20% tax is deducted at source
- As a higher rate taxpayer, Gordon will have a further tax liability to pay personally
- This will be 20% of the gross interest

(iii)
- This would be recommended
- The interest would be tax free, which is particularly attractive for a higher rate taxpayer
- The investment is just as secure as the existing deposit account, and so fits in with his attitude to risk
- There would be no loss of access

5 Question 2

Question 2 of the CF5 paper will focus primarily on building a portfolio to meet specified objectives of the client(s). However, the first part of the question may ask for a calculation, for example of the yield of a gilt or the maximum contributions permitted to a personal pension.

This should be dealt with in the same way as discussed above in relation to Question 1.

5.1 Designing a portfolio

You will then be asked to make **recommendations for a portfolio** for the client(s). You may be given details of an existing portfolio, or you may be asked to consider the investment of entirely new money, possibly arising from something like an inheritance or a pools win.

Details given may relate to:

- Requirements, eg a need to reserve money for a planned holiday
- Risk attitude

- Income need, generally that the portfolio needs to produce an income of at least a given amount

There may also be constraints, for example, that the client does not want to invest in National Savings & Investments products. You must take account of these constraints in making your recommendations (even if you feel they are not entirely logical or appropriate).

It is important to set out your recommendations clearly, preferably in the form of a table. You must specify how all of the available money will be invested, and, if the scenario concerns a couple, set out clearly the details of whose name each investment will be held in.

Your answer should also include details of **where all money will be held** even if it is known that it will only be available temporarily for investment, for example, money for an imminent house move.

5.2 Product list and tax tables

The CF5 examination paper includes a **Product List** and **Tax Tables**.

The **Tax Tables** may be useful in dealing with some or all of the questions. As well as details of income tax, inheritance tax and capital gains tax, the tables include some explanation of the workings of the taxes, for example, indexation for CGT purposes. It would be unusual to have to complete a full income tax calculation in CF5, but you will need to take account of tax in working out the income generated by a portfolio.

Remember that £3,600 per year can be paid into a personal pension without reference to income, with tax relief, provided that the individual concerned is aged less than 75. This means that such a contribution may be relevant in constructing a portfolio, even where there is no earned income. If earlier parts of the question asked candidates about contributions or benefits under personal pension rules, clearly it is likely to be expected that a contribution would be included as part of the portfolio.

Look through the content of the tables before you start the exam, so that you know what is available to you.

The **Product List** gives investment limits for some products where appropriate. Do not go over these limits, eg £15,000 in any one issue of NS&I Savings Certificates. You will lose marks if these limits are exceeded, or if you use an incorrect rate of return in your answers, so again check what information you are given.

Although the Product List does not cover all possible products and investments, **only those included on the list should be used in your answers**. You will not be awarded marks for product recommendations not taken from the list, however suitable they might otherwise be.

5.3 Recommendations

You need to invest the money available, but you must also **explain your recommendations**. Your technique should be as follows.

Step 1.	Establish objectives
Step 2.	Identify products which meet the objectives
Step 3.	Justify your recommendations

The approach to take is best covered with question practice but we can outline some basic priorities.

Most portfolios will have the following components.

- Emergency fund
- NS&I products
- ISAs
- Equity backed products such as unit trusts, often using ISAs (dependent upon risk profile)

This is not an opportunity to sell products, so do not just include commission earning products. If your portfolio does not include any National Savings & Investments products, there should be a good reason.

Take careful note of the **risk profile of the clients involved**. Your portfolio must conform to the clients' attitudes to risk.

The following proportions are a guide only, but they reflect the equity weightings shown in examination guides for the FP3 examination (which was the predecessor of CF5).

	Equity exposure
Nil risk profile	0%
Low risk profile	20%
Balanced risk profile	30 – 40%
Willing to accept risk	Up to 60%

Unless the details given to you suggest otherwise, it is unlikely to be wise to **put the whole of the portfolio into equity/asset backed investments.**

Always take account of what you are told about existing investments. Sometimes the clients will say that they already have an adequate emergency fund, and you do not then need to add to it. Sometimes they will already have used their ISA allowances, and then it would not be appropriate to include an ISA in your portfolio.

If the clients have partially used their ISA allowances, think about topping the ISAs up to maximum permitted levels.

5.4 Accessibility

One of the primary considerations you should take into account is the extent to which an investor is likely to require **access to the money** he has invested. This is one factor which will be important in determining how much is available to invest in assets which are not immediately accessible but which are geared to provide the best possible return in the longer term, in particular, equity linked investments.

A first priority in virtually all cases will be the establishment of an adequate **emergency fund** available immediately. A useful guide is to use around 10% of the portfolio as an emergency fund, and place this in an instant access deposit account with a bank or building society. However, it would be unwise to invest more than around £20,000 in this way. If the portfolio is a very large one, use an account requiring notice, which still provides a secure base for the portfolio, but achieves a higher level of interest for part of the amount to be held in cash.

Sometimes there will be one or more specific requirements which affect the need for accessibility, such as a planned major holiday, or the replacement of an expensive item such as a car. This will require further cash to be held, often in a notice account, to provide for the need.

Even after establishing these aspects, further consideration needs to be given to accessibility to all investments. If the investment is not accessible, this fact may need to be included and justified in your comments on the portfolio.

5.5 Income and capital growth

The need to draw regular amounts by way of **income** from the investment will also be an important factor in determining the portfolio overall.

The balance between income and capital growth will be determined by:

- Tax considerations
- Growth considerations
- Attitude to risk

There are many possible approaches to **generating income**, but the following guidelines are useful.

(a) If possible, use **secure products**, preferably NS&I products (Income Bond, Pensioners Bond), for the majority of the income. Use can also be made of guaranteed income bonds from the product list.

(b) Generally avoid **annuities**, which (although included in the Product List) are usually not sufficiently flexible. In particular, access to the capital used to purchase the annuity is lost, which is not the case with other income producing products.

(c) Take account of income from investments in unit trusts, OEICs or investment trusts, but make sure you deal with **tax** correctly. The product list shows gross yield, so you must allow for the fact that income is paid net of a 10% tax credit, even for non-taxpayers, and higher rate taxpayers have to pay a further 22.5% in tax (ie 32.5% in total). (This assumes the product is equity based; fixed interest unit trusts and OEICs provide income treated as savings income and paid net of 20% tax deducted at source. This is reclaimable by non-taxpayers, and higher rate taxpayers have a further liability of 20%, just as with deposit interest.)

(d) Do not count income from investing the **emergency fund**, or money required for specific purposes (such as a holiday or replacement car) towards the income target. This is money that may be, or definitely will be used, and so in the long term the income will not be available.

(e) Be especially careful not to use products which **roll-up interest** as part of the income requirement. These include the NS&I's Savings Certificates and Capital Bond. This is an easy trap to fall into, and one which catches a lot of candidates out.

You do not need to produce the exact amount of income required, but you should not under-provide. If you greatly over-provide, you will probably not have a sufficiently diversified portfolio, so you should aim for a figure that is reasonably close to the required amount.

Example

Mrs Smith, aged 62, needs £3,500 more in net income each year.

She is a basic rate taxpayer with other income of £8,000. She has £120,000 to invest.

To provide the income, you might suggest:

£65,000 NS&I 5 year Pensioners Bond
Gross interest is £65,000 @ 4.00% = £2,600
Net interest is £2,400 × 0.8 = £2,080

£30,000 Solid Ins 3 year Guaranteed Income Bond
Income (net of basic rate tax) is £30,000 @ 5.2% = £1,560

Total net income £3,640

Notes

1 Not all of the £120,000 is used to provide income. She will have other objectives, and you will want to add an emergency fund, but we have achieved her income requirement.

2 The savings income from the Pensioners Bond falls in the basic rate band and is taxed at 20%. Note that the Pensioners Bond will usually be preferable to the Income Bond where the client is eligible (ie is over 60). The interest rate is guaranteed and is usually higher than the interest rate under the Income Bond. Although currently the interest rate on the Income Bond is slightly higher for investments over £25,000, the guarantee is worth having to be sure the income target is met for a sustained period. You should state this in your answer, or, if you feel the Income Bond is better because of the higher rate, argue that instead.

3 The income from the Solid Insurance bond is treated as being net of basic rate tax.

4 In general, avoid generating part of the income target from tax efficient investments. The marking guides of the CII tend to imply that such income should be retained within the tax efficient wrapper.

5.6 Risk profile

The table below gives a broad indication of the risk profile of various investments.

	Negligible risk	Low risk	Cautious	Medium risk		High risk	Speculative
Deposit based and similar investments	National Savings & Investments	Bank/ Building Society deposit Cash ISA TESSA-only ISA Annuities					
Gilts *	Gilts (income) Gilts (redemption)		Gilts (pre-redemption capital value)				
Life insurance linked		Non-profit Guaranteed Income/ growth bonds	With profit	Unit-linked (managed) Unit-linked (UK funds)		Unit-linked (overseas funds)	
Equity investment				Unit trusts (UK) Investment trusts (UK)		Single UK equities Unit trusts (overseas funds) Investment trusts (overseas)	
Derivatives*							Futures Options

* Note there are no gilts or derivatives on the Product List and therefore they will not feature in a specific portfolio. You may however get generic questions on such products in Question 1, or possibly at the start of Question 2.

5.7 Diversification

The portfolio will need to be diversified. This **diversification** will be **across asset type and provider**. Consequently if you are placing significant funds in life assurance products or unit trusts ('significant' meaning more than about £10,000), consider using more than one provider.

If substantial sums will be invested in equity based products (in excess of, say, £20,000), consider international diversification.

You may get marks for recognising the need to diversify. However, choice of provider is not generally relevant to the marking scheme, so do not spend to much time deciding which providers to use.

5.8 Taxation

Investments producing a **tax free return** will be more attractive to higher rate taxpayers than to basic rate or indeed to non-taxpayers, and the higher rate taxpayer will therefore be more inclined to accept any accompanying limitations on accessibility or flexibility in return for those tax advantages.

It is often said that tax delayed is tax saved, and where the taxation position is likely to change in the foreseeable future, an arrangement such as an investment bond, which has the effect of deferring taxation liability might be extremely attractive.

For example, the investor might be a higher rate taxpayer now, but expects to be a basic rate taxpayer in the future, so an investment bond could be very tax efficient in deferring tax on gains now. It could be encashed after he becomes a basic rate taxpayer, in which case there would be no personal tax liability (provided the gain, after top-slicing relief, does not take him back into higher rate).

An important aspect of some portfolio questions is the ownership of assets. For example, if the clients are a married couple, with one a higher rate taxpayer, and the other a non-taxpayer, you should aim to put investments producing taxable income in the ownership of the non-taxpayer. You are usually asked specifically to indicate who owns which investments.

There will often, in real situations, be emotional issues about asset ownership. For example, if the husband is a higher rate taxpayer and has received an inheritance, it makes tax planning sense to transfer money or assets to the wife, if she is not a taxpayer, or pays only basic rate. The emotional issue is whether he wants to do this. However, in CF5, you can assume that the tax position predominates, unless you are told he does not want to transfer assets.

5.9 Costs

Different investments incorporate different levels of **cost** and inevitably this will be a factor which influences overall portfolio design.

Particularly if investment is intended only for the short term, any significant initial costs would seriously erode or even eliminate any potential return. On the other hand, longer term investments should have time to recoup initial charges and their level taken into account in any recommendations.

Costs are also an important factor in deciding whether or not a portfolio should be reorganised. Switching costs often outweigh the potential increase in yield or growth from new alternative investments.

5.10 The effect of capital gains tax

When a portfolio is revised, any tax liability should be fully taken into account. This does not just mean only the taxation of the investments themselves, and any income they produce, but also includes the effect of **CGT** at the time of the revision.

If assets such as shares or unit trusts are sold, then a CGT liability can occur as a result. Any potential gain from investment performance may be substantially reduced by any CGT liability that arises, and which could have been deferred or even avoided, had the sale of some of the assets been at least delayed.

So, for example, a move from direct shareholdings to unit trusts, in order to improve the spread of investments and to benefit from professional management, could be achieved in stages to make use of the annual CGT exemption over a number of years.

5.11 Justification

You will be asked to **justify your recommendations**. Usually, the Question will ask you to justify your choices of product types (ie the groupings used in the Product List, for example, Bank and Building Society Accounts) rather than individual products or providers.

You are likely to be asked for comments in specific areas, most commonly:

- To justify the amount to be invested
- To comment on the risks involved, and
- To explain why the investment is suitable

These are largely basic, factual points, though you must relate them to the portfolio you have recommended, and the clients concerned, particularly as regards suitability. For example, if you have recommended NS&I Savings Certificates for a higher rate taxpayer, you should state 'the investment return is tax free, which is particularly attractive for Mr X who is a higher rate taxpayer'.

5.12 Review

It is likely that the final part of the Question will ask you what you would cover in a **review** of your clients' position perhaps a year after your recommendations are implemented. This may have a particular focus, for example, on ensuring that their position is as tax efficient as possible.

Amongst the factors you might consider (depending on the context of the specific question) are the following.

- The actual performance of the portfolio

- Whether their need for income has changed

- Whether they wish to take up their ISA and pension allowances for the new tax year

- Whether they are comfortable with the level of risk in the portfolio

- Whether there have been any changes in the external environment, for example, interest rates and economic conditions generally

- Whether there has been a change in health, which might trigger a different set of priorities

- Any actual use of the emergency fund (or expected use) which might need topping up as a result

- Any change in legislation

6 Question 2 Example

The following is an example of a typical CF5 Question 2 case study. Attempt it under exam conditions, allowing yourself one hour. You should use the Product List which appears towards the end of this Study Text in preparing your portfolio. Then compare your answer with the model answer which follows, and mark your answer according to the marking scheme.

Case history: Simon and Sandy	**Married:** Aged 68 and 63 respectively
Need: Income but with potential for capital growth over the long term	

Information

Simon and Sandy both retired five years ago. They decided to retire at the same time so that they could enjoy travelling around the world together whilst they were still young enough to do so. They both love travelling and wish to be able to afford three or four trips abroad each year, paid for from their income.

Financially they are 'comfortable'. Simon receives an occupational pension from the Civil Service (which is index linked) as well as the State Pension. His total income is £23,500 gross. Sandy was a Lecturer in History at Cleverland University and has a total annual pension income of £10,000, partly from the University occupational pension scheme and part from the state.

They had a large house close to the University which they recently decided to sell. The proceeds enabled them to buy a smaller house in the Cotswolds, with a balance left over which they have put in their Townshires Building Society Reserve Account.

Now they have a total of £230,000 in their account with Townshires, which is in joint names. They have always been concerned about tax efficiency and they each have stocks and shares ISAs with £7,000 invested during the tax year 2005/06, but have not invested in ISAs in the current year.

They have asked you to advise them on the investment of their total available capital.

Simon and Sandy wish to create an extra income of at least £450 net per month from their investments. They ask that you also have consideration for capital growth in the long run. Simon is concerned that should he die, his occupational pension will only provide an income of 50% his current pension to Sandy. He would like the capital to be available to create an income for Sandy in this event.

They are both cautious to moderate risk investors. They are prepared to invest in equity related investments, but do not wish to have any great exposure to higher risk overseas markets as they feel that they cannot afford to take this risk at their 'time of life'. They wish to continue with the theme of tax efficient investment.

Questions

(a) (i)   Explain how Simon's pension benefits are taxed   **(5 marks)**

    (ii) Explain how much Simon and Sandy could invest in personal pensions in 2006/07, commenting on the way in which tax relief would affect their contributions   **(6 marks)**

    (iii) How would benefits from the personal pensions be taxed when they are drawn?   **(3 marks)**

(b) Using the Product List towards the end of this Study Text, recommend a portfolio of products which would be suitable to meet Simon and Sandy's requirements. You should show in whose name each investment is held, and explain how their specific need for income from the portfolio is met, detailing the tax position on the income.
                                                                                                              (12 marks)

(c) Justify the inclusion of each of the products you have included in your recommendations for the couple's portfolio, commenting under each of the following headings:

    (i)   The amount to be invested
    (ii) The risk profile
    (iii) The suitability of the investment   **(18 marks)**

(d) Assuming they take your advice, list six factors which you would take into account in reviewing the portfolio in a year's time.   **(6 marks)**

Total marks available for this Question: 50

Model answer

(a) (i)
- The pension from the university scheme is taxed as earned income
- The tax is deducted under PAYE
- The state pension is paid gross
- It is however taxable as earned income
- Tax is generally collected through an adjustment to PAYE code

(ii)
- They would both be regarded as non-earners, but are under 75
- They are therefore able to contribute to PPs with tax relief
- The maximum is £3,600 pa gross
- They could each pay this amount for the current tax year
- The payments would be made net of basic rate tax relief at 22%, and no further relief would be available as neither is a higher rate taxpayer
- The actual cost to them would therefore be £2,808 each if they paid the maximum

(iii)
- Part of the fund (25%) would be available as a tax free lump sum
- The rest would provide an income, taxed as earned income
- The tax would be payable through PAYE

(b) Many different portfolios could be constructed to meet the needs identified, and the following is an example. You should mark your portfolio in the light of the marking scheme described below rather than by comparison with the example.

Owner	Investment	Amount £
Joint	Townshires BS Reserve Account	24,400
Sandy	NS&I 5 year Pensioners Bond	85,000
Simon	NS&I 5 year 81st Issue Fixed Interest Certificates	15,000
Sandy	Fairplay Ins 4 year G'teed income Bond	40,000
Simon	Countryside UK Blue Chip Maxi-ISA	7,000
Sandy	Fairplay UK Tracker Maxi-ISA	7,000
Simon	Solid Pension UK Equity Personal Pension	2,800
Sandy	XYZ UK Index Tracker Personal Pension	2,800
Sandy	PDQ With Profits Bond	25,000
Sandy	Interglobal UK Income Unit Trust	8,000
Sandy	XYZ Equity Income Unit Trust	8,000
Sandy	PDQ Fixed Interest Unit Trust	5,000
	Total invested	230,000

The income generated is as follows:

Pensioner's Bond £85,000 @ 4.00% = £3,400 gross

This is taxable, and will fall in Sandy's basic rate band, and is therefore taxable at 20%. Net income is therefore £3,400 × 0.8 = £2,720

Fairplay G'teed Inc Bond £40,000 @ 5.4% = £2,160 net of basic rate tax

There would be no further tax liability as Sandy is a basic rate taxpayer.

Income from Unit Trusts	£
Interglobal UK Inc Unit Trust (£8,000 @ 3.2% × 0.9)	230.40
XYZ Equity Inc Unit Trust (£8,000 @ 3.6% × 0.9)	259.20
PDQ Fixed Int Unit Trust (£5,000 @ 4.3% × 0.8)	172.00
Total	661.60

The distributions from the equity unit trusts are paid net of a 10% tax credit, which discharges the tax liability of basic rate taxpayers like Sandy. The net income is therefore found by multiplying the gross income by 0.9.

The Fixed Interest Unit Trust pays income in the form of interest, taxable at 20% for a basic rate taxpayer. The net income is therefore found by multiplying the gross income by 0.8.

Total net income generated by the portfolio is therefore £5,541.60, which meets their requirement of £450 per month (£5,400 per year).

Marks

Correct income calculation – 3, with one deducted for each mistake
Explanation of tax aspects – 3
All or most investments producing taxable income in Sandy's name – 1
Emergency fund of between £20,000 and £30,000 – 1
Use of ISA allowances – 1
Use of PP allowances – 1
No overseas investment – 1
NS&I products used – 1
Max 6 if income need not met

(c)   **The details given will reflect the portfolio construction, so the answers below are given as an example**.

(Max 3 marks per product type, overall maximum 18)

Building Society Account

- The amount is approximately 10% of their total portfolio, and is adequate as an emergency fund

- The investment is secure

- This provides for access to capital if needed unexpectedly. Tax is deducted at source at 20% and as neither is a higher rate taxpayer, there is no further tax liability.

NS&I Pensioners Bond

- The amount is sufficient to generate the bulk of the income required

- The investment is secure and the income is guaranteed for 5 years

- The income need is a major requirement and this addresses this need without risk of fluctuation of income or capital

NS&I Savings Certificates

- The amount is the maximum permitted in this issue

- The investment is secure and government-backed

- The investment is in line with their attitude to risk and provides a good level of return combined with security

Guaranteed Income Bond

- The amount is designed to generate the majority of the balance of income required
- The income is guaranteed for 4 years, and the capital is guaranteed

- This addresses the remainder of the need for income, but at the same time provides security of capital at the end of the term

Maxi-ISAs

- The amounts are the maximum permitted for each spouse

- The investments are medium risk, and are equity based, so they could reduce in value, but offer good potential growth

- The ISA funds grow free of tax on income and gains, except that dividend tax credits cannot be reclaimed. This therefore provides a good prospect of growth, within their risk tolerance

Personal Pensions

- The amounts are within and are close to the maximum permitted for those with no earned income

- These investments are also medium risk, and are equity based, so they could reduce in value, but offer good potential growth

- These are attractive because of the tax relief on contributions and the tax advantaged growth. (Contributions attract basic rate relief at source – this is reclaimed by the product provider and added to the net amounts invested. The fund grows free of tax on income and gains, but tax credits cannot be reclaimed.) They can take benefits at any time with up to 25% of the fund available as a tax free cash sum, with the rest providing an income taxable as earned income. This is therefore available to boost their income when required, as inflation increases the income level required.

With Profit Bond

- The amount is reasonable to create balance in the portfolio

- The investment is low to medium risk, with a guarantee that the value cannot fall, though a market value adjustment could be applied on surrender

- This provides the prospect of growth from a managed and diversified portfolio, but with limited risk, in line with their tolerance of risk

Unit Trusts

- The amounts are reasonable in the light of the portfolio as a whole and the couple's attitude to risk

- The equity related investments are medium risk; the fixed interest unit trust is low to medium risk and provides high income, but modest growth potential

- These provide strong growth prospects and are UK based, in line with the couple's requirements. They also contribute to the income requirement.

(d)   Factors to review:

- Any change in income needs
- Any change in health
- Any change in attitude to risk
- Performance of the portfolio to date
- Changes in legislation
- Changes in economic conditions and interest rates

[other valid points would score]

Key chapter points

- The CF5 examination requires technique as much as knowledge. A different approach is required to each of the two Questions in the paper.

- Use a bullet point style to highlight your points succinctly. Bullet points are grammatically correct sentences which generally make a single point. Give brief justifications for recommendations.

- Read the questions you must answer before you read the case study details, so that you consider the details in a focused way. Plan your time.

- Question 1 tests your ability to factfind and to apply technical knowledge.

- Technical aspects of Question 1 may cover any area of the knowledge you built up in studying for the other units of the Certificate in Financial Planning. Update this knowledge in your preparation for CF5.

- Ensure that your recommendations are always affordable for the client.

- Question 2 will focus primarily on building a portfolio to meet specified objectives of the client. The first part of the question may ask for a calculation. You will be provided with a Product List and Tax Tables.

- Your technique should involve three steps: (1) Establish objectives (2) Identify products which meet the objectives (3) Justify your recommendations.

- One of the primary considerations you should take into account is the extent to which an investor is likely to require access to the money he has invested.

- The balance between income and capital growth will be determined by tax considerations, growth considerations, and attitude to risk.

- The portfolio will need to be diversified, across asset type and provider.

Multiple Choice
Case Studies

You may use the Tax Tables at the end of this Study Text.

Including reading time, it is recommended that you spend about

70 minutes on Case Study A

and 40 minutes each on Case Studies B and C

The total marks available are 95, divided as follows:

Case Study A	45 marks
Case Study B	25 marks
Case Study C	25 marks

Case Study A

Robert (aged 30) and Sue (aged 28) are married with two children, Sandra (aged 9) and Adam (aged 5). All four are in good health.

Robert is employed as a designer, by a local engineering firm and has a basic salary of £30,000, in addition to which he earns overtime pay, which is reasonably consistent at around £250 per month before tax. He is covered by a group Income Protection (PHI) arrangement paid for by the employer, but has no other additional benefits associated with his job.

Sue works part-time as a legal secretary at a local solicitor's practice, and earns £7,600 per annum. The hours she works allows her to take the children to and from school each day.

Robert has a building society account with a balance of around £8,000. This fluctuates, because he pays in around £350 each month from his earnings, but uses the account to pay for their holiday each summer. Sue has a cash mini-ISA, established a couple of years ago, with a current value of £2,300, which is with the same building society as Robert's account. She pays in £50 per month on a regular basis by direct debit, and occasionally puts in further amounts when she can afford to do so.

Robert pays £60 per month into an investment trust regular savings plan, and has done so for a number of years. The total value of his holding is now just over £3,000.

The couple own their own house, and it is currently valued at £120,000. The mortgage is £48,000, and is on a low cost with profits endowment basis. The mortgage and the endowment started 6 years ago and there are 19 years still to run. The mortgage and the endowment policy are in joint names, and the policy is assigned to the lender. The endowment premium is £75 per month and the mortgage interest is currently £220 per month.

The couple also have a joint life second death whole of life policy with a sum insured of £50,000, which they took out to provide money for the children if they died. They have no other personal protection arrangements in place.

The couple are concerned that they do not have very much saved, and are prepared to commit themselves to a regular monthly savings arrangement. They want to be in a position to stop work when Robert is 55, and will then want access to their savings and investments. They are particularly keen to travel in the years immediately after stopping work and would not want to tie up money beyond that point.

Additional information

Robert has recently received a valuation of his investment trust regular savings plan, and the value of the shares has fallen sharply since the previous valuation. He is uneasy about this, and tells you that he does not like to see the value of his investments go down. This is the only savings arrangement he has where this has happened. He took the plan out for medium term savings, without any particular timescale in mind.

Question 1 [2 marks]

Which of the following would be relevant in considering the suitability of the investment trust regular savings plan which Robert has?

I	Was the plan established for a specific purpose?	✓
II	Have the amounts contributed fluctuated?	
III	Where is the investment trust invested?	✓
IV	Has Robert invested any lump sums?	
V	How large is the investment trust?	
VI	How volatile is the price performance of the shares?	✓

A   I, II, V, VI only
B   I, III, VI only
C   II, IV, V only
D   III, IV, VI only

Question 2 [1 mark]

Which factors tend to increase the risk inherent in an investment trust compared to a similarly invested unit trust?

A   An investment trust is closed-ended and can gear
B   An investment trust is closed-ended and cannot gear
C   An investment trust is open-ended and can gear
D   An investment trust is open-ended and cannot gear

Question 3 [2 marks]

Which of the following factors might tend to suggest that the investment trust savings plan is not a suitable savings vehicle for Robert?

I	His cash emergency fund
II	There is no indication of a fixed term
III	His attitude to risk ✓
IV	His investment experience ✓
V	His income tax position
VI	His CGT position

A   II, III, IV only
B   II, IV, V, VI only
C   I, III, IV only
D   I, III, V, VI only

Question 4 [1 mark]

Which of the following would necessarily improve the investment return to investors in an investment trust?

A   Increase in the number of investors
B   Increase in the number of companies invested in by the investment trust
C   Decrease in a discount
D   Decrease in a premium

Additional information

Robert and Sue feel that their whole of life policy is useful, but that the cover is not sufficient for their needs. They are using indexation options under the policy to increase the cover in line with the RPI, and premiums increase each year as a result of this. However, the insurer has written to them to say that the first policy review is due and premiums will need to increase further. The policy is a non-qualifying unit-linked plan and the current value of units held is less than £300.

Question 5 [2 marks]

Which of the following factors would you need to take into account in quantifying their need for additional life insurance?

I	The amount of their mortgage
II	The amount of any other loans or debts ✓
III	Potential funeral costs ✓
IV	Changes in income and outgoings which would arise on death ✓
V	The period for which the children are likely to remain dependent ✓
VI	Potential State benefits payable on death ✓

A	I, II, III only
B	I, II, III, IV, V only
C	II, III, IV, V, VI only
D	II, IV, V, VI only

Question 6 [1 mark]

If Robert were to die tomorrow, what income benefit(s) would you expect to be payable by the State as a direct result?

A	An income for the rest of Sue's life
B	An income for the rest of Sue's life, but reducing when the children are older
C	An income payable only whilst the children are young
D	An income payable only for a period of 12 months

Question 7 [1 mark]

What particular disadvantage does the existing whole of life policy have in relation to the need for life insurance for family protection?

A	No benefit would be payable on the first death
B	No tax relief is available on premiums
C	Cover reduces as the couple's age increases
D	The insurer can refuse to continue cover at any review

Question 8 [2 marks]

Which of the following additional factors would you need to take into account in considering the suitability of the existing whole of life policy?

I   As the policy is non-qualifying, the sum insured would be subject to income tax

II   The indexation options offer a good means of increasing cover without further medical evidence

III   It is likely to be possible to increase cover beyond the indexation options, but medical evidence would be needed

IV   Further medical evidence is required at each review

V   The policy can also be used for savings and this would be very tax efficient

A   I, V only
B   II, III, V only
C   I, III, IV only
D   II, III only

Question 9 [1 mark]

Robert and Sue tell you that they are surprised that the premiums for the whole of life policy need to increase. Why is this likely to have occurred?

A   The investment performance has been below expectations
B   The indexation options have been greater than expected
C   The policy was established on a maximum cover basis
D   The taxation basis of insurance companies has changed

Question 10 [2 marks]

The existing whole of life policy is not written in trust. Which of the following are disadvantages directly resulting from this?

I   The sum assured could be subject to IHT if the nil rate band had already been used

II   The insurer could choose to whom the proceeds were paid

III   The tax treatment of the underlying investment fund is less favourable

IV   There could be a delay in the proceeds becoming available

V   The policy proceeds would not be protected from creditors

A   I, IV, V only
B   I, II, IV only
C   II, III, IV only
D   II, IV, V only

Additional information

Robert will shortly be eligible to enter the occupational pension scheme of his employer, on his 31st birthday. This is a contracted out final salary scheme, with contributions of 4% of basic pay required from members. The pension benefit is 1/60th of final pensionable salary (which is basic salary) for each year of membership, and the retirement age is 65. On death in service, there is life cover of twice basic salary and a 50% spouse's pension based on all potential service to retirement age.

Question 11 [2 marks]

Robert is concerned about the cost of the contributions to the scheme, and asks what the advantages of joining the pension arrangement would be for him. Which of the following comments are valid?

I   The employer must contribute to the scheme, so Robert's own contributions are likely to represent good value for money ✓

II   The scheme provides benefits at maximum levels which qualify for tax advantages, and the scheme is therefore very good

III   The true cost of his contributions will be reduced because he will benefit from tax relief ✓

IV   The true cost of his contributions will be reduced because his NI contributions will be lower ✓

V   The investment returns under the scheme will be taxed at basic rate, so there is little advantage in terms of investment growth

VI   He can withdraw from the scheme at any time if he wishes, and would receive a refund of his contributions

A   I, II, III, IV only
B   I, III, IV only
C   II, III, VI only
D   III, IV, V, VI only

Question 12 [1 mark]

Could Robert choose not to join the scheme when he becomes eligible?

A   Yes, but he may not be able to change his mind later
B   Yes, and he will then have the option to join at any time he chooses in the future
C   Only if he makes equivalent arrangements personally
D   No, he must join the scheme

Question 13 [1 mark]

What would be his expected benefit from the scheme based on his current earnings and assuming he joins the scheme and stays in it until retirement age?

A   £17,000
B   £18,700
C   £20,000
D   £20,000

Question 14 [2 marks]

Robert wants your advice on the extent to which retirement benefits under the scheme are likely to be flexible, bearing in mind the plan to stop work at 55 and travel. Which of the following points would be relevant?

I   Benefits can be taken at 55 if the trustees of the scheme agree ✓

II   If benefits are taken before normal retirement age, they will be reduced by an early retirement factor ✓

III   If income benefit is taken early, there will be no increases in the amount payable until the scheme's normal retirement age

IV   He is likely to be able to exchange part of the pension for a tax free cash sum ✓

V   He should be able to take the cash benefit and defer the income if he wishes

VI   Instead of taking benefits, he could continue to pay contributions after stopping work and would build up greater benefits

A   I, II, IV only ✓
B   III, IV, VI only
C   I, II, V, VI only
D   II, III, IV, V only

Question 15 [1 mark]

Robert is enthusiastic about the scheme, because he is conscious that he has no pension provision so far. Once he joins the scheme, if he wants to top up his benefits, using the AVC arrangements within the scheme, which of the following statements would be correct?

A   The AVC arrangements under a defined benefit scheme must provide added years
B   The employer must contribute to the AVC arrangements as well as the main scheme
C   His contributions attract full tax relief at his highest rate(s) ✓
D   No benefits can be provided in the form of a cash sum at retirement

Question 16 [2 marks]

Which of the following needs of Robert and Sue will be affected if he joins the pension scheme?

I   Long term savings
II   Short term savings
III   Income protection for Robert
IV   Income protection for Sue
V   Life insurance on Robert's life
VI   Life insurance on Sue's life

A   I, II, V only
B   I, V only ✓
C   III, V only
D   III, IV, V, VI only

Question 17 [2 marks]

One means of increasing savings for the couple could be for Robert to pay contributions to a personal pension after he has joined the scheme. Which of the following would be correct and relevant for him to take into account in considering this option?

I   Contributions to the PP must be regular in order to qualify for tax relief

II   The benefits built up must be taken at the same time as those under the occupational scheme

III   The employer must agree to Robert's choice of PP provider

IV   The limit on contributions with tax relief takes account of his contributions to the occupational scheme as well as the PP

V   Contributions to the PP would have to cease if he stopped work in the future

VI   The earliest he will be able to take benefits (assuming he remains In good health) will be age 55

A   I, III, VI only

B   II, III, IV, V only

C   III, IV, V only

D   IV, VI only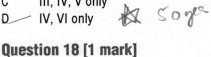

Question 18 [1 mark]

Robert is aware that the scheme is contracted out. Assuming he joins the scheme, this means that, in respect of service whilst in the scheme:

A   He will not build up any State pension benefits

B   He will build up rights to the State basic pension but not to S2P benefits

C   He will build up rights to S2P benefits but not to the State basic pension

D   He will receive full State pension benefits in addition to those under the scheme

Question 19 [2 marks]

The couple want to consider what extra financial provision they should make for the time when they plan to stop work. Assuming the couple do as they plan, and based on the current legislative position, which of the following are correct and relevant in assessing their needs?

I   Robert will be able to draw his State pension benefits immediately

II   Sue will not be able to draw her State pension benefits immediately

III   They will no longer be paying mortgage interest

IV   The children should be financially independent by then

V   They will no longer be paying premiums to the endowment policy

VI   Robert will have a higher income tax allowance because he will not be working

VII The couple will be entitled to an additional married couple's allowance

A   I, II, IV, V, VI only

B   IV, V, VII only

C   II, III, IV, V only

D   III, IV, VI, VII only

Question 20 [1 mark]

Robert asks whether there would be an income tax liability on the benefits payable under the scheme if he died before retirement. Which of the following is correct?

A   All benefits would be subject to income tax

B   Only the lump sum would be subject to income tax

C   Only the pension payable to Sue would be subject to income tax

D   None of the benefits would be subject to income tax

Additional information

The couple have read about some cases where endowment mortgages have failed to pay out as much as expected at the end of the term and are concerned about their mortgage as a result. They have asked the insurance company about their policy and have been told that the current surrender value is £5,000.

Question 21 [2 marks]

Which of the following statements are true in relation to the mortgage arrangements?

I   The minimum death benefit payable is £48,000 ✓
II   The minimum amount payable at maturity is £48,000
III   If the policy runs to maturity, there would be no personal tax charge on the proceeds of the policy ✓
IV   The loan amount outstanding reduces through the term ✓
V   The mortgage could be changed to a repayment basis, if the lender was agreeable
VI   If the endowment policy was surrendered now, Robert and Sue would have a tax liability on part of the surrender value

A   I, III, V only
B   I, II, III, VI only
C   III, IV, V, VI only
D   II, IV, V only

Question 22 [1 mark]

To what extent is a terminal bonus normally guaranteed under a low cost endowment linked to a mortgage?

A   No terminal bonus is payable on a mortgage related policy
B   There may be a terminal bonus, but it is not guaranteed until added at maturity
C   There is a guaranteed minimum bonus, but insurers hope to exceed this
D   The amount of terminal bonus is guaranteed from outset

Question 23 [2 marks]

In considering the mortgage, and whether further protection should be put in place to cover it, which of the following points would you need to consider?

I   The endowment policy would provide enough to pay off the amount borrowed if either Robert or Sue died

II   If Robert was incapacitated, he would not be able to use the Income Protection arrangement at work to meet repayments

III   If Sue was incapacitated, the reduction in the couple's joint income could make it difficult to meet their mortgage repayments

IV   Income protection policies usually include a deferred period before benefits are payable, and mortgage payments would need to be continued during this period

V   Critical Illness cover could be arranged on both Robert and Sue to allow the mortgage to be paid off if a condition covered by the policy arose

VI   In the event of incapacity, it would be possible to suspend endowment premiums until recovery

VII   Some State benefits may be payable in the event of incapacity, and in some cases, mortgage interest may be covered to an extent

A   II, IV, V, VII only
B   I, II, V, VI only
C   II, III, V, VI, VII only
D   I, III, IV, V, VII only

Question 24 [2 marks]

Robert asks if it would be a good idea to use the money he has saved in his investment trust regular savings plan to reduce the amount outstanding on the mortgage. Which of the following factors should you consider in advising him?

I   He could have a CGT liability on encashing the plan
II   There could be a penalty on encashing the plan early
III There could be an interest penalty on early repayment of part of the mortgage
IV   The endowment policy would no longer be suitable to cover the loan
V   The money used to repay part of the mortgage would no longer be accessible for other purposes
VI   The saving in interest would in effect provide a tax free return on the money used for repayment

A   I, III, IV, VI only
B   III, V, VI only
C   II, IV, VI only
D   I, IV, V, VI only

Question 25 [1 mark]

Would any tax relief be available in relation to the couple's mortgage arrangements?

A   No, there would be no relief on either the interest or the endowment premiums
B   There would be some relief on the interest but not the endowment premiums
C   There would be some relief on the endowment premiums but not the interest
D   There would be some relief on both the endowment premiums and the interest

Question 26 [1 mark]

Assuming the premiums to the endowment policy are kept up, could there be an income tax charge on benefits arising on the death of Robert or Sue?

A   Only if the death occurs before the policy has been in force for 10 years
B   Only if the deceased was a higher rate taxpayer
C   Only on any excess over the loan outstanding
D   No, there would be no liability

Additional information

Sue's mother, Edith, has suffered a fall, and will need to go into a nursing home to receive the care she needs. Edith is 62 years old and a widow. Up to now, Edith has been self-sufficient financially, although Sue has always said to Edith that she should let her know if she needs anything. Edith has a State pension and a small private pension from her deceased husband's occupational scheme, and lives in her own house, which is free of any mortgage.

Question 27 [2 marks]

Sue is not sure whether her mother will need financial help following her fall, though she has always preferred to be independent. Which of the following questions would be relevant in determining whether this is likely?

I   What are the fees charged by the nursing home? ✓
II   How long is Edith expected to stay in the home? ✓
III   How many people reside in the nursing home?
IV   How long has the nursing home been in operation?
V   How much pension income does she receive? ✓
VI   Does she have any other sources of income? ✓
VII   Does Edith have capital invested? ✓

A   I, II, III, IV only
B   I, V, VI, VII only
C   I, II, V, VI, VII only
D   I, III, IV only

Question 28 [1 mark]

If Sue pays all or part of the fees for her mother, how would this affect her protection needs?

A   It would not affect them
B   Her need for life insurance would increase, but otherwise there would be no effect
C   Her need for income protection would increase, but otherwise there would be no effect
D   Her need for both life insurance and income protection would increase

Question 29 [2 marks]

In considering the savings needs of the couple, which of the following factors are likely to be increased in importance by the possible need to help with Edith's fees?

I   Short term growth
II   Long term growth
III   Access ✓
IV   Fixed term
V   Security of capital ✓

A   I, II, V only
B   II, III, IV only
C   III, V only
D   IV, V only

Question 30 [1 mark]

If Edith sold her house in order to help fund her fees, what would be the tax position of any profit she made on the sale?

A   It would be subject to income tax
B   It would be subject to income tax, but only at higher rate
C   It would be subject to capital gains tax
D   It would be exempt from tax

Case Study B

Victoria is 29 years old, and is employed as marketing manager by a local hotel group, where she is responsible in particular for expanding sales to business users nationwide. This includes accommodation and conference facilities, and she has been successful in the role to date. She is single, with no dependants and lives in a rented flat, near the town centre. She likes the freedom this brings, without the responsibility of a mortgage to tie her down, and she has always liked to be self-sufficient and independent.

Victoria's total income from her job in the current tax year will be £38,500, including a bonus of £7,500. Although the bonus is not guaranteed, it has been at consistent levels each year since she became marketing manager. She does not anticipate any substantial change to her total income in the foreseeable future either, though her bonus could improve if she increases business substantially. Her earnings comfortably cover her expenses and she can save a little from time to time. She has no debts or outstanding credit card balances.

There are no pension rights associated with her job, but Victoria is covered for life insurance of twice basic salary. She currently contributes on a monthly basis to a personal pension which she took out three years ago. She also has a cash mini-ISA, which she has funded at maximum levels for the last three years from her bonuses, though she has not made a contribution to this or any other ISA this tax year. She feels that the amount built up in the ISA (now around £10,000) is sufficient as a cash emergency fund.

Victoria also has about £4,000 spread between three OEICs, which she invested in at different times over the last five years. She has achieved good growth on these, and likes the potential for a high return on these investments. She is aware that values go down as well as up, and indeed has seen this happen, and she only invests amounts she can believes she can afford to leave invested for the long term.

A major concern at present is what would happen if Victoria were unable to work as a result of illness or injury. She has no arrangements on a personal basis, and her employer does not make any provision beyond that required by law. A friend of Victoria's has been involved in a car accident, and almost died. In fact, although he has been off work for an extended period, he is now on the way to a full recovery and expects to start back at work within the next three months.

Additional information

Victoria has decided that she should review her financial affairs and utilise her surplus income each month, which she has calculated as being about £150 per month after tax.

Question 1 [2 marks]

Which of the following would you feel are of the highest priority for Victoria at present?

I	Term insurance
II	Whole of life insurance
III	Income protection ✓
IV	Increasing her emergency fund
V	Critical illness cover ✓
VI	Private medical insurance ✓
VII	Starting to save for house purchase

A	I, II, III only
B	III, V, VI only
C	III, IV, V, VII only
D	III, IV, VI, VII only

Question 2 [1 mark]

If she takes out a personal Income Protection (PHI) arrangement and makes a claim, how will the benefits be taxed?

A   They will be free of tax

B   They will be taxed as earned income, and NI contributions will also be payable

C   They will be taxed as earned income, but no NI contributions will be payable

D   They will be taxed as savings income

Question 3 [2 marks]

In deciding the basis of income protection cover to recommend to Victoria, which of the following would be relevant?

I   The deferred period chosen should take account of the employer's obligation to pay Statutory Sick Pay

II   The termination date should tie in with the earliest age at which she can access her pension benefits

III   The benefit level should be 100% of her earnings to ensure her standard of living is not affected

IV   The definition of incapacity should not require her to be incapacitated from doing any work

V   Increases in benefit in payment should be included to offset the effect of inflation over a potentially lengthy claim period

A   II, IV, V only

B   I, II, III only

C   III, IV, V only

D   I, IV, V only

Question 4 [1 mark]

Victoria has been influenced by the experience of the friend who was in a road accident, and she asks what happens to Income Protection cover if benefits are paid and then the person insured recovers and goes back to work. Which of the following is correct?

A   Benefits cease and cover ceases

B   Benefits cease and cover can be restored, but only subject to medical evidence

C   Benefits cease and cover is restored automatically

D   Benefits continue until the agreed termination date

Question 5 [2 marks]

Which of the following features differentiate Critical Illness cover from Income Protection and should be considered in Victoria's case?

I   Benefit is payable as a lump sum

II   Benefit is taxable

III   A claim can be paid on diagnosis of a relevant condition

IV   To claim, the insured must be incapacitated

V   The cover lapses if a claim is paid

VI   Benefit must be repaid in the event of full recovery

VII   The existence of cover will limit the income protection cover available

A   I, II, III, VI only

B   I, II, III, VII only

C   I, III, V only

D   I, III, IV, V, VII only

Additional information

Victoria has £5,000 in a building society instant access account, which is paying net interest of 3.6% pa. She funded this from her bonus this year. She plans to invest this for the long term, and wants it to help towards her retirement planning, though she is concerned that the capital should not be wholly inaccessible to her if she needs it before retirement. She is keen to generate good capital growth, and wants to ensure that the gains would not be taxable in any circumstances either within the investment product, or on a personal basis.

Question 6 [1 mark]

How much tax will she have to pay personally on the building society interest (in addition to any deducted at source) assuming the capital is invested for a full year and the interest rate does not change?

A None
B £30
C £45
D £60

Question 7 [2 marks]

Which of the following products would be appropriate for the investment of all or part of her lump sum?

I Personal Pension
II Stakeholder Pension
III Cash ISA
IV Stocks & shares ISA
V Investment bond
VI Unit trust
VII Investment trust

A I, II, III, IV, V only
B I, II, IV only
C I, II, IV, VI, VII only
D I, II, IV, V only

Question 8 [2 marks]

In comparing a stocks & shares ISA with a personal pension for this investment, which of the following aspects might make the ISA preferable in Victoria's circumstances?

I Higher contribution limit
II Ability to access investment at any time
III No restrictions on the form in which benefits are taken
IV More favourable treatment of investment income
V Wider choice of investments
VI Ability to top-up investment later
VII No tax liability on benefits

A I, II, III only
B I, II, III, IV only
C II, III, VII only
D II, IV, VI only

Question 9 [2 marks]

What factors should be considered in deciding whether it would be advisable for Victoria to contract out of S2P using a personal pension?

I   The NI rebate is the same at all ages and so is particularly attractive at young ages

II   The rebate must be used to buy Protected Rights which are subject to some restrictions

III   She could not access the Protected Rights benefits until she reaches State Pension Age

IV   She would decrease her potential reliance on the State in retirement

V   If she was single at retirement she could use the Protected Rights fund to provide income benefits for herself alone

VI   She would not receive higher rate tax relief on the employee portion of the NI rebate

VII   She could be worse off in retirement as a result of contracting out

A   I, II, IV, VII only
B   II, IV, V, VI, VII only
C   II, III, V, VI only
D   III, V, VI only

Question 10 [1 mark]

In what circumstances could Victoria access benefits under her personal pension before she reached age normal minimum pension age?

A   In no circumstances
B   If she was incapacitated
C   If she was unemployed
D   If she was incapacitated or unemployed

Question 11 [2 mark]

If Victoria contributed a lump sum to her personal pension, which of the following statements are relevant to the tax relief available?

I   She would contribute net of basic rate tax relief

II   Higher rate relief would be available

III   Higher rate relief would be restricted if the contribution exceeded the amount of income which otherwise would fall into higher rate tax

IV   She could carry back part of the contribution to the preceding tax year, subject to some restrictions regarding timing

V   Contributions may be carried forward to a later tax year if this increases the tax relief available

A   I, II, III only
B   I, II, III, V only
C   I, II, IV only
D   I, II, V only

Additional information

Victoria has received a small lump sum inheritance of £15,000, following the death of her uncle. She wants to invest this separately from her other arrangements, and has different objectives in relation to it. Her uncle wanted her to have the chance to set up in business on her own, and the bequest was made with this in mind. Victoria has decided that she wants to invest it without any personal tax liability arising on it. She will want the money to be accessible in 5 years' time.

Question 12 [2 marks]

If she wants the security of NS&I products for her investment, which of those listed below would be suitable to meet her objectives?

I Fixed Rate Savings Certificates
II Index-linked Savings Certificates
III Income Bond
IV Capital Bond
V Premium Bonds
VI Fixed Rate Savings Bonds

A I, II only
B III, V, VI only
C I, III, V, VI only
D I, II, V only

Question 13 [2 marks]

After talking to a friend, she is keen to consider investing part of the inheritance in a unitised with profit investment bond. Which of the following points should be considered in deciding whether this would be suitable?

I The underlying investment fund invests entirely in equities
II The fund pays tax on capital gains
III The fund is taxed on income
IV The price of units never reduces
V A Market Value Reduction factor may apply on surrender
VI There could be a terminal bonus added on surrender
VII There would be no personal tax liability on surrender after 5 years

A I, II, IV, VI only
B II, III, IV, V, VI only
C I, III, V, VI, VII only
D III, IV, VI, VII only

Question 14 [2 marks]

Although Victoria intends to leave the money invested throughout the five year period, she realises that circumstances can change and that she might need to take some money out. Which of the following statements are correct regarding the availability of withdrawals from a unitised with profit investment bond?

I   There is no maximum imposed on withdrawals

II   If withdrawals exceed certain limits, a chargeable event arises ✓

III   Amounts withdrawn within limits are ignored when calculating the gain on surrender ✓

IV   Any excess over limits is treated as a chargeable gain ✓

V   Top-slicing relief is not available for withdrawals

A   I, II, IV only
B   I, II, IV, V only
C   II, III, IV, V only ✓
D   III, IV, V only

Question 15 [1 mark]

If a tax charge arises on a chargeable gain under a with profits investment bond, at what rate is the charge calculated, assuming Victoria is a higher rate taxpayer at the time?

A   18%
B   20% ✓
C   22%
D   40%

Case Study C

George is 55 years old, and is a senior executive at a local manufacturing business. He has a salary of £70,000 per year and various benefits, including membership of an occupational pension scheme, a tax advantaged share option scheme, and a good quality company car.

He has a substantial investment portfolio, mostly invested in direct equity holdings, spread across 40 or so different companies, and he also has a few unit trust holdings. He does not deal actively in the shares, but tends to hold them for the long term. He also has some money on deposit at the building society, for emergencies, and this totals around £25,000. It is all held in an instant access account, and although there are other accounts on offer, he has never bothered to move the money.

George's wife died ten years ago, and he has been living with Mary for 6 years now. He regards the relationship as stable, though the couple are not legally married. Mary is 50, and works part-time in the local library, earning around £5,000 per year.

George owns the house that he and Mary live in, and there is no mortgage, because this was paid off by life insurance on his wife's death. The house is worth £450,000.

Additional information

George's employer has been taken over by a larger competitor, and George has been made redundant as a result. He received a lump sum redundancy payment, and a further sum from a share option scheme. After tax, this means he has £120,000 available to invest. This is currently held in his Building Society account.

Question 1 [2 marks]

If George decides to invest this amount to produce income without eroding capital, which of the following products would be suitable as part of the portfolio?

I	Cash ISA
II	Corporate Bond ISA
III	NS&I Savings Certificates
IV	NS&I Premium Bonds
V	NS&I Income Bonds
VI	Gilts
VII	Zero dividend preference shares

A II, III, VI, VII only
B I, IV, VII only
C III, IV, V, VI only
D I, II, V, VI only

Question 2 [1 mark]

Are capital gains resulting from an investment in gilts subject to CGT?

A No
B Only if the gilt was disposed of before redemption
C Only if the gilt was held to redemption
D Yes

Question 3 [2 marks]

If George wants to restructure his existing portfolio to generate more income, which of these strategies would be suitable to address this objective?

I   Switch from direct equity holdings into equity unit trusts
II   Move investments from UK equities to overseas equity holdings
III   Reinvest part of the portfolio in fixed interest securities
IV   Use ISAs to the maximum extent possible for fixed interest securities
V   Transfer some income producing assets to Mary to reduce the impact of tax
VI   Place assets into trust to reduce taxation

A   I, III, IV, VI only
B   II, V, VI only
C   III, IV, V only
D   IV, V, VI only

Question 4 [2 marks]

If George reorganises his portfolio, which of the following should be taken into account in deciding how this should be achieved?

I   The impact of CGT might be reduced if disposals are spread over a number of tax years
II   Transferring assets to Mary would not be regarded as a disposal for CGT purposes and would allow her annual exemption to be used
III   The costs of reorganisation can outweigh the advantages, and must be considered carefully
IV   Switching between unit trust funds does not crystallise a gain for CGT purposes
V   Taper relief reduces gains for CGT purposes on assets held for long periods
VI   Indexation allowance may be available on some investments

A   I, III, V, VI only
B   I, II, III, V, VI only
C   II, IV, V, VI only
D   III, IV, V, VI only

Question 5 [1 mark]

For what minimum period must a unit trust holding acquired in the current tax year be held in order that any gain qualifies for the maximum possible level of CGT taper relief on disposal?

A   Two years
B   Two complete tax years
C   Ten years
D   Ten complete tax years

Additional information

George has a preserved pension under his employer's occupational pension scheme, which he can draw immediately if he chooses, or he can leave the benefits to be drawn later, at any time up to the scheme normal retirement age (which is his 65th birthday). The scheme was on a defined benefit basis and so does not allow income withdrawals, but the trustees are prepared to be as flexible as possible in George's case.

Question 6 [2 marks]

Which of the following points should be considered in deciding whether he should draw benefits from the scheme now?

I   If benefits are taken, no future contributions to any pension arrangements are permitted
II   Once started, the benefits cannot be stopped even if George finds a new job
III   The benefits are likely to be reduced if they are drawn before normal retirement age
IV   The income benefits drawn would be taxable
V   Drawing the pension benefits could reduce the means-tested State benefits available

A   III, IV, V only
B   I, II, III only
C   II, III, IV only
D   I, III, V only

Question 7 [1 mark]

Is the scheme required by law to provide a pension benefit for Mary if George draws his pension from the scheme and then dies before she does?

A   No, this depends entirely on the scheme rules
B   Only if the scheme was contracted out of S2P
C   Only if there is such a provision for legal spouses
D   Yes, this is required

Question 8 [2 marks]

George asks whether he can achieve a greater degree of control by transferring his pension rights to a personal pension (PP). Which of the following factors would be important in considering this possibility?

I   The PP could allow him to take benefits by means of income withdrawals

II   Phased retirement is not allowed because the benefits originally accrued under an occupational scheme

III   He could take benefits anytime up to age 75

IV   He would have to include escalation if he purchased an annuity with the PP fund

V   If the occupational scheme was contracted out, the contracted out rights would not be able to be transferred

VI   If he transfers, he would lose the guarantee of a known benefit under the occupational scheme

VII   After transfer and prior to drawing benefits, the full fund value would be available to provide benefits on George's death

A   I, III, VI, VII only
B   II, III, V, VI, VII only
C   I, IV, VI only
D   III, IV, V, VII only

Question 9 [2 marks]

What factors would be important in deciding whether the transfer value offered by the scheme was a favourable option for George?

I   The level of benefits that could be guaranteed by the transfer
II   The critical yield needed to match the benefits under the occupational scheme
III   George's attitude to risk in relation to his pension rights
IV   The importance of flexibility in drawing benefits
V   The importance of death benefits to George
VI   The extent to which George intends to make further pension provision in future

A   I, II, IV, V, VI only
B   III, IV, V only
C   I, III, VI only
D   II, III, IV, V only

Question 10 [1 mark]

George was made redundant 3 months into the current tax year. If he does not find another job in the same tax year, could he contribute to a PP?

A   No, he is not eligible
B   Yes, up to a maximum of £2,700 gross
C   Yes, up to a maximum of £3,600 gross
D   Yes, up to 100% of his earnings

Question 11 [2 mark]

A few months after being made redundant, George starts to work for a small local firm, though the salary is considerably less than he earned previously. The employer offers a Stakeholder Pension arrangement which George can join and George does want to make further pension contributions. Which of the following factors should be taken into account in deciding whether he should join the employer's scheme or take out his own arrangement?

I   Can George use the scheme to contract out of S2P?
II   Does the employer contribute to the scheme?
III   What maximum contributions are permitted?
IV   What investment choices are available?
V   How good is the investment manager's performance record?
VI   When can retirement benefits be taken?
VII How is tax relief given on the contributions?

A   I, II, VI, VII only
B   II, IV, V only
C   I, III, IV, V only
D   II, IV, VI, VII only

Additional information

George tells you that neither he nor Mary have made a will, but they would like to ensure that on the death of either, the survivor would receive the estate of the deceased. Mary has no family apart from her mother, who is over 80, but George has two children, each adult, with their own families, and financially independent of him.

Question 12 [2 marks]

Which of the following comments regarding intestacy are correct and relevant in this case?

I   The nil rate band for IHT is not available in cases of intestacy

II   If George dies intestate, Mary would receive the house, but nothing else from his estate

III   George's children would be beneficiaries under the intestacy rules

IV   If Mary dies intestate, her entire estate would pass to her mother

V   If George and Mary got married, there would be no need for wills because the survivor would automatically inherit the estate of the deceased on the first death

A   I, II, III only
B   I, III, IV only
C   III, IV only
D   III, IV, V only

Question 13 [2 marks]

George wants to give some money to each of his three grandchildren, to be invested for them. Which of the following points should be borne in mind when arranging this?

I   Any income produced by the investments would be taxed as belonging to the children, and their personal allowances would be available

II   Dividend tax credits are not reclaimable

III   Interest deducted at source from deposit interest is not reclaimable

IV   Capital gains are taxable as if they had accrued to George himself

V   There would be no tax implications for George's children

VI   If not covered by exemptions, the gifts to the children would be potentially exempt transfers

A   I, II, V, VI only
B   II, III, V only
C   I, IV, V, VI only
D   III, IV, V only

Question 14 [2 marks]

George intends to pass quite substantial sums of money to his two children in order to reduce the potential inheritance tax liability on his estate. Which of the following points should be considered in arranging this?

I   To be effective, the gifts must be outright, with no reservation of benefit by George

II   Outright gifts would not generate any immediate inheritance tax liability

III   The gifts would still be regarded as part of George's estate for inheritance tax purposes if he died within ten years of making them

IV   Taper relief could reduce the inheritance tax in respect of the gifts if death occurs more than 3 years after they are made

V   He could make the gifts via a trust in order to retain an element of control over them

VI   He should ensure that he retains sufficient capital for his own purposes after making the gifts

A   I, II, III, VI only
B   I, II, IV, V, VI only
C   II, III, IV, V only
D   III, IV, V, VI only

Question 15 [1 mark]

George wants to provide for the remaining potential inheritance tax liability on his death. Assuming he and Mary are still unmarried, but they have made wills reflecting their wishes, which of the following would be the best approach to take?

A   10 year term insurance, on an own life basis
B   10 year term insurance, written in trust for Mary
C   Whole of life insurance, on an own life basis
D   Whole of life insurance, written in trust for Mary

Multiple Choice
Case Studies:
Answers

Case Study A

1 B Any consideration of suitability needs to take account of the purpose of the plan, which may be specific, in which case the timescale is important or non-specific and intended to build a reserve over time. Flexibility of investment is important, but whether contributions have fluctuated or included lump sums in the past does not affect suitability. Where the investment trust invests is important in determining risk, as is the extent of volatility in share price. Its size does not affect suitability directly, though this might affect how easily the trust can react to changing conditions.

2 A Investment trusts are closed-ended and this means that the number of shares in issue cannot be adjusted to balance supply and demand. As a result, shares can trade at a premium or discount to net asset vale (NAV) which increases risk and potential reward. Gearing (the ability to borrow to invest) also increases risk and potential reward, because it magnifies performance (both positive and negative).

3 C The investment trust carries a relatively high degree of risk, and given that he has very limited cash resources, it may be unsuitable to hold savings in an investment which fluctuates in value and which can be quite volatile. This is reinforced by his attitude to risk, and his statement that he does not like to see the value of his savings fall. Also his lack of experience of investments suggests this may be a step too far at the moment. Term is not relevant, because although not fixed, he does realise the need to leave the money invested for the medium term. His tax position does not suggest a lack of suitability, because there would be no further tax on income (he is a basic rate taxpayer) nor would he be subject to CGT as any gains would be within the CGT annual exemption for the foreseeable future.

4 C Investment trusts often trade at a discount and if this reduces, it means that the share price performs better than the value of the underlying assets.

5 C The mortgage is already covered by the associated endowment policy and so does not figure in the calculation of the need for additional cover. All the other items are relevant however.

6 C The bereavement benefits from the State consist of a lump sum of £2,000 and an income which is payable only whilst the children are eligible for Child Benefit, or for 12 months if the widow or widower is not responsible for any children.

7 A Although second death cover is common to provide for an IHT liability, for family protection, it is likely that cover is needed primarily on a first death basis. Currently, if Robert died before Sue, the household income would be dramatically reduced, but apart from the mortgage related endowment, there would be no life insurance benefits payable.

8 D The policy is non-qualifying, which gives a great deal of flexibility, but the sum assured would not be subject to income tax. Any investment gain would be subject to higher rate tax however (if applicable), and the underlying fund is subject to tax on income and gains, so this would not be a tax efficient savings arrangement. Indexation is a good means of providing basic cover increases, but further medical evidence would be required for additional increases. The review deals with premium levels, but does not result in a requirement for further medical evidence.

9 C These policies are very flexible, and allow a high level of cover to be established for a modest premium, but on the maximum cover basis, the premiums will increase at each review, to reflect advancing age. The profile of premiums is similar to that under a series of renewable term insurance policies. The low surrender value indicates that the policy is likely to be on, or close to, a maximum cover basis.

10 A One of the main advantages of using a trust is that the proceeds fall outside the estate of the deceased (in this case, the second of Robert and Sue to die), and are not therefore subject to IHT. They also pass direct to the intended beneficiaries without the possibility of being delayed by the need for probate. The policy is in general protected by the trust from creditors, because it does not belong to Robert and Sue. There is however no effect on the tax treatment of the fund. If not in trust, the insurer must pay the proceeds to the estate and does not have any discretion over this.

11 B   It is a condition of the tax approval of an occupational scheme that the employer must contribute, and Robert's contribution will also benefit from tax relief. Because the scheme is contracted out, there will be a reduction in his NI contributions too, which will reduce the real cost to him. Benefits are at a good level, but are well below the maximum permitted with full tax advantages. The investment return is tax advantaged, because no tax is paid on income (but dividend tax credits cannot be reclaimed) nor on capital gains. Robert can withdraw from the scheme at any time, but if he does so after a period of more than two years, he would not be able to take a refund, but would have a preserved benefit instead.

12 A   Employees have a right not to join the scheme, but if they decide against joining, the employer is under no obligation to allow them to join later.

13 A   His expected benefit is 34/60 x basic salary of £30,000 = £17,000.

14 A   Benefits can be taken before the normal retirement date provided the employee is at least 50 (55 from April 2010, which will affect Robert), but most schemes require the trustees to agree. There will be a reduction to reflect the fact that the benefits are payable for longer. Schemes generally offer the option to commute part of the pension benefit for a cash sum which is free of tax under current legislation. However, the cash and income benefits must be taken at the same time. Increases to the pension in payment will apply in the normal way, and the benefit will qualify for LPI (Limited Price Indexation) increases. It is not generally possible to continue to pay contributions and accrue benefits after leaving however.

15 C   Contributions are relieved through the net pay arrangements which mean that the contributions are deducted from his pay before tax is calculated. Most AVC arrangements are on a money purchase basis and are funded entirely by employees. There is no restriction on taking benefits in cash at retirement (thought this used to apply before April 2006.

16 B   The pension scheme provides for long term savings rather than short, given the period of time before benefits are available, and Income Protection is provided already for Robert, outside of the scheme. There is also life insurance under the scheme on Robert's life, but no life insurance or income protection on Sue.

17 D   There is no requirement for regularity of PP contributions in order to qualify for tax relief, and the benefits are controlled only by Robert (within the limitations of pensions legislation) so he can take benefits anytime between 55 and 75. The employer has no say in the choice of provider, though the employer can limit the option to have contributions deducted from pay to the PPs of one or more chosen providers. The contribution limits do take account of all contributions, but can continue as long as Robert remains eligible, including any time as a non-earner.

18 B   Contracting out means giving up rights to S2P benefits, but it is not possible to contract out of the basic pension. (In some cases, contracted out employees continue to build up some rights under S2P, but this would not be the case at Robert's earnings level.)

19 C   State benefits cannot be drawn before State Pension Age, which will be 65 for both Robert and Sue. Their outgoings should have reduced because the mortgage will be paid off, and the children should also be independent. (The adviser would need to keep these points under review, because the future is always uncertain.) The endowment has only 19 years to run, so this outgoing would also have stopped. Higher income tax allowances are available to the over 65s, but not to younger people even if they have stopped work. The married couple's allowance is only available to couples where at least one spouse was born before 6 April 1935, and so this will not be available.

20 C   Income benefits from pension schemes are taxed as earned income, whether paid to the member or a spouse, registered civil partner or dependant. The lump sum would be free of income tax and is usually free of IHT too.

21 A   Low cost endowment policies set the sum insured on death equal to the loan, but there is no guarantee that the policy will pay out enough to discharge the loan at maturity. These policies are qualifying policies and there would be no personal tax charge on death. There is a possibility of a higher rate tax charge (at 20%) if the early surrender proceeds exceed the premiums and the policy is surrendered before premiums have been paid for ten years, or, if less, three quarters of the term. In this case, the surrender value is less than the premiums paid, and neither Robert nor Sue appears to be a higher rate taxpayer anyway. With endowment mortgages, the amount

outstanding does not reduce through the term, but is designed to be paid off in one lump sum at the end of the term, from the endowment policy proceeds. A change to repayment could be considered, but the lender would have to agree.

22 B This creates an element of risk with these policies, because the terminal bonus is uncertain until maturity. In general, reliance on terminal bonuses has tended to increase, but they may not be payable at all, or may be payable at a level which is below expectations in weak stock market conditions, as have applied over the last few years.

23 D The endowment policy guarantees a death benefit equal to the amount borrowed and would pay out on the first death. Income protection is important however, and Robert's cover at work could be used, but a policy for Sue should certainly be considered. How the couple would deal with the mortgage during the deferment period is an important issue, and if it would be difficult to do so, a short deferred period should be considered, though this increases cost. Similarly critical illness cover would be useful. Endowment premiums cannot be suspended (without the policy being paid-up) during incapacity or for any other reason, and the need to continue premiums should be built into the consideration of the position on incapacity. There are State benefits payable on incapacity, though the incapacity test is stringent. In some cases, mortgage interest can be paid, but generally only after a period of 39 weeks.

24 B As the value of the plan is only £3,000, any gain would be within the CGT annual exemption, so there will be no CGT liability, and there would be no penalty as these plans do not have a fixed term. There could however be an interest penalty on early repayment of part of the mortgage and this would need to be checked. Although the endowment policy would have a death benefit in excess of the loan amount, it would not be unsuitable, and should continue in force. Using capital to repay part of the loan would mean that the capital was no longer available for other purposes, but the interest saved would constitute a tax free return on the money.

25 A Tax relief was available on mortgage interest on the first £30,000 borrowed at one time, but this is no longer the case. Neither is there any relief on endowment premiums, though this was also available (Life Assurance Premium Relief or LAPR) at one time and continues to apply to some policies started before 14 March 1984.

26 D The policy is a qualifying policy and no income tax liability arises on death provided premiums are still being paid.

27 C This is a difficult situation, and one where the people involved may not have all the information they need to determine the chance of their needing to help the elderly relative. Essentially, the information concerns the costs involved – fees and probable duration – compared to income and other usable assets.

28 D Because Edith would be partially dependent on Sue, there is a need to protect this liability if Sue is unable to continue payments. This therefore affects the need for both life insurance and income protection.

29 C The possible need to help with fees emphasises accessibility of savings above all other things, but security is also important given the potential need to draw on the savings, possibly regularly. Growth, whether short or long term, is secondary, and a fixed term would be a hindrance rather than a help.

30 D The house is Edith's main residence, and this therefore falls within one of the most important CGT exemptions.

Case Study B

1 B Life insurance seems of little concern to Victoria, as she has no debts or dependants, and the life cover at work will cover funeral costs and any other small requirements arising on death. Income protection is a major priority, and is clearly a concern of hers, but critical illness cover and private medical insurance are also relevant. She has an adequate emergency fund, and does not seem to want to plan for a property purchase at this stage in her life.

2 A Benefits under personal Income Protection (PHI) arrangements are free of income tax, although those under group arrangements funded by the employer are taxable.

3　D　The deferred period should take account of Statutory Sick Pay, as benefits would be limited taking into account income from the employer and indeed some State benefits. Termination date should be chosen to tie in with her intended retirement age rather than the earliest possible age, to give time for her pension fund to build up to a level where it can replace the Income Protection benefits. She should therefore budget to continue the PP contributions unless waiver of contribution is in place. Benefits are limited by insurers to between 60 – 65% of pre-incapacity income, so 100% cover would not be available. The incapacity definition should be realistic and not require her to be unable to work at all, but rather should be based on suitable jobs for her, based on her experience and training, and increases are important given her young age.

4　C　Income Protection is also known as Permanent Health Insurance and permanent means that the cover continues even if one or more claims have been made (though it ceases at the agreed termination date).

5　C　Critical illness cover meets a separate and distinct need, and provides a lump sum which could be used to make necessary modifications to a house, for example to accommodate a wheelchair. It is tax free and paid on diagnosis, without a requirement for incapacity. Once a claim is paid, cover lapses, but there is no question of repayment being required if the insured recovers – being diagnosed as subject to the condition is sufficient to justify the claim. There is no effect on income protection limits which are in place to provide a financial incentive to return to work.

6　C　The net interest is £180, and this is equivalent to gross interest of £225 with 20% tax (£45 deducted at source). She must pay a further 20% tax, because she is a higher rate taxpayer, which amounts to £45.

7　B　Personal and Stakeholder Pensions are tailor-made for retirement planning and offer growth free from tax on capital gains, and so would be suitable for part of her investment, though limited access would not make them suitable for the whole amount. ISAs also offer growth with the same tax advantages, but only stocks & shares ISAs offer capital growth. Investment bonds are taxed internally on gains and unit trusts and investment trusts may give rise to a personal CGT liability.

8　C　The main attraction of the ISA is the ability to access the investment at any time and in any form, without the restriction to use most of the fund to provide income. Benefits are tax free, whereas the income benefits from a PP are taxable. The contribution limit for the ISA is lower than for a PP, but both exceed the amount available, so the limit has no relevance here. Both types of investment allow top-up payments, and the investment choice is slightly wider under a PP. The treatment of investment income is now the same for PPs and ISAs (free of tax except that dividend tax credits cannot be reclaimed.

9　B　The NI rebate is age related, and is not over-generous, so she could be better off in retirement, but could be worse off – there are no guarantees. The rebate buys Protected Rights and these are restricted, but are available from 50 (55 from 2010, which will affect Victoria) rather than State Pension Age (which will be 65 for Victoria). There are other restrictions, including a requirement to include a survivor's pension if married or with a registered civil partner (though not if unmarried), and annuity rates must not differentiate by sex. The rebate is grossed up for basic rate relief, but no higher rate relief is available.

10　B　There is no minimum age in cases of incapacity, but otherwise, benefits cannot be taken before age 50 (55 from 2010). Some people with PPs established before 6 April 2006, based on earnings from certain special occupations (mostly professional sportspeople), were able to have earlier pension ages, but this does not apply here.

11　A　All contributions by individuals are paid net of basic rate tax relief and higher rate relief is claimed through self-assessment. Higher rate relief can only be effective as far as higher rate tax would otherwise have been paid, ie to the extent that income would otherwise have fallen into the higher rate band. Carry back is no longer possible after 5 April 2006, and there is no provision to carry contributions forward either.

12　D　Savings Certificates of both types, and Premium Bonds provide a tax free return, but the other products listed produce taxable interest.

13　B　The fund invests in a mixture of assets, which generally include equities, fixed interest securities and cash deposits, and often property. The fund is taxed on income and gains, broadly in the same way as a basic rate taxpayer, and any gain on surrender would be subject to higher rate tax – relevant here as Victoria is a higher rate taxpayer. The units do not reduce in price, but it is important to remember that the insurer can apply a Market Value Reduction factor if investment conditions are poor at the time of encashment. Units increase in value, usually daily (or sometimes units remain at a fixed price and additional units are added to give effect to growth) and a terminal bonus may apply at the time of surrender, but is not guaranteed.

14 A Withdrawals can be taken without limit (though from an investment point of view, large withdrawals may be unwise). Within a limit of 5% per year of the amount invested for a maximum of 20 years, there will be no immediate personal tax liability, but such amounts are included in the calculation of gain on surrender. Any excess is a chargeable gain subject to tax at higher rate (but not basic rate). Top-slicing relief applies to all chargeable events, whether arising on a withdrawal, or on surrender.

15 B The tax paid by the life fund is regarded as discharging the basic rate liability, and the gain is subject to higher rate tax at 20% as a result. Up to 5 April 2004 the rate was 18%, but this increased to 20% from 6 April 2004. There would be no liability for a basic rate taxpayer, unless the gain pushed the investor into higher rate (after allowing for top-slicing relief).

Case Study C

1 D Cash and corporate bond ISAs would produce tax free income, and NS&I Income Bonds and gilts are also good income producing investments, although the income would be taxable. Interest on NS&I Savings Certificates is rolled up rather than paid out, and Premium Bonds may produce no return if the investor is unlucky in the monthly draw. Zero dividend preference shares by definition produce no income.

2 A Income from gilts is taxable, but capital gains are exempt from CGT, and losses cannot be offset from taxable gains for CGT purposes.

3 C Fixed interest securities produce more income than equities, which is where the existing portfolio is held predominantly, so this would be effective, and holding them within ISAs would mean the income would be free of tax. Transferring assets to Mary would increase her income and make use of her basic rate band, rather than income falling into higher rate if it remains with George (particularly if he gets another job). Placing assets into trust would not reduce the impact of tax of itself. Moving from direct equities to equity unit trusts will not increase income generally, and overseas equities tend to produce less income than UK equities.

4 A The annual exemption for CGT purposes is a very useful way of reducing the impact of the tax, but if a portfolio undergoes a large reorganisation in a single year, only one exemption is available. It can therefore make sense to spread the disposals over a number of years to use the exemptions for each year. If George and Mary were married, a transfer to Mary would not be a disposal for CGT purposes, but as they are not married, it is a disposal, which could trigger a gain for CGT purposes. Costs always need to be weighed carefully against the advantage achieved. Switching between unit trusts is a disposal. Taper relief can reduce the impact of CGT, and indexation allowance applies to any assets acquired before April 1998.

5 C Two years is sufficient in the case of business assets, but unit trusts are non-business assets and so require ten years. It is not necessary for there to be ten complete tax years however.

6 C Future contributions would be permitted, though the benefits under the old employer's scheme would count towards the lifetime allowance. Income benefits are payable for life and cannot stop once started. If income withdrawals were available, it would be possible to reduce these to zero, but they are not available under the scheme. Reductions do generally apply where benefits are drawn early, although sometimes special terms are offered in cases of redundancy, and this should be checked. Income benefits are taxable, which could create tax problems if George gets a new job on a substantial salary. George's assets would preclude means-tested benefits whether or not he drew the pension.

7 A A spouse's pension is required if the scheme is contracted out, but there is no requirement in respect of common law spouses.

8 A Income withdrawals could be attractive to George because of their flexibility and the investment control. His investment experience should mean that he understands the risk involved, though there would no longer be a guarantee of a specific level of benefit. Phased retirement is also possible (it is under occupational schemes too, at least in theory, but is often not permitted by the rules of individual schemes), and contracted out rights can be transferred provided that the receiving PP has the necessary provisions in its documentation. There is no requirement to include escalation under the PP if an annuity is purchased, and the full fund would be available for death benefits prior to his drawing benefits.

9 D The transfer would be used to provide benefits on a money purchase (ie defined contribution) basis, at least for the most part (GMP benefit could be provided if he had pre-1997 contracted out rights and transferred to a s32 buy-out policy rather than a PP). The critical yield is an important measure of value for money, and it would need to be at a level George felt could be achieved, in the light of his attitude to risk, in order to make the transfer worthwhile. The possibility of ultimately receiving poorer benefits could be counterbalanced by the increased flexibility and death benefits to an extent. However, further provision would not make any difference to the value for money the transfer value represents.

10 D He is eligible because he is under 75. The maximum is the greater of 100% of his earnings and £3,600 and in this case, even if he does not find another job, the 100% of earnings basis would given the higher limit this year.

11 B Contracting out is not likely to be relevant for George, because at his age, the terms are unattractive. If he wanted to contract out, Stakeholder Pension arrangements must allow this anyway. Employer contributions would provide an important incentive to join, if available. George would want to consider the investment choices and track record, particularly in the light of his own investment experience. Maximum contributions and tax relief limits, the timing of retirement benefits and the method of giving tax relief are common to all Stakeholder Pension arrangements, and would not therefore be issues affecting his decision.

12 C The nil rate band is available in the normal way in cases of intestacy, and the rules are concerned with who benefits rather than altering the tax provisions. The rules of intestacy make no provision for common law spouses, so Mary would not benefit at all. As there is no spouse, the estate would be divided between George's two children. In Mary's case, her mother, as the only surviving relative would inherit. This illustrates why a will is particularly important for those who live with an unmarried partner. If they were married, the spouse would not necessarily inherit everything. In George's case, his wife would inherit personal chattels and the first £125,000 of the estate, plus a life interest in half the rest. As George owns the house, this would fall into his estate with his other assets. The balance would go to the children, who would also receive the capital in which Mary initially had a life interest. In Mary's case, George would receive the personal chattels and the first £200,000 of her estate. The remainder would be divided equally between George and Mary's mother.

13 A Although there are anti-avoidance provisions in relation to parental gifts, these do not extend to gifts from grandparents, and the income would be treated as belonging to the children. Tax deducted from interest is reclaimable, but tax credits on dividends are not. Gains are taxed as the children's and the gifts are PETs for IHT purposes unless exempt, for example under the annual exemption, or as small gifts.

14 B If a reservation is retained by George, the gifted assets are still regarded as part of his estate for inheritance tax purposes, so this would not be effective in reducing the potential liability. The gifts, if outright, would be potentially exempt transfers (PETs) and would fall out of account after 7 years (not ten years), and taper relief applies after 3 years to reduce any tax on the PET. A trust would be an effective way of retaining control, for example over the investment, and the entitlements of the beneficiaries, without this constituting a reservation. George could be a trustee. An important aspect of inheritance tax planning is always to ensure that the individual retains sufficient wealth to maintain their desired living standards.

15 D Whole of life insurance is the natural way of providing for inheritance tax, because the timing of death is not predictable. Putting the policy in trust avoids the proceeds falling into George's estate and increasing the tax liability, though care with the wording of the trust would be needed following the changes announced in the 2006 Budget.

Written Case Studies

PRACTICE EXAMINATION 1

All questions in this paper are based on English law and practice, as applicable in the 2006/07 tax year, unless otherwise stated, and should be answered accordingly.

INSTRUCTIONS

You are allowed two hours for this paper.

The paper consists of two questions. You should answer both of them. Read the questions and the information provided carefully.

You are advised to spend approximately 60 minutes on Question 1 and 60 minutes on Question 2.

You are strongly advised to attempt ALL parts of each Question in order to gain the maximum possible number of marks. The available marks for each part are shown in all cases.

You should use the Product List provided in answering Question 2. You may also find it useful to refer to the Tax Tables provided in answering both Questions.

It is important to show all the steps in any calculations you do, even if you use a calculator.

Questions

1   Philip is a designer in a successful plastic mouldings business, where he has worked for about three years. He is 38 years of age and his basic salary is £39,000, with bonuses averaging around £3,000 per year.

He is a member of his employer's occupational pension scheme, which is a final salary scheme. A spouse's pension is provided, which is payable on the death of a member, and there is also a lump sum death benefit. Philip contributes 4% of basic salary to the scheme. There are no other work-based benefits.

Philip tells you that retirement planning is a priority, because he has not been at the company long, and so will not have particularly high benefits under the scheme.

Philip is married, and his wife, Kathy, is 32. Kathy is a writer, but only works part-time at present because she is also looking after the couple's children. They have two children under 5, and they have been considering life cover to protect the children should either Philip or Kathy die whilst they are dependent. They have asked you for ideas as to how they might provide this cover, but have emphasised that cost is a prime concern.

They live in a house purchased with a repayment mortgage of £80,000 and have sufficient life cover in place in relation to this.

(a)   List the questions you would want to ask Philip and Kathy so that you would have all the information you need to advise them on his retirement planning needs.   (10 marks)

(b)   (i)   List two options which are open to Philip as ways of increasing his pension provision, together with one non-pensions alternative that might also be suitable, and for each option, give *one* advantage and *one* disadvantage relative to the other options.   (9 marks)

      (ii)   For each option you identified in (i), explain whether tax relief would be available, and if so, how it would be obtained, commenting on any applicable limitations on the relief.   (12 marks)

      (iii) Philip has £100 per month available with which to top-up his retirement provision, and is confident that he will not need to access this before retirement. Which of the options identified would you recommend, and why?   (3 marks)

(c)   Explain how a Family Income Benefit policy works, and comment on whether this would be a suitable means of providing the life cover they require.   (7 marks)

(d)   Suggest three other protection products the couple should consider. Explain why each should be considered and give details of the benefit levels you would recommend in each case.   (9 marks)

                                                          (Total marks for question: 50)

2   Jim, who is 64, and his wife, Annie, who is 62, are approaching retirement, and have asked you for some advice regarding investment. They will have a lump sum of around £140,000 to invest, which will partly come from Jim's pension scheme at work and partly from their plan to sell their house and move to a smaller property.

They realise that they need to ensure that their immediate income needs in retirement are met, but also want to build into their plans some protection against future inflation. After taking into account Jim's pension, they feel they will need an extra £2,400 per year (after any tax liability).

Jim is a basic rate taxpayer. Annie has not worked for a number of years, and has no taxable income, nor any pension rights. The couple have no debts.

Annie has about £10,000 invested in an ISA, part linked to a UK Equity unit trust, and part to a Fixed Interest unit trust. She took this out two years ago. There is also a Building Society Account in joint names with £20,000 reserved as an emergency fund, and they feel that this is adequate for this purpose. Jim has a cash mini-ISA which is currently worth about £3,500 and was taken out at the same time as Annie's ISA, but there are no other investments.

They regard their attitude to risk as being moderate, and they realise that low risk investments do not generally provide the best returns. They are therefore prepared to take a degree of risk in their overall investment strategy, to achieve some capital growth.

As well as the income needed from their investments, they also want to keep £10,000 available to replace their car, which they will need to do at some time over the next 18 months or so.

(a)   **Explain the tax treatment of the two unit trusts within Annie's ISA, and comment on the suitability of each.**

                  (13 marks)

(b)   **Using the Product List at the end of the book, recommend a portfolio of products which would be suitable to meet Jim and Annie's requirements. You should show in whose name each investment is held, and how their need for income from the portfolio is met.**

                  (12 marks)

(c)   **Justify the inclusion of each of the product types you have included in your recommendations, commenting under each of the following headings:**

        (i)   **The amount to be invested**

        (ii)   **The risk profile**

        (iii) **The suitability of the investment**   (15 marks)

(d)   **When you return to see Jim and Annie after they have retired and sold their property, what aspects of their circumstances would you need to review before confirming your recommendations?**   (10 marks)

(Total marks for question: 50)

PRACTICE EXAMINATION 1

ANSWERS

Answers

1

> **Tutorial notes**
>
> In part (a), remember that the question sequence must be written in the form of direct questions, and should use wording that will be understandable for the clients. Questions are addressed to both Philip and Kathy, because retirement planning must take account of the situations of them both.
>
> In (b) (i), the advantages and disadvantages should focus on differences between the options. So, for example, stating that a PP qualifies for tax advantaged growth would not score, because all three options have this advantage.
>
> In part (b) (ii), note that relief on in-house AVC contributions is given through the net pay arrangements under PAYE. However, relief on PP contributions is given by payment net of basic rate tax relief, with any higher rate relief being claimed through the Inspector of Taxes. The recommendation in part (b) (iii) picks up on the information given that Philip is confident that he will not need to access the money before retirement.
>
> In your answer to part (d), you should justify the cover levels suggested in the context of the case study, although there is room for differences of opinion as to the precise levels which would be recommended.

(a)
- Philip, could I please see the booklet describing your pension scheme and your latest benefit statement?
- Exactly when did you join the scheme?
- Do you expect to work for this employer until you retire, or are you likely to move on?
- When do you plan to retire?
- What level of income would you want to have at that time, in today's terms?
- Do you have any pension benefits from earlier employments, or which you have paid into yourself?
- Are there any other investments that you expect to be available to help with your financial position in retirement?
- Have you any particular plans for retirement which might influence your needs, such as a major holiday?
- Kathy, do you intend to retire at the same time as Philip?
- Do you have any pensions or other savings for your retirement?
- How much do you feel that you both could comfortably put aside for your retirement?
- How much of this do you feel you should place where it would be accessible in an emergency?

(b) (i) In-house AVCs:

Advantage
- Costs are generally low, because they are subsidised by the main scheme

Disadvantage
- Choice of funds may be limited

Personal Pensions or Stakeholder Pensions:

Advantage

- Entirely outside of the main scheme, ensuring privacy, whilst still benefiting from pension tax advantages

Disadvantage

- This needs to be arranged by Philip, either direct or with the help of a financial adviser

ISA:

Advantage

- Allows access to the accumulated savings at any time

Disadvantage

- No tax relief is available on contributions

(Other valid points would score)

(ii) In-house AVCs

- Relief is available on contributions
- The maximum relievable contribution by Philip is 100% of his earnings (which is well above what he wants to contribute)
- Less his contributions to the main scheme
- Tax relief is given through the net pay arrangements under PAYE
- This means that the contributions are deducted from income before tax is calculated
- The result is immediate tax relief at the appropriate rate

Personal Pension/Stakeholder Pension

- Relief is available
- The maximum relievable contribution is the same as for AVCs
- Contributions are paid net of basic rate relief
- Higher rate relief is applicable in Philip's case and, it is claimed from the Inspector of Taxes through self-assessment

ISA

- No tax relief is available on ISA contributions
- The maximum Philip could contribute would be £7,000 per year

(iii) • A Stakeholder Pension is most suitable.

- This gives flexibility and privacy since the arrangement is independent of the occupational scheme.

- Tax relief is particularly valuable as Philip is a higher rate taxpayer, and access is not an issue for him.

(c) • It is a form of decreasing term assurance

- The benefit is expressed as a monthly income

- It is payable following death for the remainder of the policy term

- The payments are free of tax, because they are instalments of a sum insured rather than true income

- Most policies allow the income to be exchanged for a discounted lump sum

- This is a cheap method of providing cover and fits with their requirement to protect the children whilst they are dependent

- It is therefore a suitable product

(d) Income Protection Insurance (also known as PHI)

- There is no work-based protection for either, so the couple could be in financial difficulty if either was incapacitated

- Cover should be the maximum possible in both cases (around 65% of earned income in both cases)

Critical Illness Benefit

- It would be useful to cover the mortgage and provide additional cash for any necessary alterations to the home in the event of either suffering a serious condition such as heart attack or stroke

- Cover should match the mortgage of £80,000 as a minimum and if possible within affordability constraints provide an additional £40,000 for alterations

Private Medical Insurance

- This would allow the family to receive private medical treatment, which would minimise the disruption caused if treatment was needed but NHS waiting lists are long

- Cover should be for medical expenses for conditions with long NHS waiting lists, reflecting conditions in the local area; this would provide good cover at reasonable cost

2

Tutorial notes

There are 13 marks available for part (a), so some detail will be expected. It is important to justify your comments on suitability in relation to the circumstances of this couple.

Many different portfolios could be constructed to meet the needs identified for part (b), and the one we have given is an example. Mark your portfolio using our *Marking guide* rather than by comparison with our example.

For part (c), the details given will reflect the portfolio construction, so our answers are given as an example. It is not always easy to justify exactly the amount invested where there is no maximum allowed amount. Wording similar to that shown in our part (c) answer has been acceptable in the past.

The examiner will generally regard a with profit bond as low to medium risk.

(a)
- Gains made within the equity unit trust are exempt from tax.

- Within the ISA, any gains on disposal of the holding are also exempt.

- Income is distributed net of a 10% tax credit and there is no additional tax to pay on this.

- The tax credit cannot be reclaimed however, even though it is within an ISA and irrespective of the fact that Annie is a non-taxpayer.

- The fixed interest unit trust is similarly exempt from tax on gains within the unit trust

- And on disposal because it is within an ISA.

- Income is payable net of 20% tax deducted at source.

- This can be reclaimed by the ISA manager under normal ISA rules.

- Both are potentially suitable within their overall attitude to risk and in the light of their objectives.

- However, the ability to reclaim tax deducted from interest under the fixed interest unit trust makes this particularly attractive.

- In the context of balance of the overall portfolio, equity unit trust holdings could lie outside the ISA utilising the couple's CGT annual exemptions, without reducing tax efficiency.

- In the light of the new investment, it might therefore be worth considering switching the equity unit trust holding to fixed interest.

- As well as tax efficiency and suitability, the potential cost of switching (eg a new initial charge) must be taken into account.

(b)

Owner	Investment	Amount £
Annie	Tinytown Bank 60 day Account	10,000
Jim	NS&I 39th issue 5 year Index-linked Certificates	15,000
Jim	NS&I 11th issue 3 year Index-linked Certificates	15,000
Annie	NS&I Income Bond	60,000
Jim	XYZ Life with Profit Bond	26,000
Jim	Countryside UK Income Maxi ISA	7,000
Annie	Interglobal UK income Maxi ISA	7,000
		140,000

Income need is met from the Income Bond, which yields 4.2% gross (£60,000 × 4.2% = £2,520pa), but with the ability to supplement this if required from income generated by the ISAs, and by withdrawals from the With Profit Bond. There will be no tax to pay of the income from the Income Bond, as Annie is a non-taxpayer and the income is within her personal allowance.

Marking guide

Correct income calculation – 4, with one deducted for each mistake

Effective split of ownership to use Annie's tax allowance – 1

No taxable income for Jim – 1

No further emergency fund – 1

Suitable investment for money to replace car – 1

Allowance made for inflation proofing (Index-linked certs and/or asset backed investments) – 1

Use of ISA allowances – 1

Diversified portfolio – 1

No more than £40,000 directly asset-linked – 1

Maximum 6 if income need not met

(c)   *(Maximum 3 marks per product type, overall maximum 15)*

Tinytown Bank 60 Day Account

- The amount is the minimum required to open the account

- The investment is secure

- The amount is what is required to provide for the replacement car and is held in Annie's name so that there will be no tax to pay on the interest

NS&I Index-linked Certificates

- This is the maximum permitted investment in each issue

- The investment is government backed and is totally secure, with the return exceeding inflation

- These investments meet the requirement for inflation protection within the portfolio, and do so on a guaranteed basis. The return is tax free so there is no disadvantage in their being held by Jim

NS&I Income Bond

- The amount invested provides for the minimum required income, with a small surplus to provide some cushion against possible future interest rate changes

- The investment is government backed and totally secure, though the interest rate is variable

- The interest is paid gross and, as Annie is a non-taxpayer, and the total income generated for her from the portfolio is within her personal allowance, there will be no tax liability. The investment meets the couple's income need

XYZ Life With Profit Bond

- The amount is reasonable in the context of the portfolio as a whole, in order to provide some diversification

- The bond is low to medium risk, and allows Jim to participate in a diversified portfolio, with the insurance company smoothing returns

- The investment fund is taxed, but assuming he remains a basic rate taxpayer, Jim would have no further personal tax liability on returns, and 5% pa of the original capital can be withdrawn with no immediate personal liability in any event. The with profit basis gives the potential for a good return, but with a degree of security too, in line with their attitude to risk

Maxi ISAs

- The recommended amounts are the maximum permitted

- These are equity related investments, involving risk

- The risk level is acceptable given their attitude to risk and the overall portfolio construction, and these holdings address their wish to see growth to counteract inflation

(d)
- The actual benefits produced by the pension scheme
- The capital made available when the mortgage was paid off
- The capital made available as a result of their trading down
- Whether there is any change to their net income requirement from the portfolio
- Their state of health
- Current returns available from investments, particularly the NS&I Income Bond
- Their attitude to risk
- Whether the cash required for the car replacement is still the same
- Whether they have any other capital needs other than the need to replace the car
- Their view of the likely effect of future inflation

(Other valid points would score)

PRACTICE EXAMINATION 2

INSTRUCTIONS

You are allowed two hours for this paper.

The paper consists of two questions. You should answer both of them. Read the questions and the information provided carefully.

You are advised to spend approximately 60 minutes on Question 1 and 60 minutes on Question 2.

You are strongly advised to attempt ALL parts of each Question in order to gain the maximum possible number of marks. The available marks for each part are shown in all cases.

You should use the Product List provided in answering Question 2. You may also find it useful to refer to the Tax Tables provided in answering both Questions.

It is important to show all the steps in any calculations you do, even if you use a calculator.

Questions

1   Lindsay is 28, and is single. She works as a conveyancer in a local law practice and earns £25,000 per year. She is not a member of an occupational pension, but she has been thinking of starting her own personal pension, or alternatively an ISA. She understands that both are very tax efficient, but is undecided between the two.

She has also been a bit confused by her father who has said to her that she should consider investing in a qualifying endowment policy. He had such a policy and said that it performed very well, giving him a very useful lump sum when it matured. She has asked you for advice on this.

Lindsay has a personal IPI (Income Protection Insurance, also known as Permanent Health Insurance) arrangement but is not sure exactly how it works.

(a)   **List the questions you would want to ask Lindsay so that you would have all the information you need to advise her on her retirement planning needs.**   (8 marks)

(b)   **List the advantages and disadvantages of PPs and ISAs for Lindsay.**   (16 marks)

(c)   (i)   **Describe the tax treatment of a qualifying endowment policy, and state the conditions that must be fulfilled in order for the policy for Lindsay to be regarded as qualifying.**   (11 marks)

       (ii)   **Do you think that a qualifying endowment policy would be more suitable for Lindsay than a personal pension or ISA? Explain your answer.**   (4 marks)

(d)   **Describe the main features of personal IPI arrangements, including tax treatment and any limitations on benefit.**   (8 marks)

(e)   **What other types of insurance protection should she consider?**   (3 marks)

(Total marks for question: 50)

2   Ingrid works as a computer programmer and is 33 years old. She is not married, nor in a long term relationship, though she does have a young son, Josh, who is 4 years old. She has no other dependants.

She has been left a substantial sum of money in the will of an uncle and she will shortly receive £200,000. She has asked you to advise her on the investment of this.

She intends to reduce her working hours to spend more time with Josh. This will mean a reduction of £6,500 per year in her gross salary (from £32,500 to £26,000). She will save £1,700 per year in child-minding fees but will need to replace the remainder of the reduction in her income from her investments.

The second objective is to provide more long term security for herself and her son. She will spend £7,000 on a short holiday with Josh, and some new furniture, and then wants to invest £40,000 specifically for her son, in his name. The rest should provide for her in the long term, with the emphasis on growth rather than on any further income.

She has an ISA, to which she contributes £100 per month. This is linked to the Montgomery Worldwide Investment Trust. She understands the risk involved in this investment, and that she must be prepared to take on an element of risk to have the prospect of good long term returns. However, she is not an experienced investor and describes her attitude to risk as balanced.

Apart from the ISA, she has no other investments or savings arrangements. She does however have a number of life assurance and health protection arrangements in force, and she does not wish this aspect of her financial planning to be considered by you.

(a)   List two NS&I products which would be suitable to invest in for Josh, and describe their main features.

(6 marks)

(b)   Ingrid asks for advice on establishing a personal pension for Josh. Comment on this, with details of the tax relief available, and any points which are particularly relevant given Josh's age.   (6 marks)

(c)   Using the Product List at the end of the book, recommend a portfolio of products which would be suitable to meet Ingrid's requirements. You should show which assets are in Ingrid's name, and which in Josh's, and how her need to replace the reduction in income is met from the portfolio.

(14 marks)

(d)   Justify the inclusion of each of the product types you have included in your recommendations for Ingrid's personal portfolio, commenting under each of the following headings:

(i)   The amount to be invested
(ii)   The risk profile
(iii)   The suitability of the investment

You are not required to comment on those in Josh's portfolio.   (18 marks)

(Total marks for question: 50)

PRACTICE EXAMINATION 2

ANSWERS

Answers

1

(a)
- Lindsay, when are you planning to retire?
- What level of income would you want to have at that time, in today's terms?
- Are you likely to want a lump sum in addition at that time?
- Are you likely to become eligible for a pension arrangement at work at some time in the future?
- Do you have any pension benefits from earlier employments?
- Do you have any other savings or investments which would help towards your financial position in retirement?
- How much do you feel that you could comfortably save towards your retirement planning?
- How important is it that the amount is flexible, so you can increase or decrease it, or even suspend it for a period?
- How much of this do you feel you should place where it would be accessible in an emergency?

(b) PP Advantages
- Contributions attract tax relief at Lindsay's highest rate of tax (basic rate currently).
- The fund grows free of tax on income and capital gains,
- Except that dividend tax credits cannot be reclaimed.
- Part of the benefit at retirement can be taken as a tax free lump sum.

PP Disadvantages
- Retirement benefits are not available until age 50, unless Lindsay suffers incapacity (this will increase to 55 in 2010, which will affect Lindsay).
- Retirement benefits are largely in the form of income, which limits flexibility.
- The income benefit is taxable.
- Contribution limits will reduce if her earnings reduce or particularly if she stops work.

ISA Advantages

- The fund grows free of tax on income and capital gains, except that dividend tax credits cannot be reclaimed.

- The accumulated fund is accessible at any time.

- All withdrawals are free of tax.

- There is no restriction on the form of benefits.

ISA Disadvantages

- There is no tax relief on contributions.
- Investments cannot be switched between components.
- Contribution limits are less than for PPs.
- On death, the ISA fund falls into the estate and could be subject to IHT and/or probate delay.

(Other valid points would score)

(c) (i) Tax treatment

- There is no tax relief on contributions.

- The fund pays tax on its income and its capital gains, at a rate broadly equivalent to that paid by a basic rate taxpayer.

- However, there is no personal allowance or annual exemption to set against income and gains respectively.

- The proceeds of the policy on death or maturity would be free of any personal income tax and capital gains tax.

- Surrender proceeds are free of personal tax provided premiums have been paid for at least ten years, or if less, for three-quarters of the term.

- Otherwise, any gain on surrender would be subject to higher rate tax (but not basic rate) if Lindsay was a higher rate taxpayer at the time.

Qualifying conditions

- The premium paying term must be at last 10 years.
- The sum assured must be at least 75% of the total premiums payable.
- Premiums must be payable at least annually.
- The premiums payable in any one year cannot be more than double those in any other year,
- Nor more than 12.5% of those payable in total.

(ii) • No. The tax treatment is less favourable than for either a PP or ISA.

- In particular, she would be paying tax through the life fund on capital gains.

- The freedom from personal tax on the proceeds is of no value unless she becomes a higher rate taxpayer, and the restrictions implied by the qualifying rules are therefore not compensated by a worthwhile advantage.

(d) • The IPI policy is designed to replace earned income in the event of incapacity.

- The definition of incapacity varies from policy to policy and often a modest premium means a stringent definition incapacity which might be hard to meet.

- Benefits will start at the end of a set period (the deferred period) following incapacity.

- They will continue until an agreed date (usually set to correspond to planned retirement date) unless she recovers (or dies) in the meantime.

- Benefits are usually limited to around 65% of pre-incapacity earnings.

- Under most policies, this limit is reduced by any payments from the employer, other policies and State Incapacity Benefits.

- Incapacity resulting from some causes is likely to be excluded (eg participation in a criminal act, pregnancy, misuse of alcohol or drugs).

- Proportionate benefits are usually payable if Lindsay were to return to work in a more junior capacity, or part-time, and so received lower salary payments.

- The policy cannot be cancelled by the insurer (assuming Lindsay keeps up premiums).

- There is no tax relief on the premiums,

- But no tax on the benefits.

(e) • Critical illness cover to help with accommodation etc if she suffers a serious condition

- Private Medical Insurance to allow rapid treatment of any serious conditions

- Modest life cover to deal with funeral costs and any outstanding debts

2

> **Tutorial notes**
>
> The obvious product choices are given in our answer to part (a), though others are possible. Where you can, it is best to choose the most obvious products, which is most likely to be included in the examiner's marking scheme.
>
> In part (b), although the availability of tax relief is important, it is the tax advantaged growth which is most relevant to Josh's age.
>
> Part (c): many different portfolios could be constructed to meet the needs identified, and the one we have constructed is an example. Mark your portfolio in the light of the *Marking guide* given rather than by comparison with the example. Remember to show how the portfolio meets the income need in detail, so that if you make an arithmetic mistake, you will still have a chance of marks for your method.
>
> The details given to part (d) will reflect the portfolio construction, so our answers is given as an example.

(a) • One suitable product would be the NS&I Children's Bonus Bond.

- The Bond would be taken out by Ingrid, for Josh's benefit.

- Control of the bond passes to Josh at age 16.

- It matures on Josh's 21st birthday.

- Interest is guaranteed for 5 years, after which a new guaranteed rate is specified (and so on until his 21st birthday) and is free of tax.

- The limit is £3,000 per issue of the bond.

- Another would be Premium Bonds

- The Bonds can be bought on Josh's behalf by Ingrid

- Bonds participate in a monthly prize draw, with prizes of up to £1m

- No interest accrues (the prizes are provided instead)

- Capital is secure however

- The maximum investment is £30,000

(b) • Josh is a non-earner, but can pay PP contributions with tax relief.

- The maximum relievable contribution is £3,600 gross per year.

- The net contribution payable is £2,808 per year as 22% relief is given through the Relief At Source (RAS) system.

- The PP would be established by Ingrid on his behalf

- The tax advantaged growth is particularly attractive over the long period before Josh reaches retirement age.

- On the other hand, the loss of accessibility could be a disadvantage given that Josh's circumstances could change considerably over the years.

(c)

		£
Josh	XYZ UK Equity Unit Trust	6,000
Josh	Interglobal UK Income Unit Trust	6,000
Josh	PDQ Recovery Unit Trust	6,000
Josh	XYZ Europe Unit Trust	6,000
Josh	NS&I Children's Bonus Bond	3,000
Josh	Personal pension (Index Tracker Fund)	2,800
Josh	Townshires BS 90 Day Account	10,200
		40,000
Ingrid	Tinytown Bank Deposit Account	16,000
Ingrid	Townshires BS Reserve Account	10,200
Ingrid	NS&I 39th Issue 5 year Index-linked Certificates	15,000
Ingrid	Central Insurance 5 year Guaranteed Income Bond	65,000
Ingrid	Personal pension (Fairplay Insurance Managed)	8,000
Ingrid	PDQ With Profit Bond	25,000
Ingrid	ISA top-up (Montgomery Worldwide)	5,800
Ingrid	Interglobal UK Growth Unit Trust	5,000
Ingrid	Fairplay UK Tracker	5,000
Ingrid	Countryside UK Blue Chip	5,000
		160,000

- Income lost is £6,500 gross

- Ie £5,070, net of tax at 22%

- £1,700 is saved in child-minding fees, so the portfolio must provide £3,370.

- The investment in the Central Insurance Bond will provide 5.5% of £65,000 = £3,575 per year on a guaranteed basis.

- Additional income will be available from the unit trust investments and could also be taken if required from the with profit bond, thus providing a safety margin.

Marking guide

Diversified portfolio – 1

Tax efficient and secure income for Ingrid – 1

Use of ISA allowance – 1

Use of PP allowance – 1

Suitable short term investment for £7,000 spending money – 1

Emergency fund between £10,000 and £20,000 – 1

Correct income loss and replacement calculation (5, with one deducted for each mistake)

Suitable investments for Josh, with mix of risk rating – 1

Maximum 6 marks if lost income not replaced

(d)   *(Maximum 3 marks per product type, overall maximum 18)*

Bank and Building Society Accounts

- The amount is appropriate for an emergency fund plus the £7,000 required for short- term spending.

- The investment is secure.

- These amounts are accessible, as necessary for the emergency fund and the amounts needed for short term expenditure, but earning interest at a reasonable rate until called upon.

NS&I 5 year Index-linked Certificates

- This is the maximum permitted investment.

- The investment is government backed and is totally secure, with the return exceeding inflation.

- This provides some security, in line with her attitude to risk, but with guaranteed returns in excess of inflation.

Guaranteed Income Bond

- The amount invested is sufficient to meet her need for income from the portfolio.

- The income is guaranteed for the 5 year term of the bond, and the capital will be returned in full.

- This meets her income need, whilst safeguarding the capital at the end of the term of the bond.

Personal Pension

- The amount shown is net of basic rate tax and is well within the maximum relievable amount for Ingrid of 100% of her earnings (the amount shown in net of basic rate tax relief).

- The managed fund is medium risk, and the value of the investment may fluctuate, but with the potential for long term growth.

- Contributions attract tax relief, and the fund grows free of tax except that dividend tax credits cannot be reclaimed, so this investment is attractive to build long term savings for Ingrid's retirement.

PDQ With Profit Bond

- The amount is reasonable in the context of the portfolio as a whole, in order to provide some diversification.

- The bond is low to medium risk.

- This allows Ingrid to participate in a diversified portfolio, with the insurance company smoothing returns, to provide good growth prospects, but with limited risk.

Montgomery Worldwide Maxi ISA

- The recommended amount is the maximum permitted, taking into account her monthly investments.

- These are equity related investments, involving risk, but would be acceptable given her attitude to risk and the overall portfolio balance.

- The investment return is free of tax except that tax credits cannot be reclaimed so the good long term are enhanced by the tax advantages and the risk, in the context of her portfolio, is in line with her tolerance of risk, particularly as she is already familiar with this investment trust.

Unit trusts

- The amounts are suitable to provide diversification within the portfolio as a whole, and good growth potential.

- These are equity linked funds and are medium risk, whose values can fluctuate, and should be regarded as medium to long term investments.

- These are also focused on the long term, in line with her objectives and with an acceptable level of risk in the overall portfolio context; she is not using her CGT annual exemptions currently and so there is scope here for gains without tax liability.

PRACTICE EXAMINATION 3

All questions in this paper are based on English law and practice, as applicable in the 2006/07 tax year, unless otherwise stated, and should be answered accordingly.

INSTRUCTIONS

You are allowed two hours for this paper.

The paper consists of two questions. You should answer both of them. Read the questions and the information provided carefully.

You are advised to spend approximately 60 minutes on Question 1 and 60 minutes on Question 2.

You are strongly advised to attempt ALL parts of each Question in order to gain the maximum possible number of marks. The available marks for each part are shown in all cases.

You should use the Product List provided in answering Question 2. You may also find it useful to refer to the Tax Tables provided in answering both Questions.

It is important to show all the steps in any calculations you do, even if you use a calculator.

Questions

1   You have recently been to see Andrew and Margaret, who are married. Andrew has recently changed careers and is a chemistry teacher at the local comprehensive school; he is 50 years old. He is doing well and has been told he should be able to progress in seniority quite rapidly, given his past experience. He intends to retire at 60 and will draw his benefits at that time from the Teachers Pension Scheme.

Andrew's current earnings are £32,000 a year and he will have completed 10 years service as a teacher by the time he reaches age 60.

Before becoming a teacher, Andrew worked as an industrial chemist, and he has a preserved pension as a result of this employment, payable at 65. He is interested in making further provision for retirement, because he feels that his pension rights built up so far will not meet his income needs.

Margaret is 48 years old. She is self-employed and works as a music teacher. Her income for the current tax year is £12,000 pa, though this has been higher in the past. She is also keen to make retirement provision, because she has not made any pension provision at all to date.

The couple have no children, but Andrew has a son, Rory, by a previous marriage and he pays maintenance of £300 per month to his ex-wife for Rory's benefit. This will continue until Rory reaches the age of 18. Andrew wants to protect this with life assurance, and has been told that a Family Income Benefit policy would be ideal. He has asked you if you agree.

Andrew and Margaret have a whole of life policy, on a joint life first death basis, intended to provide financial protection if either were to die. The sum assured is £250,000, which would repay the mortgage of £60,000 and leave a capital sum left over for the use of the survivor. They have just received a letter from the insurer telling them that the policy is coming up to a review date, and stating that the premium must increase.

(a)   **List the questions you would want to ask so that you would have all the information you need to advise Andrew and Margaret on their retirement planning needs** (11 marks)

(b)   **What options are open to Andrew regarding his preserved pension rights from the earlier period of employment?** (6 marks)

(c)   **State two possible ways in which Andrew could top-up his pension benefits, briefly explaining the advantages of each. Which one would you recommend and why?** (10 marks)

(d)   **Name one other tax-advantaged product which could be used to provide for retirement, stating its tax treatment, the contribution limits that apply, and whether this might be an alternative to the arrangements discussed in your answer to part (c).** (10 marks)

(e)   (i)   **Explain why review dates occur under whole of life policies and why the premium sometimes needs to increase.** (8 marks)

      (ii)   **Explain what is meant by a 'joint life first death' policy.** (2 marks)

      (iii)   **Define a 'joint life second death policy' and state when might it be appropriate to utilise such a policy?** (3 marks)

(Total marks for question: 50)

2   Martha is 52 years old and has recently been unexpectedly widowed following a car accident involving her husband Bill. She needs to rearrange her finances as a result of this with a view to ensuring that she has a reasonable income for the rest of her life. At the same time, she wants to ensure that her capital is invested with a realistic prospect of some capital growth to offset the effects of inflation.

She has some awareness of investment and risk, and although her husband used to deal with their investment decisions, she also took an interest. She therefore understands that equity related investment offers the best opportunities for long term growth, but also carries a degree of risk. Overall, she regards her attitude to risk as moderate.

The available capital in relation to which she needs your advice relates primarily to life assurance benefits. They amount to £200,000 in total. She will need an income of £4,000 per year net of tax from her investments, to supplement the widow's pension of £7,000 pa which she will receive from Bill's occupational scheme. She has asked that this is provided by a combination of at least three products, to ensure she has some diversification.

The mortgage on the house she lives in was repaid by a further life policy on Bill's death, and she has no intention of moving.

She has a Townshires Building Society Reserve Account, with £8,000 invested. She wants to top this up to £20,000, which she feels would then be an adequate emergency fund.

She also has a small holding of Treasury 5% 2012 stock. The current price of this in the newspapers is £107.91. She has no other assets, though she knows she will receive a State bereavement allowance for a year, and intends to invest this.

(a)   **Calculate the current yield on the gilt holding and comment on whether the redemption yield will be higher or lower.**
                                                                                                          (4 marks)

(b)   **Give two possible options for the investment of her income from the State bereavement benefit, and give one advantage and one disadvantage of each.**
                                                                                                          (6 marks)

(c)   **Using the Product List provided, recommend a portfolio of products which would be suitable for the investment of Martha's capital. You should explain how her specific need for income from the portfolio is met, detailing the tax position on the income.**
                                                                                                          (14 marks)

(d)   **Justify the inclusion of each of the product types you have included in your recommendations for Martha's portfolio, commenting under each of the following headings:**

       (i)   **The amount to be invested**

       (ii)   **The risk profile**

       (iii) **The suitability of the investment**
                                                                                                          (21 marks)

(e)   **Assuming that Martha takes your advice, list five factors which you would take into account in reviewing her portfolio in a year's time.**
                                                                                                          (5 marks)

                                                                    (Total marks for question: 50)

PRACTICE EXAMINATION 3

ANSWERS

Answers

1

(a)
- Andrew, when you retire, what level of income would you want to have, in today's terms?
- What lump sum are you likely to need in addition?
- Can I see the statement of the benefits available from your old employer's scheme, and any other details you may have such as a scheme booklet?
- Could I see the details of your pension benefits from earlier employment?
- How much do you feel that you could comfortably save towards your retirement planning?
- How much of this do you feel you should place where it would be accessible in an emergency?
- Margaret, how much income do you feel you will need when you retire?
- When do you think you are likely to retire?
- How much do you feel you can put aside for your retirement planning?
- Given that your income has fluctuated in the past, how important is it that the contributions are flexible so that you can increase or decrease them, or even suspend them for a period in the future?
- Have you obtained details of the State pension you can expect at retirement?
- Do either of you have any other savings or investments which would help towards your financial position in retirement?

(b)
- He can leave them where they are, and take benefits at 65.
- He could take benefits early (at any time) subject to the rules of the scheme and (possibly) the discretion of the trustees.
- Or he could defer benefits, again subject to the rules of the scheme.
- He could transfer the value of the rights to the Teachers Pension Scheme and receive extra benefits under the Scheme as a result.
- He could transfer to a Personal Pension.
- He could transfer to a Section 32 buy out policy.

(c) • In-house AVCs – under the Teachers Pension Scheme

• Andrew is eligible because he is accruing benefits under the Teachers Pension Scheme.

• This is an attractive route for Andrew, because it is low cost

• There is a defined benefit (added years) basis available, which could represent very good value

• Personal pension

• It is now possible for occupational scheme members to also contribute to a PP, without restriction, though the available allowances apply to total benefits and contributions.

• If so, this could be an attractive alternative to in-house AVCs, particularly if he wants a defined contribution arrangement.

• He would personally have control over the arrangements and would retain privacy in relation to them.

• Of the possible routes, in-house AVCs on an added years basis seem most attractive.

• This reflects the fact that Andrew is doing well in his job and should enjoy good salary progression. The known relationship to final earnings could therefore be attractive and will make planning easier.

(d) • ISA
• There is no tax relief on contributions
• The fund grows free of tax on income and capital gains
• But dividend tax credits can no longer be reclaimed
• Maximum contributions are £7,000 pa to a maxi-ISA
• This could be an attractive alternative because of its flexibility
• Contributions can be varied at will
• Benefits can be taken at any time
• And in any form
• Benefits are free of tax

(e) (i) • In setting the initial premium level, the insurance company will indicate the minimum premium it will accept for the chosen level of cover.

• This will be enough to meet the cost of the insurance cover for a set period, known as the review period, but not beyond.

• At the end of the review period, the policy will be reviewed and a new premium set for a further review period.

• This will be based on the then age of the insured life/lives.

• The increased cost of life insurance as age increases is the reason minimum premiums increase on review.

• But no further medical evidence is required.

• A higher premium than the minimum can be paid if this is desired.

• This may reduce or eliminate the need for an increase on review.

(ii) • The policy has two lives insured.

• It pays out on the death of the first of the two to die.

(iii) • This type of policy also has two lives assured,

• But pays out on the death of the last of the two to die.

• It is useful to provide for inheritance tax which will arise on the death of the longest survivor of a married couple if the estate of the first to die passes wholly or mainly to the survivor.

2

(a)
- The income per £100 nominal value is £5.
- Current yield is (£5/£107.91) x 100 = 4.63% (to 2 decimal places).
- The redemption yield is lower.
- This is because it takes account of the loss of value between its current value (£107.91) and its redemption value (£100).

(b)   ISA
- Advantage: Investment returns are free of all tax, except that dividend tax credits cannot be reclaimed
- Disadvantage: The accumulated fund would fall into Martha's estate on death and is likely to be subject to inheritance tax

Personal Pension
- Advantage: Contributions attract tax relief
- Disadvantage: Only 25% of the benefits can be taken in the form of tax free cash, with the balance providing an income, which will be taxed as earned income

(c)

	£
Townshires Building Society Reserve Account	12,000
Tinytown Bank 60 day Account	10,000
NS&I 5 year Index-Linked Certificates 39th Issue	15,000
NS&I Income Bond	50,000
Solid Insurance 3 yr G'teed Inc Bond	40,000
XYZ Life With-Profits Bond	36,000
Countryside UK Income Maxi-ISA	7,000
Countryside UK Blue Chip Unit Trust	10,000
Interglobal UK Growth Unit Trust	10,000
Fairplay UK Tracker Unit Trust	10,000
	200,000

Income generated is:

Tinytown Bank 60 day Account: £10,000 @ 4.0% = £400 gross
Net income for Martha as a basic rate taxpayer = £400 × 0.8 = £320
NS&I Income Bond: £50,000 @ 4.2% = £2,100 gross
Net income for Martha as a basic rate taxpayer = £2,100 x 0.8 = £1,680

Solid Insurance 3 yr G'teed Inc Bond: £40,000 @ 5.2% = £2,080

221

Withdrawals regarded as net of basic rate tax, so there is no further tax liability as Martha is a basic rate taxpayer.

Total net income: £4,080, which meets her requirements.

Further income, if needed, could be taken as income from the unit trusts, or withdrawals from the with profit bond, or the ISA.

Marking guide

Correct income calculation – 6, with 1 deducted for each mistake
Explanation of tax aspects – 3
Top-up to Reserve Account of £12,000 – 1
Some directly asset-backed investments, max £50,000 – 1
Some secure investments – 1
Diversified portfolio –1
Use of ISA and/or PP allowances – 1

Maximum 6 if income need not met, or less than three products used for income

---

(d)   Building Society and bank accounts

- The Reserve Account is built up to the level specified by Martha as an adequate emergency fund and a further secure investment is made in the 60 day account

- These are secure investments.

- This provides the required top-up to her emergency fund and a further secure cash investment, accessible at notice with a contribution to income from the 60 day account

NS&I Index-linked Certificates

- The amount is the maximum permitted investment

- The investment is government backed and is totally secure, with the return exceeding inflation.

- This gives a guaranteed return in excess of inflation and provides a good boost to growth within the portfolio

NS&I Income Bond

- The amount invested provides for the bulk of the required income and qualifies for the higher interest rate for investments of £25,000 or more.

- The investment is government backed and totally secure, though with a variable interest rate.

- The income need is a vital aspect of her requirements and this provides security, accessibility and a competitive rate, compensating for the variability of interest rate

Guaranteed Income Bond

- The amount invested provides for most of the remaining income requirement

- The income is guaranteed for four years and capital is guaranteed at maturity

- This provides for the rest of her income need, at a competitive rate, which makes up for the fact that access terms would be unfavourable during the term

With Profit Bond

- The amount invested provides for balance within the portfolio as a whole.

- The investment is low to medium risk, with the returns smoothed by the insurance company

- This provides a good return based on a diversified portfolio, but with modest risk, in line with her attitude to risk

Maxi ISA

- The recommended amount is the maximum permitted, and assumes no ISA investment is made from income.

- These are diversified equity related investments, involving medium risk

- The risk is acceptable given Martha's attitude to risk and meets her wish for growth

Unit trusts

- The amounts are reasonable to give balance to the portfolio.

- These are medium risk diversified investments restricted to the UK, to limit risk

- These investments offer good growth prospects at acceptable risk and will allow her to use her annual CGT exemption

(e)
- Any change in her need for income

- Any change in the income produced by the portfolio, for example as a result of interest rate changes

- The availability of a new year's ISA allowance

- The possibility of using her annual CGT exemption to crystallise a tax free gain

- Any change in her health creating different priorities, for example a need for long term care

(Other valid points would score)

PRACTICE EXAMINATION 4

All questions in this paper are based on English law and practice, as applicable in the 2006/07 tax year, unless otherwise stated, and should be answered accordingly.

INSTRUCTIONS

You are allowed two hours for this paper.

The paper consists of two questions. You should answer both of them. Read the questions and the information provided carefully.

You are advised to spend approximately 60 minutes on Question 1 and 60 minutes on Question 2.

You are strongly advised to attempt ALL parts of each Question in order to gain the maximum possible number of marks. The available marks for each part are shown in all cases.

You should use the Product List provided in answering Question 2. You may also find it useful to refer to the Tax Tables provided in answering both Questions.

It is important to show all the steps in any calculations you do, even if you use a calculator.

Questions

1   Dennis is 44 years old, and is beginning to think about his retirement and the financial position he will find himself in at that time. He is currently employed as a stores manager on a salary of £24,000.

He does not belong to an occupational pension. He does however have two pension arrangements which he has started himself. Both are personal pension plans, one of which he started in 1988. He has been contributing to it at the rate of £60 per month since then. The investment performance has been sluggish however, and he has asked for your advice as to whether he should transfer the accumulated fund to the other personal pension, which he started more recently, and it has performed better from an investment point of view. The fund now stands at around £15,000.

Dennis tells you that his employer provides a private medical insurance scheme, of which he is a member. The company pays two thirds of the cost and the members of the scheme pay the other third. Dennis values this benefit particularly as his wife, Elizabeth, is covered as well as him.

Elizabeth works as a dental receptionist, on a part-time basis, earning about £10,000 per year. She has no pension arrangements, but feels that she prefers the flexibility and access of ISAs as a means of long term saving. She has invested £500 in a cash mini-ISA at a local building society this year. Having put some money aside in cash, she now wants to maximise the extent to which she invests in equity related investments within an ISA wrapper.

The couple have also asked you about Critical Illness Benefit, having read an article on the subject in the weekend press. Elizabeth is particularly interested in this, because a number of her relations have suffered from heart problems. The couple want some further information before deciding if this cover is appropriate for them, possibly as an alternative to Income Protection Insurance (IPI, also known as Permanent Health Insurance or PHI), which they have already researched.

(a)   List the questions you would want to ask so that you would have all the information you need to advise Dennis and Elizabeth on their retirement planning needs.   (11 marks)

(b)   (i)   Explain the operation of the lifetime allowance introduced in April 2006 in relation to pension schemes, and comment on its relevance to Dennis.   (10 marks)

        (ii)   List *six* factors which Dennis should take into account in deciding whether or not to transfer his fund from one PP to the other.   (6 marks)

(c)   Explain the tax and NI treatment of the private medical insurance scheme.   (6 marks)

(d)   (i)   Explain the limits that would apply to further investments by Elizabeth in ISAs during the current tax year.   (3 marks)

        (ii)   Give *two* advantages and *two* disadvantages of investing in ISAs rather than personal pensions for retirement planning in Elizabeth's circumstances.   (4 marks)

(e)   (i)   What are the main features of Critical Illness Benefit?   (6 marks)

        (ii)   Would you recommend this cover as an alternative to IPI? Explain your answer.   (4 marks)

(Total marks for question: 50)

2   Eric and Anita are married and are aged 73 and 69 respectively. Eric is receiving a pension from his former employer's scheme, which amounts to £16,000 per year. He also receives a State Pension of £7,500.

Anita has never worked and has no pension rights, though she does feel that she would like to have more independence in terms of having her own income.

The couple live in a bungalow in a small coastal town, and there is no mortgage on the property.

Eric has saved money over the years in building society accounts and he now has a total of £90,000 invested, split between £30,000 in the Townshires BS Reserve Account and £60,000 in the Tinytown Bank Deposit Account. In addition, he invested £10,000 in a unit-linked bond, all in a UK Equity fund. He has taken no withdrawals and the value is now £12,000.

The building society interest has been used to supplement their income since Eric retired a few years ago (they have a separate emergency fund which they consider adequate). However, interest rates have fallen, and they now need to increase the income they receive by at least £750 pa after tax. He does not want to use the investment bond at this stage to supplement income. Eric also says that they should make some allowance for increasing the income in future, though he has no fixed target for this.

They have a fairly cautious attitude to risk, but do accept that some risk may be necessary to achieve their goals.

They have no immediate requirements for cash sums, though they would not be prepared to lose access to all of their capital, and similarly, they would not be prepared to invest in an annuity to any great extent.

(a)   **Explain how the investment bond is taxed, including the effect of withdrawals or encashment, and comment on the suitability of the investment in this case.**   (16 marks)

(b)   **Using the Product List provided, recommend a portfolio of products which would be suitable for the investment of Eric and Anita's capital. You should show who owns each investment, and explain how their specific need for an increased income and for further future increases from the portfolio is met, detailing the tax position on the income.**   (18 marks)

(c)   **Justify the inclusion of each of the product types you have included in your recommendations for the couple's portfolio, commenting under each of the following headings:**

     (i)   **The amount to be invested**

     (ii)   **The risk profile**

     (iii)   **The suitability of the investment**   (12 marks)

(d)   **Assuming they take your advice, list five factors which you would take into account in reviewing the portfolio in a year's time, with particular regard to tax efficiency.**   (4 marks)

(Total marks for question: 50)

BPP
PROFESSIONAL EDUCATION

PRACTICE EXAMINATION 4

ANSWERS

Answers

1

> **Tutorial notes**
>
> For part (a), spread your questions sensibly between both spouses, and cover joint issues as well. Although you should get one mark for each valid question, it is a good idea to include one or two 'extra' questions. This can also help to establish a logical sequence and provides complete coverage of relevant areas.
>
> Part (b) picks up knowledge that you should have from earlier exams, and this is worth revising. Where rule changes occur, as is the case for 2006, you should ensure you are fully familiar with the new rules.
>
> Always read the question carefully. For example, part (c) of this question asks for the tax and NI treatment, which includes IPT. The question is not limited to income tax.
>
> Part (d) is quite routine, but you should clearly indicate which are advantages and which are disadvantages.

(a)
- Dennis, when you retire, what level of income would you want to have, in today's terms?
- What lump sum are you likely to need in addition?
- Can I see the latest statements showing the value of your pension arrangements?
- Are you aware of any special terms, such as guaranteed annuity rates, which apply under the older arrangement?
- Are you likely to become eligible for any pension arrangements at work in the future?
- Do you have any pension benefits from earlier employments?
- How much do you feel that you could comfortably save towards your retirement planning?
- How much of this do you feel you should place where it would be accessible in an emergency?
- Elizabeth, how much income do you feel you will need when you retire?
- When do you think you are likely to retire?
- How much do you feel you can put aside for your retirement planning?
- Do either of you have any other savings or investments which would help towards your financial position in retirement?

(b) (i)
- The lifetime allowance places a limit on the extent to which benefits can be built up under registered pension schemes with full tax advantages
- It covers all benefits built up under all arrangements, whether before or after its introduction on A-Day (6 April 2006)
- The limit is tested when benefits crystallise, generally through taking benefits on retirement
- Or their being paid out on earlier death
- If the total fund exceeds the lifetime allowance, a lifetime allowance tax charge applies
- This is at 55% if the excess is taken as a lump sum
- Or 25% if the excess is used to provide income• The income would however be taxable as earned income
- There is little chance of Dennis' fund building up to the level of the lifetime allowance (£1.5m in 2006/07) unless he increases contributions considerably, or has other benefits from earlier employments

- The build up of the fund should be monitored to ensure that he can consider the position carefully if the allowance is approached in later years

(ii)
- There may be surrender penalties under the RAP
- There may be entry costs under the PP
- The level of management charge may differ
- There is no guarantee that the better performance of the newer PP will continue
- There could be a guaranteed annuity rate under the RAP, which would be lost on transfer
- Death benefit under the RAP may not be a full return of fund

(Other valid points would score)

(c)
- The premiums paid by the company are a deductible business expense
- But they are treated as a benefit in kind for the members and are subject to income tax
- They are also subject to employer NI contribution liability
- But there is no NI liability for employees
- The premiums are subject to Insurance Premium Tax (IPT)
- The benefits are payable free of tax

(d) (i)
- She can only invest in mini-ISAs this tax year.
- She can contribute up to a further £2,500 into the cash mini-ISA to bring the total to the maximum of £3,000.
- She can contribute up to £4,000 to a stocks & shares mini-ISA.

(ii) Advantages
- The accumulated fund is available at any time if needed
- There is no tax on benefits

Disadvantages
- There is no tax relief on contributions
- Death benefits would be paid to the estate and could be subject to inheritance tax if Margaret dies before taking benefits (though the inter-spouse exemption would apply if the money passed to Dennis)

(e) (i)
- The benefit is paid as a lump sum
- Following diagnosis of any one of a number of conditions specified in the policy
- These generally include cancer, heart attack, coronary artery bypass surgery, stroke, cancer, major organ transplant and total permanent disability, though the details vary from provider to provider
- There is no requirement for the insured to be unable to work (except in cases of total permanent disability), though there is often a minimum survival period
- There is no tax relief on premiums
- There is no tax on the benefits

(ii)
- No. The cover is different and serves a different purpose
- IPI is intended to replace income if the insured is unable to work
- Critical Illness Benefit provides a lump sum which could be used (for example) to repay a mortgage, finance specialist treatment or make necessary modifications to a residential property

2

Tutorial notes

Part (a) has a detailed answer but, with 16 marks available, this is to be expected. Your assessment of the suitability of the product must take into account the position of these individuals, so their currently unused CGT exemptions are important.

Many different portfolios could be constructed for part (b), to meet the needs identified. Mark your own answer using the *Marking guide*. For part (c), the details given will reflect the portfolio construction.

Part (d): questions asking for points to review in relation to a particular aspect of financial planning are inevitably more difficult to answer, and require additional thought, as always taking into account the position of the clients.

(a)
- The funds in which the investment bond invest pay tax both on income and capital gains
- The rates of tax are 10% on dividends (discharged by the tax credit) and 20% on other income
- The rate of tax on capital gains is 20%
- There are no annual allowances which can be set against income or gains in the way that personal income tax and CGT allowances can
- Indexation relief is available on gains however
- Withdrawals can be made without an immediate tax liability up to 5% of the amount originally invested (ie £10,000 in this case) each year for 20 years
- If unused, the ability to withdraw these amounts can be carried forward indefinitely
- On encashment, the gain (ie the surrender proceeds plus any withdrawals within the 5% allowances, less the amount invested) is subject to higher rate, but not basic rate tax
- There is therefore no personal liability unless the investor is a higher rate taxpayer, or is pushed into higher rate by the gain
- Top-slicing relief may reduce the liability in these circumstances
- Any withdrawals in excess of the 5% allowances are treated in the same way as a gain (but on ultimate surrender of the bond, are not added into the calculation of gain)
- The bond allows diversified investment into equities, which could be attractive
- However, the tax paid by the fund, particularly on gains is unattractive
- If assets were held personally, for example through a unit trust, similar diversification could be achieved, but with the ability to use the CGT annual exemption of both spouses
- The bond does not therefore seem suitable
- Care is needed over encashment however, particularly if this could affect the Age Allowance (including Married Couple's Allowance available to the couple)

(b)

Owner	Investment	Amount £
Anita	Townshires BS Reserve Account	11,400
Anita	Townshires BS 90 day Account	10,000
Anita	NS&I 5 year Pensioners Bond	49,000
Eric	Personal pension - XYZ With Profits	2,800
Anita	Personal pension – XYZ With Profits	2,800
Eric	XYZ Gilt Maxi-ISA	7,000
Anita	PDQ Fixed Interest Maxi-ISA	7,000
		90,000

Current income:

Reserve Account: £30,000 @ 3.5% = £1,050 pa gross

Bank deposit £60,000 @ 2.2% = £1,320 pa gross

Total: £2,370 gross

Total net: £2,370 × 0.8 = £1,896 pa (As Eric is the account holder, and is a basic rate taxpayer, there is a 20% tax liability.)

Income from new portfolio (all in Anita's name):

Reserve Account: £11,400 @ 3.5% = £399 pa

90 day Account: £10,000 @ 3.8% = £380 pa

Pensioners Bond: £49,000 @ 4.0%= £1,960 pa

Total income: £2,739 which falls within Anita's personal allowance, so there is no tax liability.

Increase: £843 pa net, which exceeds their requirement

Future increases

- Building up funds in PPs will provide a future income for both Eric and Anita

- ISAs will also allow future income increases to be provided for by drawing on these investments

- Both offer significant tax advantages, particularly through growth free of tax on gains and income (although dividend tax credits cannot be reclaimed)

- And allow control of timing

Marking guide

Correct income calculation on existing basis, allowing for tax – 3, with one deducted for each mistake.

Correct income calculation on new basis – 4, with one deducted for each mistake

Explanation of tax aspects – 3

Use of Anita's allowances – 1

Largely secure assets (min £60,000) – 1

Use of ISA allowances – 1

Use of PP allowances – 1

Future increases in income and explanation – 4

Maximum 9 if increased income need not met

(c)   *(Maximum 3 marks per product type, overall maximum 12)*

Building Society Accounts

- The amount in the Reserve Account maintains access, and the amount in the 90 day Account gives a useful capital resource if required, but offers a higher interest rate

- Secure

- This is secure and familiar, but increasing the interest rate by allowing for a notice period gives a greater contribution to income and the tax is saved by putting the holdings into Anita's name

NS&I Pensioners Bond

- This amount provides for the bulk of the increase in income

- Capital is secure and the interest rate is guaranteed for 5 years

- The combination of secure capital and a guaranteed rate of interest payable as income is very much in line with their objectives

Personal Pensions

- These amounts are close to the maximum permitted net contributions for the current year

- They are low to medium risk investments

- The with profits fund smoothes growth giving the opportunity of growth but at a low to medium risk level, in line with their requirements

Maxi ISAs

- The recommended amounts are the maximum permitted.

- Although these funds can fluctuate in value, they are less volatile than equity funds, and are low to medium risk.

- Although a higher level of risk than other investments within the portfolio, the diversified and managed nature of the unit trusts moderates this whilst meeting their wish for some growth prospects within the portfolio

(d)   - The availability of new ISA allowances

- The availability of new PP allowances

- Possibility of encashing the investment bond to move to more tax efficient investments

- Income position relative to age allowance income limit to ensure there is no loss of allowances if the bond is encashed

Product list

PRODUCT LIST

The Product List for use in answering **written Case Study questions** in this Study Text is set out below.

1 Bank and Building Society Accounts – UK

	Gross yield/AER
Tinytown Bank Cheque Account (min £1)	1.8%
Tinytown Bank Deposit Account (min £10)	2.2%
Townshires Building Society Reserve (min £4,000)	3.5%
Townshires Building Society 90 Day (min £5,000)	3.8%
Tinytown Bank 60 Day Account (min £10,000)	4.0%

2 Offshore Accounts - Channel Islands

	Gross yield/AER
Channel Bank Offshore Deposit Account (min £20,000)	4.2%
Townshires Building Society Offshore Account (min £20,000)	4.8%
Tinytown Bank Offshore Account (min £5,000)	4.7%

3 National Savings & Investments (NS&I)

	Gross yield
Investment Account (£20 to £100,000: interest rate depends on balance)	2.95% to 3.85%
Income Bond (£500 to £24,999)	3.95%
Income Bond (£25,000 to £1m)	4.20%
Capital Bond (£100 to £250,000)	4.05%
*Children's Bonus Bond (£25 to £3,000)	3.85%
*5 year Certificates 81st Issue (£100 to £15,000)	2.95%
*2 year Certificates 31st Issue (£100 to £15,000)	2.95%
*5 year Index-Linked Certificates 39th Issue (£100 to £15,000)	RPI + 1.05%
*3 year Index-Linked Certificates 11th Issue (£100 to £15,000)	RPI + 1.05%
Pensioners Bonds (£500 - £1m) 5 years	4.00%
Pensioners Bonds (£500 - £1m) 2 years	4.00%
Pensioners Bonds (£500 - £1m) 1 year	4.00%

* Tax free

4 Guaranteed Income Bonds

	Gross yield
Central Insurance 1 year Income Bond	4.2%
Solid Insurance 3 year Income Bond	5.2%
Fairplay Insurance 4 year Income Bond	5.4%
Central Insurance 5 year Income Bond	5.5%

5   Single Premium Investment Bonds

Fairplay Insurance Managed
Solid Insurance Recovery
Mutual Life Pacific
PDQ American
Central Insurance UK Growth
Mutual Life Property

6   With Profit Bonds

XYZ Life With-Profits Bond
PDQ With-Profits Bond
Central With-Profits Bond

7   Annuity rates

Single Life, guaranteed five years, level		
	Male 65	Female 60
XYZ Life	£771	£664
Solid Insurance	£795	£670
Mutual Life	£787	£656

Single Life, guaranteed 5 years, escalating at 5%		
	Male 60	Female 55
XYZ Life	£502	£402
Solid Insurance	£497	£408
Mutual Life	£508	£410
	Male 65	Female 60
Fairplay Insurance	£552	£470
XYZ Life	£547	£474
Solid Insurance	£560	£478

8   Pension Funds

	Available for Stakeholder
Fairplay Insurance Managed	Yes
Solid Pensions UK Equity	Yes
PDQ Fixed Interest	No
PDQ Recovery	No
XYZ UK	Yes
Index Tracker Fund	Yes

9 Unit trusts and OEICs (for ISA Stocks & Shares components and investment outside ISAs)

	Available as Mini-ISA	Available as Maxi-ISA	Gross yield
Interglobal UK Income	Yes	Yes	3.2%
XYZ Equity Income	--	Yes	3.6%
Countryside UK Income	Yes	Yes	3.4%
XYZ UK Equity	--	Yes	2.7%
PDQ Recovery	Yes	Yes	1.2%
Countryside UK Blue Chip	Yes	Yes	2.8%
Interglobal UK Growth	Yes	Yes	0.9%
Fairplay UK Tracker	Yes	Yes	2.8%
XYZ Gilt Fund	--	Yes	4.2%
PDQ Fixed Interest	Yes	Yes	4.3%
Solid Fixed Interest	Yes	Yes	4.6%
XYZ Europe	--	Yes	2.3%
Interglobal US	Yes	Yes	0.2%
Interglobal Japan	Yes	Yes	-
Fairplay Pacific	Yes	Yes	0.3%
Mutual Property	--	--	3.1%

10 Investment Trusts (for ISA Stocks & Shares components and investment outside ISAs)

	Gross yield
Montgomery UK	3.2%
Montgomery European	2.4%
Montgomery Worldwide	1.8%
Grimmett US	1.9%
Mountain Income	3.8%
Simmonds UK	3.1%

11 FSA Recognised Offshore Funds - Channel Islands

	Gross yield	Paid
PDQ Offshore Gilt Fund	4.6%	Monthly
Solid Gilt Fund	4.4%	Monthly
Mountain Gilt Fund	4.8%	Quarterly
Mountain UK Income	4.2%	Quarterly
XYZ European Technology	0.3%	Annually
Simmonds UK Offshore Fund	3.2%	Half-yearly

Tax Tables

Income tax rates

2006/07		2005/06	
Rate %	Band £	Rate %	Band £
10	1 – 2,150	10	1 – 2,090
22	2,151 – 33,300	22	2,091 – 32,400
40	Over 33,300	40	Over 32,400

Income tax reliefs

		2006/07 £	2005/06 £
Personal allowance	– under 65	5,035	4,895
	– 65 – 74	7,280	7,090
	– 75 and over	7,420	7,220
Married couple's allowance	– 65 – 74 (see note 1)	6,065	5,905
	– 75 and over (see note 1)	6,135	5,975
	minimum for 65+	2,350	2,280
Age allowance income limit		20,100	19,500
Blind person's allowance		1,660	1,610
Enterprise investment scheme relief limit (see note 2)		400,000	200,000
Venture capital trust relief limit (see note 3)		200,000	200,000

Notes

1 Ages relate to the elder spouse or civil partner. MCA is available to only those couples where at least one spouse or civil partner was born before 6 April 1935. Relief is restricted to 10%.

2 EIS qualifies for 20% relief.

3 Tax relief is at 30% for VCT shares issued on or after 5 April 2006 (previously 40%).

Pensions

	Annual Allowance £	Lifetime Allowance £
2006/07	215,000	1,500,000
2007/08	225,000	1,600,000
2008/09	235,000	1,650,000
2009/10	245,000	1,750,000
2010/11	255,000	1,800,000

Working and child tax credits

Working tax credit	2006/07	2005/06
	£	£
Basic element	1,665	1,620
Couple and lone parent element	1,640	1,595
30 hour element	680	660
Childcare element of WTC		
Maximum eligible cost for 1 child	175 per week	175 per week
Maximum eligible cost for 2 children	300 per week	300 per week
Percent of eligible child costs covered	80	70
Child tax credit		
Family element	545	545
Baby addition	545	545
Child element	1,765	1,690
Tax credits income thresholds and withdrawal rates		
First income threshold	5,220	5,220
First withdrawal rate	37%	37%
Second income threshold	50,000	50,000
Second withdrawal rate	6.67%	6.67%
First threshold for those entitled to CTC	14,155	13,910
Income disregard	25,000	2,500

Capital gains tax

	2006/07	2005/06
Rate	Gains taxed at 10%, 20% or 40%, subject to level of income	Gains taxed at 10%, 20% or 40%, subject to level of income
Individuals - exemption	£8,800	£8,500
Trusts - exemption	£4,400	£4,250

Taper relief

Gains on business assets			Gains on non-business assets *	
Complete years after 5 April 98	% of gain chargeable		Complete years after 5 April 98	% of gain chargeable
0	100.0		0	100
1	50		1	100
2 or more	25		2	100
			3	95
			4	90
			5	85
			6	80
			7	75
			8	70
			9	65
			10 or more	60

* Non-business assets held on 17 March 1998 given additional year of relief.

Inheritance tax

Death rate	Lifetime rate	Chargeable 2006/07	Chargeable 2005/06
%	%	£'000	£'000
Nil	Nil	0 – 285	0 – 275
40	20	Over 285	Over 275

Reliefs

Annual exemption	£3,000	Marriage	– parent	£5,000
Small gifts	£250		– grandparent	£2,500
			– bride/groom	£2,500
			– other	£1,000

Reduced charge on gifts within 7 years of death

Years before death	0 – 3	3 – 4	4 – 5	5 – 6	6 – 7
% of death charge	100%	80%	60%	40%	20%

Stamp taxes

Stamp Duty Land Tax

Transfers of property (consideration paid)

Rate (%)	All land in the UK		Land in disadvantaged areas	
	Residential	Non-residential	Residential	Non-residential
Zero	£0 - £125,000	£0 - £150,000	£0 - £150,000	
1	Over £125,000 - £250,000	Over £150,000 - £250,000	Over £150,000 - £250,000	
3	Over £250,000 - £500,000	Over £250,000 - £500,000	Over £250,000 - £500,000	
4	Over £500,000	Over £500,000	Over £500,000	

New leases - Duty on rent

Rate (%)	Net present value (NPV) of rent	
	Residential	Non-residential
Zero	£0 - £125,000	£0 - £150,000
1%	Over £125,000	Over £150,000

The rate applies to the amount of NPV in the slice, not to the whole value.

Duty on lease premium is the same as for transfer of land (except special rules apply for premium where rent exceeds £600 annually).

Shares and securities

The rate of stamp duty / stamp duty reserve tax on the transfer of shares and securities is unchanged at 0.5% for 2006/07.

Retail prices index

	Jan	Feb	Mar	Apr	May	Jun	Jul	Aug	Sep	Oct	Nov	Dec
1982			79.4	81.0	81.6	81.9	81.9	81.9	81.9	82.3	82.7	82.5
1983	82.6	83.0	83.1	84.3	84.6	84.8	85.3	85.7	86.1	86.4	86.7	86.9
1984	86.8	87.2	87.5	88.6	89.0	89.2	89.1	89.9	90.1	90.7	91.0	90.9
1985	91.2	91.9	92.8	94.8	95.2	95.4	95.2	95.5	95.4	95.6	95.9	96.0
1986	96.2	96.6	96.7	97.7	97.8	97.8	97.5	97.8	98.3	98.5	99.3	99.6
1987	100.0	100.4	100.6	101.8	101.9	101.9	101.8	102.1	102.4	102.9	103.4	103.3
1988	103.3	103.7	104.1	105.8	106.2	106.6	106.7	107.9	108.4	109.5	110.0	110.3
1989	110.0	111.8	112.3	114.3	115.0	115.4	115.5	115.8	116.6	117.5	118.5	118.8
1990	119.5	120.2	121.4	125.1	126.2	126.7	126.8	128.1	129.3	130.3	130.0	129.9
1991	130.2	130.9	131.4	133.1	133.5	134.1	133.8	134.1	134.6	135.1	135.6	135.7
1992	135.6	136.3	136.7	138.8	139.3	139.3	138.8	138.9	139.4	139.9	139.7	139.2
1993	137.9	138.8	139.3	140.6	141.0	141.0	140.7	141.3	141.9	141.8	141.6	141.9
1994	141.3	142.1	142.5	144.2	144.7	144.7	144.0	144.7	145.0	145.2	145.3	146.0
1995	146.0	146.9	147.5	149.0	149.6	149.8	149.1	149.9	150.6	149.8	149.8	150.7
1996	150.2	150.9	151.5	152.6	152.9	153.0	152.4	153.1	153.8	153.8	153.9	154.4
1997	154.4	155.0	155.4	156.3	156.9	157.5	157.5	158.5	159.3	159.5	159.6	160.0
1998	159.5	160.3	160.8	162.6	163.5	163.4	163.0	163.7	164.4	164.5	164.4	164.4
1999	163.4	163.7	164.1	165.2	165.6	165.6	165.1	165.5	166.2	166.5	166.7	167.3
2000	166.6	167.5	168.4	170.1	170.7	171.1	170.5	170.5	171.7	171.6	172.1	172.2
2001	171.1	172.0	172.2	173.1	174.2	174.4	173.3	174.0	174.6	174.3	173.6	173.4
2002	173.3	173.8	174.5	175.7	176.2	176.2	175.9	176.4	177.6	177.9	178.2	178.5
2003	178.4	179.3	179.9	181.2	181.5	181.3	181.3	181.6	182.5	182.6	182.7	183.5
2004	183.1	183.8	184.6	185.7	186.5	186.8	186.8	187.4	188.1	188.6	189.0	189.9
2005	188.9	189.6	190.5	191.6	192.0	192.2	192.2	192.6	193.1	193.3	193.6	194.1
2006	193.4	194.2										

Indexation relief was frozen at 5 April 1998 and replaced by taper relief for individuals and trustees.

Main Social Security benefits

		2006/07 £	2005/06 £
Child benefit	– first child	17.45	17.00
	– subsequent child	11.70	11.40
Incapacity benefit	– short term lower rate	59.20	57.65
	– short term higher rate	70.05	68.20
	– long term rate	78.50	76.45
Attendance allowance	– lower rate	41.65	40.55
	– higher rate	62.25	60.60
Retirement pension	– single	84.25	82.05
	– married	134.75	131.20
Widowed parent's allowance		84.25	82.05
Bereavement payment (lump sum)		2,000.00	2,000.00
Jobseekers allowance (25 or over)		57.45	56.20

National Insurance contributions
2006/07 rates

	Weekly	Monthly	Yearly
Class I (employee)			
Lower Earnings Limit (LEL)	£84.00	£364.00	£4,368.00
Upper Earnings Limit (UEL)	£645.00	£2,795.00	£33,540.00
Earnings Threshold (ET)*	£97.00	£420.00	£5,035.00

Employees' contributions – Class 1

Total earnings £ per week	Contracted in rate	Contracted out rate
Below £97.00*	Nil	Nil
£97.01 - £645.00	11%	9.4%
Excess over £645.00	1%	1%
		1.6% rebate on earnings between LEL and ET

Employers' contributions – Class 1

Total earnings £ per week	Contracted-in rate	Contracted-out rate	
		Final salary	**Money purchase**
Below £97.00*	Nil	Nil	Nil
£97.01 - £645.00	12.8%	9.3%	11.8%
Excess over £645.00	12.8%	12.8%	12.8%
		3.5% rebate on earnings between LEL and ET	1% rebate on earnings between LEL and ET

* Earnings threshold below which no NICs payable. There is a zero band between the lower earnings limit (£84 pw) and the earnings threshold (£97 pw) to protect lower earners' rights to contributory state benefits such as basic state pension.

Class 1A
(employers' contributions on most benefits)   12.8% on all relevant benefits

Class 2 (self-employed)
Flat rate per week £2.10
where earnings are over £4,465 pa

Class 3 (voluntary)
Flat rate per week £7.55

Class 4 (self-employed)
8% on profits £5,035 – £33,540;
1% on profits above £33,540

Index

Name: _____

Email: _____

Date: _____

How have you used this Study Text?
(Tick one box only)

☐ home study (book only)

☐ on a course: at _____

☐ with 'correspondence' package

☐ other _____

Address: _____
_____
_____

Why did you decide to purchase this Study Text?
(Tick one box only)

☐ recommended by training department

☐ recommendation by friend/colleague

☐ recommendation by a lecturer at college

☐ saw advertising/website

☐ have used BPP products in the past

☐ other _____

Have you used the BPP Passcards ☐ **or i-Pass disk** ☐ **for this subject?** *Yes / No*

Your ratings, comments and suggestions would be appreciated on the following areas.

	Very useful	Useful	Not useful
Introductory section	☐	☐	☐
Main text	☐	☐	☐
Questions in chapters	☐	☐	☐
Chapter roundups	☐	☐	☐
Quizzes at ends of chapters	☐	☐	☐
Practice examination	☐	☐	☐
Structure and presentation	☐	☐	☐
Availability of Updates on website	☐	☐	☐

	Excellent	Good	Adequate	Poor
Overall opinion of this Study Text	☐	☐	☐	☐

Do you intend to continue using BPP study material?   ☐ Yes   ☐ No

Please note any comments or suggestions on the reverse of this page, or write by e-mail to FPQueries@bpp.com

Please return this form to: Financial Adviser Series Publishing Manager, BPP Professional Education, FREEPOST, London, W12 8BR

REVIEW FORM

Please note any further comments, suggestions and apparent errors below.